THE AMERICAN NATION
A HISTORY

GROUP III

DEVELOPMENT OF THE NATION

GROUP IV

TRIAL OF NATIONALITY

Group V

National Expansion

COMMITTEES APPOINTED TO ADVISE AND CONSULT WITH THE EDITOR

The Massachusetts Historical Society

Charles Francis Adams, LL.D., President
Samuel A. Green, M.D., Vice-President
James Ford Rhodes, LL.D., 2d Vice-Preside
Edward Channing, Ph.D., Prof. History Harvard Univ.
Worthington C. Ford, Chief of Division of MSS. Library of Congress

The Wisconsin Historical Society

Reuben G. Thwaites, LL.D., Secretary and Superintendent
Frederick J. Turner, Ph.D., Prof. of American History Wisconsin University
James D. Butler, LL.D., formerly Prof. Wisconsin University
William W. Wight, President
Henry E. Legler, Curator

The Virginia Historical Society

William Gordon McCabe, Litt.D., President
Lyon G. Tyler, LL.D., Pres. of William and Mary College
Judge David C. Richardson
J. A. C. Chandler, Professor Richmond College
Edward Wilson James

The Texas Historical Society

Judge John Henninger Reagan, President
George P. Garrison, Ph.D., Prof. of History University of Texas
Judge C. W. Raines
Judge Zachary T. Fullmore

PRINCE HENRY, THE NAVIGATOR

THE AMERICAN NATION: A HISTORY

VOLUME 1

EUROPEAN BACKGROUND OF AMERICAN HISTORY

1300–1600

BY

EDWARD POTTS CHEYNEY, A.M.

PROFESSOR OF HISTORY, UNIVERSITY OF PENNSYLVANIA

WITH MAPS

8106

NEW YORK AND LONDON
HARPER & BROTHERS PUBLISHERS

TO
MY FATHER

CONTENTS

MAPS

EDITOR'S INTRODUCTION TO THE SERIES

THAT a new history of the United States is needed, extending from the discovery down to the present time, hardly needs statement. No such comprehensive work by a competent writer is now in existence. Individual writers have treated only limited chronological fields. Meantime there is a rapid increase of published sources and of serviceable monographs based on material hitherto unused. On the one side there is a necessity for an intelligent summarizing of the present knowledge of American history by trained specialists; on the other hand there is need of a complete work, written in untechnical style, which shall serve for the instruction and the entertainment of the general reader.

To accomplish this double task within a time short enough to serve its purpose, there is but one possible method, the co-operative. Such a division of labor has been employed in several German, French, and English enterprises; but this is the first attempt to carry out that system on a large scale for the whole of the United States.

The title of the work succinctly suggests the character of the series, *The American Nation: A History. From Original Materials by Associated Scholars*. The subject is the "American Nation," the people combined into a mighty political organization, with a national tradition, a national purpose, and a national character. But the nation, as it is, is built upon its own past and can be understood only in the light of its origin and development. Hence this series is a "history," and a consecutive history, in which events shall be shown not only in their succession, but in their relation to one another; in which cause shall be connected with effect and the effect become a second cause. It is a history "from original materials," because such materials, combined with the recollections of living men, are the only source of our knowledge of the past. No accurate history can be written which does not spring from the sources, and it is safer to use them at first hand than to accept them as quoted or expounded by other people. It is a history written by "scholars": the editor expects that each writer shall have had previous experience in investigation and in statement. It is a history by "associated scholars," because each can thus bring to bear his special knowledge and his special aptitude.

Previous efforts to fuse together into one work short chapters by many hands have not been altogether happy: the results have usually been encyclopædic, uneven, and abounding in gaps. Hence in this series the whole work is divided into twenty-six volumes, in each of which the writer is free to develop a period for himself. It is the editor's function to see that the links of the chain are adjusted to each other, end to end, and that no considerable subjects are omitted.

The point of view of *The American Nation* is that the purpose of the historian is to tell what has been done, and, quite as much, what has been purposed, by the thinking, working, and producing people who make public opinion. Hence the work is intended to select and characterize the personalities who have stood forth as leaders and as seers; not simply the founders of commonwealths or the statesmen of the republic, but also the great divines, the inspiring writers, and the captains of industry. For this is not intended to be simply a political or constitutional history: it must include the social life of the people, their religion, their literature, and their schools. It must include their economic life, occupations, labor systems, and organizations of capital. It must include their wars and their diplomacy, the relations of community with community, and of the nation with other nations.

The true history, nevertheless, must include the happenings which mark the progress of discovery and colonization and national life. Striking events, dramatic episodes, like the discovery of America, Drake's voyage around the world, the capture of New Amsterdam by the English, George Rogers Clark's taking of Vincennes, and the bombardment of Fort Sumter, inspired the imagination of contemporaries, and stir the blood of their descendants.

A few words should be said as to the make-up of the volumes. Each contains a portrait of some man especially eminent within the field of that volume. Each volume also contains a series of colored and black-and-white maps, which add details better presented in graphic form than in print. There being no general atlas of American history in existence, the series of maps taken together will show the territorial progress of the country and will illustrate explorations and many military movements. Some of the maps will be reproductions of contemporary maps or sketches, but most of them have been made for the series by the collaboration of authors and editor.

Each volume has foot-notes, with the triple purpose of backing up the author's statements by the weight of his authorities, of leading the reader to further excursions into wider fields, and of furnishing the investigator with the means of further study. The citations are condensed as far as is possible while leaving them unmistakable, and the full titles of most of the works cited will be found in the critical essay on bibliography at the end of each volume. This constant reference to authorities, a salutary check on the writer and a safeguard to the reader, is one of the features of the work; and the bibliographical chapters carefully select from the immense mass of literature on American history the titles of the most authentic and the most useful secondary works and sources.

The principle of the whole series is that every book shall be written by an expert for laymen; and every volume must therefore stand the double test of accuracy and of readableness. American history loses nothing in dramatic climax because it is true or because it is truly told.

As editor of the series I must at least express my debt to the publishers, who have warmly adopted the idea that truth and popular interest are inseparable; to the authors, with whom I have discussed so often the problems of their own volumes and of the series in general; especially to the members of the committees of the Massachusetts Historical Society, Virginia Historical Society, Texas Historical Society, and Wisconsin State Historical Society, whose generous interest and suggestions in the meetings that I have held with them were of such assistance in the laying out of the work; to the public, who now have the opportunity of acting as judges of this performance and whose good - will alone can prove that the series justifies itself.

ALBERT BUSHNELL HART.

EDITOR'S INTRODUCTION

THIS first volume of the series supplies a needed link between the history of Europe and the history of early America; for whether it came through a Spanish, French, English, Dutch, or Swedish medium, or through the later immigrants from Germany, from Italy, and from the Slavic countries, the American conception of society and of government was originally derived from the European. Hence the importance at the outset of knowing what that civilization was at the time of colonization. Professor Cheyney (chapters i. and ii.) fitly begins with an account of mediæval commerce, especially between Europe and Asia, and the effect of the interposition of the Turks into the Mediterranean, and how, by their disturbance of the established course of Asiatic trade, they turned men's minds towards other routes to Asia by sea.

Thence he proceeds to show (chapter iii.) how the Italians in navigation and in map-making exhibited the same pre-eminence as in commerce and the arts, and why Italy furnished so many of the explorers of the western seas in the period of discovery. It is an easy transition in chapter iv. to

the dramatic story of the efforts of the Portuguese
to reach India round Africa.

The next step is to describe in some detail (chapters v. and vi.) the system of government and of
commerce which existed in Spain, France, and
Holland in the sixteenth century; and the book will
surprise the reader in its account of the effective and
far-reaching administration of the Spanish kingdom, the mother of so many later colonies. This
discussion is very closely connected with the account of Spanish institutions in the New World as described by Bourne in his *Spain in America* (volume
III. of the series), and we find the same terms, such
as "audiencia," "corregidor," and "Council of the
Indies" reappearing in colonial history.

A much-neglected subject in American history is
the development of great commercial companies,
which, in the hands of the English, planted their
first permanent colonies. To this subject Professor
Cheyney devotes two illuminating chapters (vii. and
viii.), in which he prints a list of more than sixty such
companies chartered by various nations, and then
selects as typical the English Virginia Company,
the Dutch West India Company, and the French
Company of New France, which he analyzes and
compares with one another. It is significant that
not one of these companies was Spanish, for that
country retained in its own hands complete control
both of its colonies and of their commerce.

Since English colonization was almost wholly

Protestant and added a new centre of Protestant influence, Professor Cheyney has, in two chapters
(ix. and x.), given some account of the Reformation
and of the religious wars of the sixteenth century.
He brings out not only the differences in doctrine but
in spirit, and shows how, by the Thirty Years' War,
Germany was excluded from the possibility of establishing American colonies, a lack which that
country has found it impossible to repair in our
day.

The mother-country for the American nation was
in greater part England; even Scotland and Ireland
contributed their numbers and their characteristics
only in the third and fourth generations of the colonies.   A considerable part of this volume, therefore
(chapters xi. to xvi.), is given up to a description of
the conditions of England at the time of the departure of the first colonists.   Everybody knows,
and nobody knows clearly, the religious questions
in England from Elizabeth to James II.   Here will
be found a distinct and vivid account of the struggle
between churchmen, Catholics, Puritans, and Independents for influence on the Church of England
or for supremacy in the state.   Why did the Catholics in general remain loyal?   Why were the Puritans punished?   Why were the Independents at
odds with everybody else?   Why did not Presbyterianism take root in England?   These are all questions of great moment, and their adjustment by
Professor Cheyney prepares the way for the account

of the Pilgrims who founded Plymouth colony in
Tyler's *England in America* (volume IV. of the
series).

An absolute essential for an understanding of
colonial history before the Revolution is a clear
idea of the political system of England, both in its
larger national form and in its local government.
Hence the importance of Professor Cheyney's chapters on English government. The kings' courts,
council, and Parliament all had their effect upon
the governors' courts, councils, and assemblies of the
various colonies. From the English practice came
the superb, fundamental notion of a right of representation and of the effectiveness of a delegated assembly. In local government the likeness was in
some respects even closer; and Professor Cheyney's
account of the English county court, and especially
of the township or parish, will solve many difficulties
in the later colonial history. In some ways Professor Cheyney's conclusions make more striking and
original the development of the astonishing New
England town-meetings.

As the volume begins with the rise of the exploring spirit, it is fitting that Prince Henry the Navigator should furnish the frontispiece. The bibliography deals more than those of later volumes
with a literature which has been a tangled thicket,
and will shorten the road for many teachers and
students of these subjects.

The significance of Professor Cheyney's volume is

that, without describing America or narrating American events, it furnishes the necessary point of departure for a knowledge of American history. The first question to be asked by the reader is, why did people look westward? And the answer is, because of their desire to reach the Orient. The second question is, what was the impulse to new habits of life and what the desire for settlements in distant lands? The answer is, the effect of the Reformation in arousing men's minds and in bringing about wars which led to emigration. The third question is, what manner of people were they who furnished the explorers and the colonists? The answer is found in these pages, which describe the Spaniard, the French, the Dutch, and especially the English, and show us the national and local institutions which were ready to be transplanted, and which readily took root across the sea.

AUTHOR'S PREFACE

THE history of America is a branch of that of Europe. The discovery, exploration, and settlement of the New World were results of European movements, and sprang from economic and political needs, development of enterprise, and increase of knowledge, in the Old World. The fifteenth century was a period of extension of geographical knowledge, of which the discovery of America was a part; the sixteenth century was a time of preparation, during which European events were taking place which were of the first importance to America, even though none of the colonies which were to make up the United States were yet in existence.

From the time of the settlement forward, the only population of America that has counted in history has been of European origin. The institutions that characterize the New World are fundamentally those of Europe. People and institutions have been modified by the material conditions of America; and the process of emigration gave a new direction to the development of American history from the very beginning; but the origin of the people, of their institutions, and of their history was none the less a European one. The beginnings of American history are therefore to be found in European conditions at the time of the foundation of the colonies.

Similar forces continued to exercise an influence in later times. The power and policy of home governments, successive waves of emigration, and numberless events in Europe had effects which were deeply felt in America. This influence of Europe upon America, however, became less and less as time passed on; and the development of the American nation has made its history constantly more independent. It is, therefore, only with some of the most important and earliest of these European occurrences and conditions that this book is occupied. The general relation of America to Europe is a subject that would require a vastly fuller treatment, and it is a subject which doubtless will increasingly receive the attention of scholars as our appreciation of the proper perspective of history becomes more clear.

In so wide a field as that of this volume, it has been necessary to use secondary materials for many statements; their aid is acknowledged in the footnotes and in the bibliography. Other parts, so far as space limits allowed, I have been able to work out from original sources. For much valuable information, suggestion, and advice also, I am indebted to friends and fellow-workers, and here gladly make acknowledgment for such assistance.

EDWARD POTTS CHEYNEY.

EUROPEAN BACKGROUND

OF AMERICAN HISTORY

EUROPEAN BACKGROUND
OF AMERICAN HISTORY

CHAPTER I

THE EAST AND THE WEST

(1200–1500)

TO set forth the conditions in Europe which favored the work of discovering America and of exploring, colonizing, and establishing human institutions there, is the subject and task of this book. Its period extends from the beginning of those marked commercial, political, and intellectual changes of the fifteenth century which initiated a great series of geographical discoveries, to the close, in the later years of the seventeenth century, of the religious wars and persecutions which did so much to make that century an age of emigration from Europe. During those three hundred years few events in European history failed to exercise some influence upon the fortunes of America. The relations of the Old World to the New were then constructive and fundamental to a degree not true of earlier or of later times. Before the fifteenth century events were only distantly preparing the way; after the seventeenth the centre of gravity of American history was transferred to America itself.

The crowding events, the prominent men, the creative thoughts, and the rapidly changing institutions which fill the history of western Europe during these three centuries cannot all be described in this single volume. It merely attempts to point out the leading motives for exploration and colonization, to show what was the equipment for discovery, and to describe the most significant of those political institutions of Europe which exercised an influence on forms of government in the colonies, thus sketching the main outlines of the European background of American history.

Many political, economic, intellectual, and personal factors combined to make the opening of our modern era an age of geographical discovery. Yet among these many causes there was one which was so influential and persistent that it deserves to be singled out as the predominant incentive to exploration for almost two hundred years. This enduring motive was the desire to find new routes from Europe to the far East.

Columbus sailed on his great voyage in 1492, "his object being to reach the Indies."[1] When

[1] Columbus's *Journal*, October 3, 21, 23, 24, etc. Cf. Bourne, *Spain in America*, chap. ii.

he discovered the first land beyond the Atlantic, he came to the immediate conclusion that he had reached the coast of Asia, and identified first Cuba and then Hayti with Japan. A week after his first sight of land he reports, "It is certain that this is the main-land and that I am in front of Zayton and Guinsay."[1] Even on his third voyage, in 1498, he is still of the opinion that South America is the main-land of Asia.[2] It was reported all through Europe that the Genoese captain had "discovered the coast of the Indies," and "found that way never before known to the East."[3] The name West Indies still remains as a testimony to the belief of the early explorers that they had found the Indies by sailing westward.

When John Cabot, in 1496, obtained permission from Henry VII. to equip an expedition for westward exploration, he hoped to reach "the island of Cipango (Japan) and the lands from which Oriental caravans brought their goods to Alexandria."[4] It is true that he landed on the barren shore of Labrador, and that what he descried from his vessel as he sailed southward was only the wooded coast of North America; but it was reported, and for a while believed, that the king of England had in this manner "acquired a part of Asia without drawing his sword."[5]

[1] Columbus's *Journal*, November 1.   [2] Columbus's will.
[3] Ramusio, *Raccolta di Navigazioni*, I., 414.
[4] Letter of Soncino, 1497, in Hart, *Contemporaries*, I., 70.
[5] *Ibid.* Cf. Bourne, *Spain in America*, chap. v.

In 1501 Gaspar Cortereal, in the service of the king of Portugal, pressed farther into the ice-bound arctic waters on the same quest, and with his companions became the first in the dreary list of victims sacrificed to the long search for a northwest passage.[1]

When the second generation of explorers learned that the land that had been discovered beyond the sea was not Asia, their first feeling was not exultation that a new world had been discovered, but chagrin that a great barrier, stretching far to the north and the south, should thus interpose itself between Europe and the eastern goal on which their eyes were fixed. Every navigator who sailed along the coast of North or South America looked eagerly for some strait by which he might make his way through, and thus complete the journey to the Spice Islands, to China, Japan, India, and the other lands of the ancient East.[2]

Verrazzano, in 1521, and Jacques Cartier, in 1534, 1535, and 1541, both in the service of the king of France, and Gomez, in the Spanish service, in 1521, were engaged in seeking this elusive passage.[3] For more than a hundred years the French traders and explorers along the St. Lawrence and the Great Lakes were led farther and farther into the wilderness by hopes of finding some western outlet which would make it possible for them to reach Cathay and India.

[1] Harrisse, *Les Cortereal.*

[2] Bourne, *Spain in America*, chap. viii.

[3] Pigeonneau, *Histoire du Commerce de la France*, II., 142–148.

Englishmen, with greater persistence than Spaniards, Portuguese, or French, pursued the search
for this northwestern route to India. To find such
a passage became a dream and a constantly renewed
effort of the navigators and merchants of the days
of Queen Elizabeth; the search for it continued into
the next century, even after colonies had been established in America itself; and a continuance of the
quest was constantly impressed by the government
and by popular opinion upon the merchants of the
Hudson Bay Company, till the eighteenth century.

A tradition grew up that there was a passage
through the continent somewhere near the fortieth
parallel. It was in the search for this passage that
Hudson was engaged, when, in the service of the
Dutch government, in 1609, he made the famous
voyage in the *Half Moon* and hit on the Hudson
River; just as in his first voyage he had tried to
reach the Indies by crossing the North Pole, and in
his second by following a northeast route.[1] Much
of the exploration of the coast of South America
was made with the same purpose. To reach India
was the deliberate object of Magellan when, in 1519
and 1520, he skirted the coast of that continent
and made his way through the southern straits.
The same objective point was intended in the
"Molucca Voyage" of 1526–1530, under the command of Sebastian Cabot,[2] as well as in other

---

[1] Asher, *Henry Hudson, the Navigator*, cxcii.–cxcvi.
[2] Beazley, *John and Sebastian Cabot*, 152.

South American voyages of Spanish explorers. Thus the search for a new route to the East lay at the back of many of those voyages of the fifteenth and sixteenth centuries, which gradually made America familiar to Europe.

The same object was sought in explorations to the eastward. The earliest voyages of the Portuguese along the coast of Africa, it is true, had other motives; but the desire to reach India grew upon the navigators and the sovereigns of that nation, and from the accession of John II., in 1481, every nerve was strained to find a route to the far East. Within one twelvemonth, in the years 1486 and 1487, three expeditions left the coast of Portugal seeking access to the East. The first of these, under Bartholomew Diaz, discovered the Cape of Good Hope; the second was an embassy of Pedro de Cavailham and Affonso de Paiva through the eastern Mediterranean to seek Prester John, a search which carried one of them to the west coast of India, the other to the east coast of Africa; the third was an exploring expedition to the northeast, which reached, for the first time, the islands of Nova Zembla.[1] The Portuguese ambition was finally crowned with success in the exploit of Vasco da Gama in reaching the coast of India by way of the southern point of Africa, in 1498; the Spanish expedition under Magellan reached the same lands by the westward route twenty years afterwards. Even after these successes, efforts con-

[1] Beazley, *Henry the Navigator.*

tinued to be made to reach China and the Indies by a northeast passage around the northern coast of Europe. Successive expeditions of Portuguese, English, French, and Dutch were sent out only to meet invariable failure in those icy seas, until the terrible hardships the explorers endured gradually brought conviction of the impracticability of this, as of the northwestern, route.

What was the origin of this eagerness to reach the Indies? Why did Portuguese, Spaniards, English, French, and Dutch vie with one another in centuries of effort not only to discover new lands, but to seek these sea-routes to the oldest of all lands? Why were the old lines of intercourse between the East and the West almost deserted, and a new group of maritime nations superseding the old Mediterranean and mid-European trading peoples? The answer to these questions will be found in certain changes which were in progress in those lands east of the Mediterranean Sea, which lie on the border-line between Europe and Asia. Through this region trade between Europe and the far East had flowed from immemorial antiquity; but in the fifteenth century its channels were obstructed and its stream much diminished.

Mediæval Europe was dependent for her luxuries on Asia Minor and Syria, Arabia and Persia, India and the Spice Islands, China and Japan. Precious stones and fabrics, dyes and perfumes, drugs and medicaments, woods, gums, and spices reached Europe by many devious and obscure routes, but all

from the eastward.   One of the chief luxuries of the
Middle Ages was the edible spices.   The monoto-
nous diet, the coarse food, the unskilful cookery of
mediæval Europe had all their deficiencies covered
by a charitable mantle of Oriental seasoning.   Wines
and ale were constantly used spiced with various
condiments.   In Sir Thopas's forest grew "notemuge
to putte in ale."[1]   The brewster in the *Vision of
Piers Plowman* declares:

> "I have good ale, gossip, Glutton wilt thou essay?
> 'What hast thou,' quoth he, 'any hot spices?'
> I have pepper and peony and a pound of garlic,
> A farthing-worth of fennel seed for fasting days."[2]

Froissart has the king's guests led to "the palace,
where wine and spices were set before them."[3]
The dowry of a Marseilles girl, in 1224, makes mention of "mace, ginger, cardamoms, and galangale."[4]
In the garden in the *Romaunt of the Rose*,

> "Ther was eek wexing many a spyce,
> As clow-gelofre, and licoryce,
> Gingere, and greyn de paradys,
> Canelle, and setewale of prys,
> And many a spyce delitable,
> To eten when men ryse fro table."[5]

When John Ball wished to draw a contrast between
the lot of the lords and the peasants, he said, "They

---

[1] Chaucer, *Sir Thopas*, line 52.
[2] Text C, passus VII., lines 355, etc.
[3] Froissart, *Chronicles*, book II., chap. lxxx.
[4] Quoted in Beazley, *Dawn of Modern Geography*, II., 433, *n.*
[5] Chaucer (Skeat's ed.), lines 1367-1372.

have wines, spices, and fine bread, when we have
only rye and the refuse of the straw." [1]   When old
Latimer was being bound to the stake he handed
nutmegs to his friends as keepsakes. [2]

Pepper, the most common and at the same time
the most valued of these spices, was frequently
treated as a gift of honor from one sovereign to another, or as a courteous form of payment instead of
money.   "Matilda de Chaucer is in the gift of the
king, and her land is worth £8, 2d., and 1 pound of
pepper and 1 pound of cinnamon and 1 ounce
of silk," reads a chance record in an old English
survey. [3]   The amount of these spices demanded
and consumed was astonishing.   Venetian galleys,
Genoese carracks, and other vessels on the Mediterranean brought many a cargo of them westward,
and they were sold in fairs and markets everywhere.
"Pepper-sack" was a derisive and yet not unappre-
ciative epithet applied by German robber-barons to
the merchants whom they plundered as they passed
down the Rhine.   For years the Venetians had a
contract to buy from the sultan of Egypt annually
420,000 pounds of pepper.   One of the first vessels
to make its way to India brought home 210,000
pounds.   A fine of 200,000 pounds of pepper was
imposed upon one petty prince of India by the
Portuguese in 1520.   In romances and chronicles, in
cook-books, trades-lists, and customs-tariffs, spices

---

[1] Froissart, *Chronicles*, book II., chap. lxxiii.
[2] Froude, *History of England*.   [3] *Festa de Nevil*, p. 16.

are mentioned with a frequency and consideration unknown in modern times.

Yet the location of "the isles where the spices grow" was very distant and obscure to the men of the Middle Ages. John Cabot, in 1497, said that he "was once at Mecca, whither the spices are brought by caravans from distant countries, and having inquired from whence they were brought and where they grew, the merchants answered that they did not know, but that such merchandise was brought from distant countries by other caravans to their home; and they further say that they are also conveyed from other remote regions." [1] Such lack of knowledge was pardonable, considering that Marco Polo, one of the most observant of travellers, after spending years in Asia, believed, mistakenly, that nutmegs and cloves were produced in Java.[2] It was only after more direct intercourse was opened up with the East that their true place of production became familiarly known in Europe. Nutmegs and mace, cloves and allspice were the native products of but one little spot on the earth's surface: a group of small islands, Banda, Amboyna, Ternäte, Tidore, Pulaway, and Prelaroon, the southernmost of the Moluccas, or Spice Islands, just under the equator, in the midst of the Malay Archipelago. Their light, volcanic soil, kept moist by the constant damp winds and hot by the beams of an overhead sun, furnished

---

[1] Letter of Soncino, in Hart, *Contemporaries*, I., 70.
[2] *Marco Polo* (Yule's ed.), book III., chap. vi., 217, *n.*

the natural conditions in which the spice-trees grew.
Here the handsome shrubs that yield the nutmeg
and its covering of mace produced a continuous crop
of flowers and fruit all the year around. Cloves
grew in the same islands, as clusters of scarlet buds,
hanging at the ends of the branches of trees which
rise to a greater height and grow with even a greater
luxuriance than the nutmeg-bushes.[1]

Pepper had scarcely a wider field of production.
The forests that clothed a stretch of the Malabar
coast of India some two hundred miles in length,
and extending some miles back into the interior,
were filled with an abundant growth of pepper-
vines. One of the earliest of European travellers
in India, Odoric de Pordenone, says: "The province
where pepper grows is named Malabar, and in no
other part of the world does pepper grow except in
this country. The forest where it grows is about
eighteen days in length."[2] John Marignolli, in
1348, also speaks of this district as "where the
world's pepper is produced."[3] Its habitat was,
however, somewhat more extensive, for in less abundance and of inferior quality the pepper-vines were
raised all the way south to Cape Comorin, and even
in the islands of Ceylon and Sumatra.

Cinnamon-bark was the special product of the

---

[1] Wallace, *The Malay Archipelago*, chap. xix.
[2] *Odoric de Pordenone* (d'Avezac's ed.), chap. x.
[3] Quoted in *Marco Polo* (Yule's ed.), II., 314, *n.*, and *Sir John Mandeville*, chap. xviii.

mountain-slopes in the interior of Ceylon, but this
also grew on the Indian coast to the westward,[1] and,
in the form of cassia of several varieties, was obtained
in Thibet, in the interior provinces of China, and in
some of the islands of the Malay Archipelago. Ginger was produced in many parts of the East; in
Arabia, India, and China. Odoric attributes to a
certain part of India "the best ginger that can be
found in the world;"[2] and Marco Polo records its
production of good quality in many provinces of
India and China.[3] A great number of other kinds
of spices were produced in various parts of the Orient, and consumed there or exported to Europe.

Precious stones were of almost as much interest
to the men of the Middle Ages as were spices. For
personal ornament and for the enrichment of shrines
and religious vestments, all kinds of beautiful stones
exercised an attraction proportioned to the small
number and variety of articles of beauty and taste
in existence.

> "No saphir ind, no rubè riche of price,
>   There lakked than, nor emeraud so grene."[4]

These were as much characteristic products of the
East as were spices. Diamonds, before the discovery of the American and African fields of produc-

---

[1] *Marco Polo* (Yule's ed.), book III., chaps. xiv., xxv.

[2] *Odoric de Pordenone* (d'Avezac's ed.), chap. x.

[3] *Marco Polo* (Yule's ed.), book II., chap. lxxx., book III.,
chaps. xxii., xxiv., xxv., xxvi.

[4] Chaucer, *Court of Love*, lines 78, 79.

tion, were found only in certain districts in the
central part of India, especially in the kingdom of
Mutfili or Golconda. Marco Polo tells the same
story of the method of getting them there that is
reported by Sindbad the Sailor.[1] Rubies, the next
most admired stone of the Middle Ages, were also
found, to some extent, in India, but more largely in
the island of Ceylon, in farther India, and, above all,
in the districts of Kerman, Khorassan, Badakshan,
and other parts of the highlands of Persia along
the Oxus and Jaxartes rivers.[2] Sapphires, garnets,
topaz, amethyst, and sardonyx were found in several of the same districts and also in the mountains
and streams of the west coast of India, from the
Gulf of Cambay all the way to Ceylon. The greatest markets in the world for these stones were the
two Indian cities of Pulicat and Calicut; the former
on the southeastern, the latter on the western shore
of the great peninsula.

Pearls were then, as now, produced only in a very
few places, principally in the strait between Ceylon
and the main-land of India, and in certain parts of
the Persian Gulf. In the native states in the south
of India they were, however, accumulated in enormous quantities, and scarcely a list of Eastern articles of merchandise omits mention of them. One
of the early European expeditions brought home

[1] *Marco Polo* (Yule's ed.), book III., chap. xix.; *Arabian
Nights.*
[2] Heyd, *Geschichte des Levantehandels*, II., App., I.

among its freight 400 pearls chosen for their size and beauty, and forty pounds of an inferior sort. The passion ot the native rajahs of India for gems had made the treasury of every petty prince a storehouse where vast numbers of precious stones had been garnered through thousands of years of wealth and civilization. This mass served as the booty of successive conquerors, and from time to time portions of it came into the hands of traders, along with stones newly obtained from natural sources. An early chronicler, in describing the return of the Polos to Venice from the East, tells how, from the seams of their garments, they took out the profits of their journeys in the East, in the form of "rubies, sapphires, carbuncles, diamonds, and emeralds." [1]

Drugs, perfumes, gums, dyes, and fragrant woods had much the same attraction as spices and precious stones, and came from much the same lands. The lofty and beautiful trees from which camphor is obtained grew only in Sumatra, Borneo, and certain provinces of China and Japan. Medicinal rhubarb was native to the mountainous districts of China, whence it was brought to the cities and the coast of that country on the backs of mules. Musk was a product of the border-lands of China and Thibet. The sugar-cane, although it grew widely in the East, from India and China to

[1] Ramusio, *Raccolta*, quoted in *Marco Polo* (Yule's ed.), book I., chap. xxxvii.

Syria and Asia Minor, was successfully managed so as to produce sugar in quantities that could be exported only in certain parts of Arabia and Persia. Bagdad was long famous for its sugar and articles preserved in sugar. Indigo was grown and prepared for dyeing purposes in India.[1]

Brazil wood grew more or less abundantly in all parts of the peninsula of India and as far east as Siam and southern China. This wood, from which was extracted a highly valued dye, made a particularly strong impression on the mediæval imagination. European travellers in India gave accounts of its being burned there for firewood, as their strangest tale of luxury and waste. It gave its name to a mythical island of Bresil, in the western seas, which was the subject of much speculation and romance. The same name was eventually applied to the South American country that now bears it, because it produced a similar dye-wood in large quantities. Sandal-wood and aloe-wood, which were valuable for their beautiful surface and fragrance when used in cabinet-work, and for their pleasant odor when burned as incense, grew only in certain parts of India.

Many articles of manufacture, attractive for their material, their workmanship, or their design, came from the same Eastern lands. Glass, of superior workmanship to anything known in Europe, came from Damascus, Samarcand, and Kadesia,

[1] Heyd, *Geschichte des Levantehandels*, II., App., I.

near Bagdad. Objects of fine porcelain came from China, and finally became known by the name of that country. A great variety of fabrics of silk and cotton, as well as those fibres in their raw state, came from Asia to Europe. Dozens of names of Eastern origin still remain to describe the silk, cotton, hair, and mixed fabrics which came to Europe from China, India, Cashmere, and the cities of Persia, Arabia, Syria, and Asia Minor. Brocade, damask, taffeta, sendal, satin, camelot, buckram, muslin, and many varieties of carpets, rugs, and hangings, which were woven in various parts of those lands, have always since retained the names of the places which early became famous for their manufacture. The metal-work of the East was scarcely less characteristic or less highly valued in the West, though its varieties have not left such specific names.[1]

Europe could feed herself with unspiced food, she could clothe herself with plain clothing, but for luxuries, adornments, refinements, whether in food, in personal ornament, or in furnishing her palaces, her manor - houses, her churches, or her wealthy merchants' dwellings, she must, in the fifteenth century, still look to Asia, as she had always done. It is true that in the later Middle Ages many articles of beauty and ornament were produced in the more advanced Western countries; but not spices nor drugs, nor precious stones, nor any great variety of dyes. Oriental rugs are even yet superior to

[1] Heyd, *Geschichte des Levantehandels*, II., App., 543–699.

any like productions of the West; and a vast number of other articles of Eastern origin then held, and indeed still hold, the markets.

In return for the goods which Europe brought from Asia a few commodities could be shipped eastward. European woollen fabrics seem to have been almost as much valued in certain countries of Asia as Eastern cotton and silk goods were in Italy, France, Germany, and England. Certain Western metals and minerals were highly valued in the East, especially arsenic, antimony, quicksilver, tin, copper, and lead.[1] The coral of the Mediterranean was much admired and sought after in Persia and India, and even in countries still farther east. Nevertheless the balance of trade was permanently in favor of the East, and quantities of gold and silver coin and bullion were used by European merchants to buy the finer wares in Asiatic markets.

There was much general trading in Eastern marts. Numbers of Oriental merchants, like Sindbad the Sailor and his company, "passed by island after island and from sea to sea and from land to land; and in every place by which we passed we sold and bought and exchanged merchandise." The articles enumerated above were almost without exception in demand throughout the whole East, and were bought by merchants in one place and sold in an-

---

[1] Birdwood, *Hand-book to the Indian Collection* (*Paris Universal Exhibition, 1878*), Appendix to catalogue of the British Colonies, pp. 1–110.

other. Marco Polo, in describing the Chinese city
of Zayton, says: "And I assure you that for one
shipload of pepper that goes to Alexandria or elsewhere destined for Christendom, there come a hundred such, aye and more too, to this haven of
Zayton." [1] Even as late as 1515, Giovanni d'Em-
poli, writing about China, says: "Ships carry spices
thither from these parts. Every year there go
thither from Sumatra 60,000 cantars of pepper and
15,000 or 20,000 from Cochin and Malabar—besides
ginger, mace, nutmegs, incense, aloes, velvet, European gold-wire, coral, woollens, etc." [2]

Nevertheless the attraction of the West was clearly
felt in the East. Extensive as were the local purchase
and sale of articles of luxury and use by merchants
throughout India, Persia, Arabia, Central Asia, and
China, yet the export of goods from those countries
to the westward was a form of trade of great importance, and one which had its roots deep in antiquity. A story of the early days tells how the
jealous brothers of Joseph, when they were considering what disposition to make of him, "lifted up their
eyes and looked, and, behold, a travelling company of
Ishmeelites came from Gilead, with their camels
bearing spicery and balm and myrrh, going to
carry it down to Egypt." [3] When the prophet cries,
"Who is this that cometh from Edom, with gar-

---

[1] *Marco Polo* (Yule's ed.), book II., chap. lxxxii
[2] Quoted in *ibid.*, book II., 188.
[3] Genesis, xxxvii. 25.

ments dyed red from Bozrah?" he is using two of
the most familiar names on the lines of west Asiatic
trade.   Solomon gave proof of his wisdom and made
his kingdom great by seizing the lines of the trade-
routes from Tadmor in the desert and Damascus
in the north to the upper waters of the Red Sea on
the south.   The "royal road" of the Persian kings
from Sousa to Ephesus made a long détour through
northern Asia Minor, which was inexplicable to
modern archæologists until it was perceived that it
was following the line of a trade-route much more
ancient than the Persian monarchy.[1]

The harbor of Berenice, named after the mother
of Ptolemy Philadelphus, was built by him as a place
of transit for goods from India which were to be
carried from the Red Sea to the Nile.[2]   Roman
roads followed ancient lines through Asia Minor and
Syria, and mediæval routes in turn, in many places,
passed by the remains of Roman stations.   Thus
the East and the West had been drawn together
by a mutual commercial attraction from the earliest
times, an attraction based on the respective natural
productions of the two continents, and favored by
the vast superiority of the East in the creation of
articles of beauty and usefulness.

[1] Ramsay, *The Historical Geography of Asia Minor*, chap. i.
[2] Hunter, *Hist. of British India*, I., 40.

CHAPTER II

ORIENTAL AND OCCIDENTAL TRADE-ROUTES
(1200–1500)

IN the fifteenth century Eastern goods regularly reached the West by one of three general routes through Asia. Each of these had, of course, its ramifications and divergences; they were like three river-systems, changing their courses from time to time and occasionally running in divided streams, but never ceasing to follow the general course marked out for them by great physical features. The southernmost of these three routes was distinguished by being a sea-route in all except its very latest stages. Chinese and Japanese junks and Malaysian proas gathered goods from the coasts of China and Japan and the islands of the great Malay Archipelago, and bought and sold along the shores of the China Sea till their westward voyages brought them into the straits of Malacca and they reached the ancient city of that name. This was one of the great trading points of the East. Few Chinese traders passed beyond it, though the more enterprising Malays made that the centre rather than the western limit of their commerce. Many Arabian traders also came there from India to sell their goods and to buy the products of the islands of the archipelago, and the goods which the Chinese traders had brought from still farther East.

The Indian and Arabian merchants who came to Malacca as buyers were mostly from Calicut and other ports on the Malabar coast, and to these home ports they brought back their purchases. To these markets of southwestern India were also brought the products of Ceylon, of the eastern coast, and of the shore of farther India. From port to port along the Malabar coast passed many coasting vessels, whose northern and western limit was usually the port of Ormuz at the entrance to the Persian Gulf. A great highway of commerce stretched from this trading and producing region, and from the Malabar ports directly across the Arabian Sea to the entrance of the Red Sea. When these waters were reached, many ports of debarkation from Mecca northward might be used. But the prevailing north winds made navigation in the Red Sea difficult, and most of the goods which eventually reached Europe by this route were landed on the western coast, to be carried by caravan to Kus, in Egypt, and then either by caravans or in boats down the line of the Nile to Cairo.

Cairo was a very great city, its population being occupied largely in the transmission of goods. A fifteenth-century traveller counted 15,000 boats in

the Nile at one time;[1] and another learned that
there were in all some 36,000 boats belonging in
Cairo engaged in traffic up and down the river.[2]
From Cairo a great part of these goods were taken
for sale to Alexandria, which was in many ways as
much a European as an African city. Thus a regular route stretched along the southern coasts of
Asia, allowing goods produced in all lands of the
Orient to be gathered up in the course of trade and
transferred as regular articles of commerce to the
southeastern shores of the Mediterranean Sea.

A second route lay in latitudes to the north of
that just described. From the ports on the west
coast of India a considerable proportion of the goods
destined ultimately for Europe made their way
northward to the Persian Gulf. A line of trading
cities extending along its shores from Ormuz near
the mouth of the gulf to Bassorah at its head served
as ports of call for the vessels which carried this
merchandise. Several of these coast cities were also
termini of caravan routes entering them from the
eastward, forming a net-work which united the various provinces of Persia and reached through the
passes of Afghanistan into northern India. From
the head of the Persian Gulf one branch of this
route went up the line of the Tigris to Bagdad.
From this point goods were taken by caravan through
Kurdistan to Tabriz, the great northern capital of

[1] Piloti, quoted in Heyd, *Geschichte des Levantehandels*, II., 43.
[2] Ibn Batuta, quoted, *ibid*.

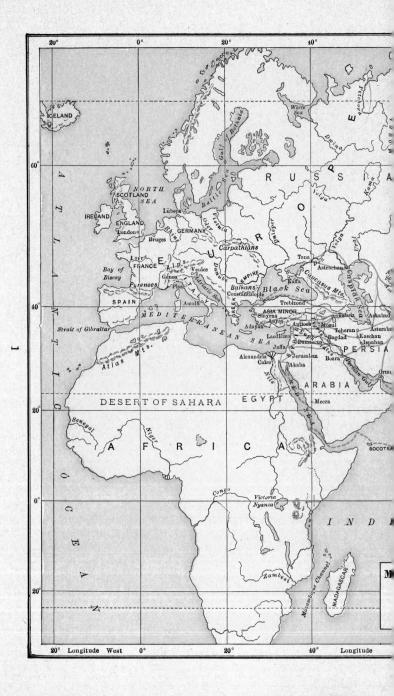

ICELAND

ATLANTIC

White Sea

Dwina

RUSSIA

Kama

E

Petchora

Gulf of Bothnia

NORTH SEA

SCOTLAND

Baltic Sea

Volga

Oka

Vistula

IRELAND

ENGLAND

London

Bruges

Lübeck

GERMANY

Oder

Dnieper

Elbe

Rhine

Don

Carpathians

Tana

Astrachan

Caspian Sea

EUROPE

Loire

FRANCE

A L P S

Venice

Bay of Biscay

Genoa

Adriatic Sea

EMPIRE

Balkans

Caucasus Mts.

Pisa

ITALY

Constantinople

Black Sea

Kaffa

Askabad

Pyrenees

SPAIN

Amalfi

Trebizond

Asterabad

Strait of Gibraltar

MEDITERRANEAN SEA

ASIA MINOR

Smyrna

Layas

Tabriz

Teheran

PERSIA

Antioch

Mosul

Kaschan

Ispahan

Adana

Laodicea

Damascus

Bagdad

Atlas Mts.

Alexandria

Cairo

Jaffa

Jerusalem

Akaba

Bozra

Orm

Persian Gulf

Red Sea

DESERT OF SAHARA

EGYPT

ARABIA

Mecca

Senegal

Niger

Nile

SOCOTRA

A F R I C A

Congo

Victoria Nyanza

I N D I

OCEAN

Zambesi

Mozambique Channel

MADAGASCAR

N

M

20°   0°   20°   40°

60°

40°

20°

0°

20°

20° Longitude West   0°   20°   40°   Longitude

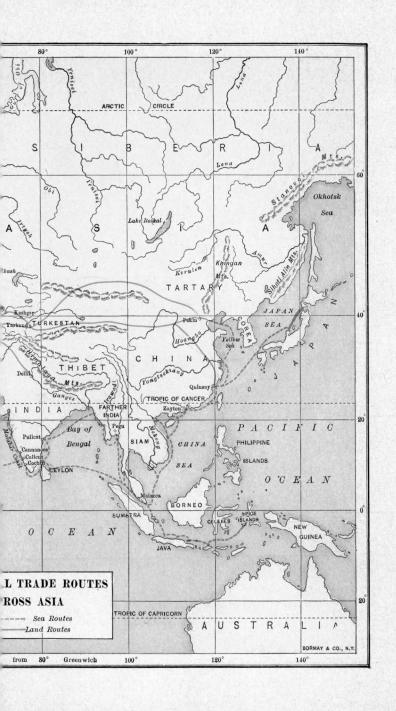

MEDIÆVAL TRADE ROUTES
ACROSS ASIA

- - - - *Sea Routes*
——— *Land Routes*

BORMAY & CO., N.Y.

from 80° Greenwich

Persia, and thence westward either to the Black Sea
or to Layas on the Mediterranean. Another branch
was followed by the trains of camels which made
their way from Bassorah along the tracks through
the desert which spread like a fan to the westward,
till they reached the Syrian cities of Aleppo, Antioch,
and Damascus. They finally reached the Mediterranean coast at Laodicea, Tripoli, Beirut, or Jaffa,
while some goods were carried even as far south as
Alexandria.

Far to the north of this complex of lines of trade
lay a third route between the far East and the West,
extending from the inland provinces of China westward across the great desert of Obi, south of the
Celestial mountains to Lake Lop; then passing
through a series of ancient cities, Khotan, Yarkand,
Kashgar, Samarcand, and Bokhara, till it finally
reached the region of the Caspian Sea. This main
northern route was joined by others which crossed
the passes of the Himalayas and the Hindoo-Kush,
and brought into a united stream the products of
India and China.[1] A journey of eighty to a hundred days over desert, mountain, and steppes lay by
this route between the Chinese wall and the Caspian.
From still farther north in China a parallel road to
this passed to the north of the desert and the mountains, and by way of Lake Balkash, to the same ancient and populous land lying to the east of the Caspian Sea. Here the caravan routes again divided.

[1] Hunter, *Hist. of British India*, I., 31.

Some led to the southwestward, where they united with the more central routes described above and eventually reached the Black Sea and the Mediterranean through Asia Minor and Syria. Others passed by land around the northern coast of the Caspian, or crossed it, reaching a further stage at Astrakhan. From Astrakhan the way led on by the Volga and Don rivers, till its terminus was at last reached on the Black Sea at Tana near the mouth of the Don, or at Kaffa in the Crimea.[1]

Along these devious and dangerous routes, by junks, by strange Oriental craft, by river-boats, by caravans of camels, trains of mules, in wagons, on horses, or on human shoulders, the products of the East were brought within reach of the merchants of the West. These routes were insecure, the transportation over them difficult and expensive. They led over mountains and deserts, through alternate snow and heat. Mongol conquerors destroyed, from time to time, the cities which lay along the lines of trade, and ungoverned wild tribes plundered the merchants who passed through the regions through which they wandered. More regularly constituted powers laid heavy contributions on merchandise, increasing many-fold the price at which it must ultimately be sold. The routes by sea had many of the same dangers, along with others peculiar to themselves. The storms of the Indian Ocean and its ad-

[1] Heyd, *Geschichte des Levantehandels*, II., 68–254.

jacent waters were destructive to vast numbers of the frail vessels of the East; piracy vied with storms in its destructiveness; and port dues were still higher than those of inland marts.

With all these impediments, Eastern products, nevertheless, arrived at the Mediterranean in considerable quantities. The demands of the wealthy classes of Europe and the enterprise of European and Asiatic merchants were vigorous enough to bring about a large and even an increasing trade; and the three routes along which the products of the East were brought to those who were able to pay for them were never, during the Middle Ages, entirely closed. They found their western termini in a long line of Levantine cities extending along the shores of the Black Sea and of the eastern Mediterranean from Tana in the north to Alexandria in the south. In these cities the spices, drugs, dyes, perfumes, precious stones, silks, rugs, metal goods, and other fabrics and materials produced in far Eastern lands were always obtainable by European merchants.

The merchants who bought these goods in the market-places of the Levant for the purpose of distributing them throughout Europe were for the most part Italians from Pisa, Venice, or Genoa; Spaniards from Barcelona and Valencia; or Provençals from Narbonne, Marseilles, and Montpellier.[1] They were not merely travelling buyers and sellers,

[1] Beazley, *Dawn of Modern Geography*, II., chap. vi.

but in many cases were permanent residents of the eastern Mediterranean lands. In the first half of the fifteenth century there were settlements of such merchants in Alexandria in Egypt; in Acre, Beirut, Tripoli, and Laodicea on the Syrian coast; at Constantinople, and in a group of cities skirting the Black Sea. Even in the more inland cities of Syria, such as Damascus, Aleppo, and Antioch, Italians were established.[1] The position of European merchants varied in the different cities on this trading border between the East and the West, from that of mere foreign traders, living on bare sufferance in the midst of a hostile community, to that of citizens occupying what was practically an outlying Venetian or Genoese or Pisan colony.

In the greater number of cases the Italian and other European merchants had quarters, or fondachi, granted to them in the Eastern cities by the Saracen emirs of Egypt and Syria, or by the Greek emperor of Asia Minor, Constantinople, and Trebizond. These fondachi were buildings, or groups of dwellings and warehouses, often including a market - place, offices, and church, where the merchants of some Italian or Provençal city carried on their business affairs according to their own rules, under permission granted to them by the local ruler. A Genoese or Venetian fondaco was usually governed by a consul or bailiff, appointed by the home government, or elected among themselves with the approval of the

---

[1] Heyd, *Geschichte des Levantehandels*, II., 67.

senate and doge at home. Two or more advisers
were usually provided by the home government to
act with the consul in negotiations with the local
government. In more important matters embassies
were sent directly from the doge to the ruler on
whose toleration or self-interest the whole settlement was dependent.

For whole centuries Italians had made up an appreciable part of the population of many cities of
the Levant; the galleys of Venice, Genoa, and Pisa
lay at their wharves discharging produce of the
West and loading the products of the East; a large
part of the income of the local potentates, or governors, was made up of export and import duties,
harbor charges, and other impositions paid by the
Western merchants. The prosperity of these Greek
and Saracen seaboard cities was as largely dependent
on this trade as was that of the merchants who came
there for its sake.[1]

We have seen how the merchandise of the far
East flowed to the Eastern cities of the Mediterranean, and how it was gathered there into the hands
of European merchants. It remains to follow the
routes by which it was redistributed throughout
Europe. Both Genoa and Venice had possessions
in the Greek Archipelago which formed stepping-
stones between the home cities and their fondachi in
the cities of the Levant. Trading from port to port

[1] Heyd, *Geschichte des Levantehandels*, I., 165, 168, 316, 363,
414, 443, etc., II., 430, 435, etc.

along these lines of connection, or sometimes carrying cargoes unbroken from their most distant points of trade, the galleys of the Italian, French, or Spanish traders brought Eastern goods along with the products of the Mediterranean islands and shores to the home cities. These cities then became new distributing-points of Eastern and Mediterranean goods as well as of their own home products.

Venice may fairly be taken as a type of the cities which subsisted on this trade. Her merchants were the most numerous, widely spread, and enterprising; her trade the most firmly organized, her hold on the East the strongest. To her market-places and warehouses a vast quantity of goods was constantly brought for home consumption and re-export. From Venice, yearly fleets of galleys went out destined to various points and carrying various cargoes. One of these fleets, after calling at successive ports in Illyria, Italy, Sicily, Spain, and Portugal, and after detaching some galleys for Southampton, Sandwich, or London, in England, reached, as its ultimate destination, Bruges, in Flanders.[1]

Other goods were taken by Venetian merchants through Italy and across the mountains by land. Most of the re-export from Venice by land was done by foreigners. Over the Alps came German merchants from Nuremberg, Augsburg, Ulm, Regensburg, Constance, and other cities of the valleys of the Danube and the Rhine. They had a large building

---

[1] Brown, *Cal. of State Pap.*, *Venetian*.

in Venice set apart for their use by the senate, the "Fondaco dei Tedeschi," much like those settlements which the Venetians themselves possessed in the cities of the Levant.[1] The goods which they purchased in Venice they carried in turn all through Germany, to the fairs of France, and to the cities of the Netherlands. Merchants of the Hanseatic League bought these goods at Bruges or Antwerp or in the south German cities, and carried them, along with their own northern products, to England, to the countries on the Baltic, and even into Poland and Russia, meeting at Kiev a more direct branch of the Eastern trade which proceeded from Astrakhan and Tana northward up the Volga and the Don.

Thus the luxuries of the East were distributed through Europe. With occasional interruptions, frequent changes in detail, and constant difficulties, the same general routes and methods of transfer and exchange had been followed for centuries. It was the oldest, the most extensive, and the most lucrative trade known to Europe. It stretched over the whole known world, its lines converging from the eastward and southward to the cities of Syria, Asia Minor, and the Black Sea coast, and diverging thence to the westward and northward throughout Europe.

With the close of the Middle Ages this ancient and well-established trade showed evident signs of dis-

[1] Simonsfeld, *Der Fondaco dei Tedeschi in Venedig*, II.

organization and decline.   The Levant was suffering
from changes which interrupted its commerce and
which made the old trade-routes that passed through
it almost impracticable.   The principal cause for
this process of decay and failure was the rise of the
Ottoman Turks as a conquering power.   About 1300
a petty group of Turks, in the heart of Asia Minor,
under a chieftain named Osman, began a career of
extension of their dominions by conquering the
other provinces of Turkish or Greek origin and
allegiance in their vicinity.[1]   Little by little the
Osmanli pushed their borders out in every direction
till they reached the Mediterranean, the Sea of Mar-
mora, and the Black Sea.   Within a century and a
half, by the close of the reign of Murad II., in 1451,
they had built vessels on the Ægean, plundered the
Greek islands and laid them under tribute, crossed
the Dardanelles and made conquests far up in the
Balkan Peninsula, pressed close upon the Christian
cities along the south coast of the Black Sea, and
reduced the possessions of the Greek Empire to a
narrow strip of land around Constantinople.[2]   The
Turkish Empire was admirably organized for military and financial purposes and governed by a
series of able sultans.

Thus a great power arose on the border-line between the Orient and the Occident, of which the
merchant states of Italy and the West evidently had

[1] Zinkeisen, *Geschichte des Osmanischen Reiches in Europa*, I.,
65–132.   [2] *Ibid.*, 184–798.

to take account. But its existence did not at first
appear to be necessarily destructive to their interests. In many cases comparatively favorable commercial treaties were made with the Turkish sultans,
and the facile Italians modified their trading to
meet the new conditions.[1] Nevertheless, with the
Turks there could be no such close connection as that
which had existed between the Western traders and
the old-established states in the East, under which
they enjoyed practical independence so long as they
paid the money. The Turks were not only Mohammedans, they were barbarians; they added to the
Moslem contempt for the Christian the warrior's
contempt for the mere merchant. They were without appreciation for culture or even for refined
luxury.

The conquests of the Turks proceeded steadily to
their completion. In 1452 Sultan Mohammed II.
built the fort of Rumili Hissari, on the European side
of the Bosporus, and gave the commander orders to
lay every trading-vessel that passed the straits
under tribute. The next year saw the final siege,
the heroic resistance, and the fall of Constantinople.

Among its defenders were Venetians, Genoese,
Florentines, and Italian colonists from various settlements, summoned to the help of their coreligion-
ists against the Mohammedans. On its capture all
their goods were plundered, their leaders beheaded,

[1] Heyd, *Geschichte des Levantehandels*, II., 259, 260, 267, 275,
284, etc.

8106

those of rank held for ransom, and the common men slaughtered or sold as slaves.[1] The neighboring colony of Pera was left to the Genoese, but humbled to the rank of a Turkish village with a sadly restricted trade. Trade was allowed to and from Constantinople, but all the old privileges were abrogated, and the city was now the capital of a semi-barbarous ruler and race, who placed but small value on things brought by trade and continually engaged in war.

Especially destructive to trade were the wars between the Turks and the Italian colonists of the eastern Mediterranean. Such wars were inevitable. In the progress of their career of conquest the Ottoman fleets early attacked the island possessions of Venice and Genoa in the Ægean and their independent or semi-independent settlements on the shores of the Black Sea. Efforts for the defence of these involved war between the home governments and the rising Eastern power. From 1463 to 1479 war between the Turkish Empire and Venice raged in Syria and Asia Minor, in the islands of the eastern Mediterranean, on the main-land of Greece, and northward to Albania. The Italian republic lost some of its best territories, including the Greek islands, and only obtained permission to take its vessels through the Dardanelles and the Bosporus on payment of a heavy annual sum.[2] The few remaining

---

[1] Pears, *The Destruction of the Greek Empire.*
[2] Heyd, *Geschichte des Levantehandels*, II., 325-332.

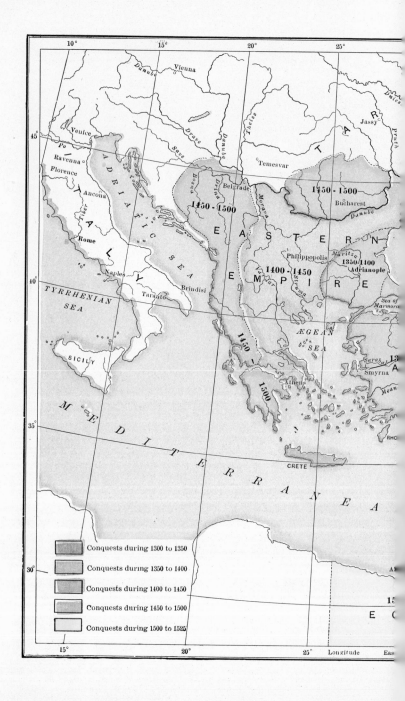

Conquests during 1300 to 1350
Conquests during 1350 to 1400
Conquests during 1400 to 1450
Conquests during 1450 to 1500
Conquests during 1500 to 1525

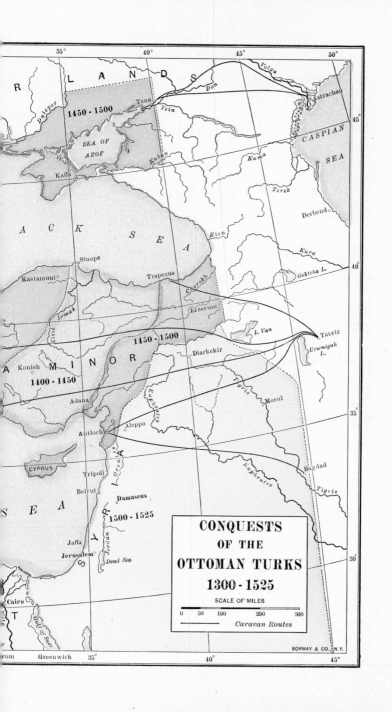

CONQUESTS

OF THE

OTTOMAN TURKS

1300 - 1525

SCALE OF MILES

0   50   100   200   300

Caravan Routes

island possessions of Genoa were also lost—Lesbos in
1462, Chios in 1466.   A brave defence of their island
homes was made by the Italians, but one after another these succumbed to the terrible attacks of the
Turks.[1]

In the mean time the possessions still farther east
had the same fate.   Immediately after the downfall
of Constantinople the Turks placed a fleet upon the
Black Sea and attacked the colonies on the north
coast at Kaffa, Soldaia, and Tana, and on the south
at Trebizond and other ports.   One after another
these cities were placed under tribute; repeated battles destroyed their possessions; their population
was enslaved and their property plundered.   In 1461
Trebizond was captured; in 1500 Kaffa was finally
conquered and the whole Christian population,
after many sufferings, carried off to live as a subject
race in a suburb of Constantinople.   In 1499 and
1500 Venice lost almost all the rest of her possessions.

Some of the cities of the West which had never had
landed possessions in the East fared better under
the Ottoman than did Venice and Genoa.   Florentines, Ragusans, and men of Ancona, for some decades, took their galleys from port to port of the
Turkish coasts and islands, or passed as individual
traders back along the trade-routes seeking goods
for export.   Nevertheless, the flow of Eastern goods
along these routes was becoming less and less; the

[1] Bury, in *Cambridge Modern History*, I., 75–81.

internal wars of rival Tartar rulers and those between Tartars and Turks threw the northern routes and parts of the central route into even more than their usual confusion; and the lessened demands at the ports of the Black Sea and Asia Minor discouraged the bringing of goods from the Eastern sources of supply.

The Turkish thirst for conquest brought under the control of that race, in the half-century between 1450 and 1500, half the western termini of the trade-routes with the East. It crushed out all semblance of independence in the settlements of the European merchants in Asia Minor and on the Black Sea, and left to them a bare foothold for purposes of trade under the most burdensome restrictions. These conquests were very destructive to life and property. Mercantile firms failed, old families died out, the mother-states were exhausted, and the flow of merchandise was dried up. The system of trade which had been in existence in these regions for centuries was quite destroyed by this violence.

The central and southern routes for a time remained open; indeed, the blocking of the more northerly outlets sent a greater proportion of the trade in Eastern products through Syria and through the Red Sea ports. The markets at Damascus, Aleppo, Beirut, and Alexandria were better filled than ever with the products of the East. Even the Genoese, who had so completely lost their prosperity, still had a fondaco in Alexandria in 1483; while the

Venetians, notwithstanding their losses in the north-eastern Mediterranean and their bitter struggles with the Turks, continued to make closer and closer trade arrangements with the Saracen emirs of the Syrian cities and the Mameluke sultans of Egypt. Under heavy financial burdens and amid constant disputes they still kept up an active trade. Ten or fifteen galleys came every year from Italy, France, and Spain to Alexandria, which in the later years of the fifteenth century was by far the greatest market for spices in the world. Even Florence, in the later years of the fifteenth century, opened up a trade with Egypt and Syria.[1]

The southeastern Mediterranean was now destined to be swept by the same storm as the other parts of the Levant. In the early years of the sixteenth century the Ottoman army invaded Syria and Egypt. In 1516 the sultan captured Damascus; in 1517 he entered Cairo as a conqueror. Syria and Egypt became a part of the Turkish Empire, as Asia Minor, the Balkan Peninsula, and the coasts of the Black Sea had already done. Treaties, it is true, were even yet formed by which Venice, at the price of humiliating conditions, obtained permission from the Ottoman government to continue a heavily burdened trade in the blighted cities of Egypt and Syria, as she was already doing in Constantinople. But the process by which Turkish conquest was attained, and the whole spirit and policy of that

[1] Heyd, *Geschicte des Levantehandels*, II., 427-494.

power, were adverse to trade between the East and West.

The old trade-routes between Asia and Europe were effectually and permanently blocked by the Turkish conquests. Not only routes of trade, but methods of exchange, forms of transportation, and, in fact, the whole system by which Eastern goods had been brought to Europe for centuries, were interrupted, undermined, and made almost impracticable. During this period the city republics of Italy, which had been the chief European intermediaries of this trade, were losing their prosperity, their wealth, their enterprise, and their vigor. This was due, as a matter of fact, to a variety of causes, internal and external, political and economic; but the sufferings in the wars with the Turks and the adverse conditions of the Levant trade on which their prosperity primarily rested were far the most important causes of their decline.

Thus the demand of European markets for Eastern luxuries could no longer be met satisfactorily by the old methods; yet that demand was no less than it had been, and the characteristic products of the East were still sought for in all the market-places of Europe. Indeed, the demand was increasing. As Europe in the fifteenth century became more wealthy and more familiar with the products of the whole world, as the nobles learned to demand more luxuries, and a wealthy merchant class grew up which was able to gratify the same tastes as the nobles, the demand of the West upon the East became more insistent than ever. Therefore, the men, the nation, the government that could find a new way to the East might claim a trade of indefinite extent and extreme profit.

This is the explanation of that eager search for new routes to the Indies which lay at the back of so many voyages of discovery of the fifteenth and sixteenth centuries. Southward along the coast of Africa, in the hope that that continent could be rounded to the southeast; northward along the coast of Europe in search of a northeast passage; westward relying on the sphericity of the earth, and hoping that the distance from the west coast of Europe to the east coast of Asia would prove not to be interminable; after America was reached, again northward and southward to round and pass beyond that barrier, and thus reach Asia—such was the progress of geographical exploration for a century and a half, during which men gradually became familiar with a great part of the earth's surface. A study of the history of trade-routes corroborates the fact disclosed by many other lines of study—that the discovery of America was no isolated phenomenon; it was simply one step in the development of the world's history. Changes in the eastern Mediterranean led men to turn their eyes in other directions looking for other sea routes to the East. When they had done so, along with much else that was new, America was disclosed to their vision.

To follow out all the remote effects of the up-
heaval in western Asia and eastern Europe would
lead too far afield: but the diversion of commercial
interest was only a part: the restless energies of the
Latin races of southern Europe turned into a new
channel; search for trade led to discovery, discovery
to exploration, exploration to permanent settlement; and settlement to the creation of a new centre
of commercial and political interest, and eventually
to the rise of a new nation.

CHAPTER III

ITALIAN CONTRIBUTIONS TO EXPLORATION

(1200–1500)

ALTHOUGH in the fifteenth century Italy lost the commercial leadership which she had so long held, she did not cease to be the teacher of the other countries of Europe. In those arts which lay at the base of exploration, as in so many other fields, Italy was far in advance of all other Western countries. Through the Middle Ages she preserved much of the heritage of ancient skill and learning; by her Renaissance studies she recovered much that had been temporarily lost; and in geographical science she early made progress of her own. "The greatness of the Germans, the courtesy of the French, the valor of the English, and the wisdom of the Italians" is the tribute paid by a fifteenth-century Portuguese chronicler to the nations of his time, and this "wisdom of the Italians" he especially connects with exploration and navigation.[1]

As a nation Italy played but a slight part in the discoveries of the fifteenth and sixteenth centuries; but through her scattered sons she used her fine in-

[1] Azurara, *Chronicle of Guinea*, chap. ii.

telligence to initiate and guide much of the work
that was completed by the ruder but more efficient
and vigorous nations of the Atlantic seaboard.
Educated men from Venice, Genoa, Pisa, and Florence emigrated to other lands, carrying with them
science, skill, and ingenuity unknown except in
the advanced and enterprising Italian city republics
and principalities. Italian mathematicians made
the calculations on which all navigation was based;
Italian cartographers drew maps and charts; Italian
ship-builders designed and built the best vessels of
the time; Italian captains commanded them, and
very often Italian sailors made up their crews; while
at least in the earlier period Italian bankers advanced the funds with which the expeditions were
equipped and sent out.

Columbus, Cabot, Verrazzano, and Vespucci were
simply the most famous of the Italians who during
this period made discoveries while in the service of
other governments. The Venetian Cadamosto led
repeated and successful expeditions for Prince Henry
of Portugal; Perestrello, the discoverer of Porto
Santo, in the Madeiras, and Antonio de Noli, the
discoverer of the Cape Verd Islands, were both
Italians.[1] This was no new condition of affairs.
In the time of Edward II. and Edward III., in the
service of England, we find the names of Genoese
such as Pesagno and Uso de Mare. Another Genoese, Emanuel Pesagno, was appointed as the first

---

[1] Ruge, *Der Zeitalter der Entdeckungen*, 217.

hereditary admiral of the fleet of Portugal, and by the terms of his engagement was required to keep the Portuguese navy provided with twenty Genoese captains of good experience in navigation. Of the sixty men who made up the complement of Magellan's fleet of 1519, in the service of Spain, twenty-three were Italians, mostly Genoese.[1] At the same time all Spanish taxes were administered by Genoese bankers, and they or other Italians had a monopoly of all loanable capital.[2]

Long before the great period of discoveries Italians contributed to the increase of geographical knowledge by travel and narratives of travel over the world as it was already known, but only known vaguely and by dim report. Down to the middle of the thirteenth century the total knowledge of the lands and waters of the globe possessed by the educated men of Europe was not appreciably greater than it had been a thousand years earlier. The disintegration of the old Roman world, the more stationary habits of life, and the narrower interests of men during the early Middle Ages were unfavorable to travel.

The later Middle Ages were not lacking in keen intellect, in large knowledge, in powers of systematization and elaboration of what has already been acquired; but they had neither the material equipment nor the mental temperament to carry the

---

[1] Navarrete, quoted in Ruge, *Zeitalter*, 466, *n.*
[2] Hume, *Spain, Its Greatness and Decay*, 87.

boundaries of knowledge further. What was known of the world to Ptolemy in the second century made up the sum of knowledge possessed by the geographers of all the following centuries to the thirteenth. Indeed, the mediæval tendency to establish symmetrical measurements, to adopt fanciful explanations, and to find analogies in all things, obscured earlier knowledge and made geographers of the twelfth and thirteenth centuries less correct in their knowledge of the world than were those of the second or the third.[1]

The discoveries, conquests, and settlements of the Northmen in the north of Europe and the northern Atlantic were so detached from the knowledge of the south and came to a pause so early in time that notwithstanding their potential value they contributed practically nothing to the general geographical knowledge of Europe. Nor did Christian, Jewish, or Arabic accounts of Eastern lands written by travellers of the eleventh, twelfth, and early thirteenth centuries become widely known or influential.[2] Even the knowledge brought home by the Crusaders was of a restricted territory, most of it already comparatively familiar; and therefore they added little to the common stock.

About the middle of the thirteenth century, however, began a series of journeys which were more fully recorded in narratives more widely circulated

[1] Beazley, *Dawn of Modern Geography.*
[2] *Ibid.,* II., chaps. i.–iv.

and in a more receptive period. Three incentives habitually carry men into distant and unknown lands—missionary zeal, desire for trade, and curiosity. Actuated by one or other of these influences, an increasing number of Europeans visited lands far beyond the eastern terminations of the trade-routes, and some of them brought back reports of which the influence was wide and lasting.

Among the earliest and most observant were a succession of Franciscan friars, sent after 1245 on missionary journeys to the court of the ruler of the great Tartar Empire, which was then so rapidly overspreading Asia and eastern Europe. The first of these was John de Plano Carpini, a native of Naples, who belonged to a Franciscan house near Perugia. He went through Bohemia, Poland, southern Russia, and the vast steppes of Turkestan, and found the Khan at Karakorum, in Mongolia. He was two years on the journey, and after his return wrote an exact and interesting account of his observations and experiences.[1]

A few years afterwards William de Rubruquis—a Fleming in this case, not an Italian—was sent to visit the Mongol emperor by Louis IX. when he was in the East. He followed a more southerly route than Carpini, skirting the northern shores of the Black Sea, the Caspian, and the Sea of Aral, and then passing northward to Karakorum. Returning he crossed the Caucasus and passed through Persia

Travels of John de Plano Carpini (d'Avezac's ed.)

and the lands of the Turks, finally reaching the Mediterranean through Syria. The account which he wrote of his adventures was much fuller than that of Plano Carpini, and gives descriptions of China as well as of the central Asiatic lands.[1]

Just at the beginning of the next century two other travellers, John de Monte Corvino[2] and Odoric de Pordenone,[3] both Italians, made journeys through Persia, India, southern Asia, and China, and later wrote accounts of these more southern lands quite as full as were those already mentioned concerning the northern parts of the great eastern continent.

The most famous of all mediæval travellers in the East were the Venetian merchants Nicolo and Matteo Polo and their nephew Marco. These enterprising traders, leaving their warehouses in Soldaia on the Crimea, in two successive journeys made their way along the northern and central traderoutes to Pekin, in northern China, or Cathay, which had become the capital of the Great Khan. For almost twenty years the Polos were attached to the court of Kublai Khan, the nephew, Marco, rising higher and higher in the graces of that ruler.

Marco Polo was one of the well-known type of Italian adventurers who appeared at foreign courts, and, with the versatility of their race, made them-

[1] *Travels of William de Rubruquis* (d'Avezac's ed.).
[2] Beazley, *Dawn of Modern Geography*, II., chap. v.
[3] *Travels of Odoric de Pordenone* (d'Avezac's ed.).

selves useful, and indeed indispensable, to their masters. He learned the languages of the East, and went upon missions for the Great Khan to all parts of his vast empire. When, in 1292, the Polos obtained permission to return home they followed the longest and most important of the three main trade-routes which have been described. They sailed from Zaiton, a seaport of China, and passing along the shores of Tonquin, Java, and farther India, made their way from port to port through the Bay of Bengal to Ceylon, then to the Malabar coast of India, along which they passed to Cambay, and thence through the Red Sea to Cairo, and so to Venice. Their journey homeward from China, with its long detentions in the East Indies, took almost three years.

All the world knows of Marco Polo's subsequent experiences in Venice, his capture and imprisonment in Genoa, the stories of his travels with which he whiled away the weary days of his captivity, and the gathering of these into a book which spread widely through Europe within the next few years and has been eagerly read ever since.[1]

Neither the travels of Marco Polo nor those of his predecessors or immediate successors disclosed any lands the existence of which was not before known to Europeans; but they gave fuller knowledge of many countries and nations of which the names only were known; and they gave this knowledge with

[1] *Marco Polo* (Yule's ed.), Introduction

astonishing freshness, minuteness, and accuracy. The writers of these books travelled over many thousands of miles, and they described, in the main, what they saw, although, of course, they repeated, with more or less of exaggeration, much which they only knew from conversation or from hearsay. Besides the written stories of such experiences, other Europeans who accompanied these travellers, or who made independent journeys to various parts of Asia, spread knowledge of the same things. The author of a later popular volume of travels, passing under the name of Sir John Mandeville, managed, by making use of a slight acquaintance with Asia, of a fuller knowledge of the writings of other travellers, and, most of all, of the resources of a fertile imagination, to weave a tissue of mendacious description which really lessened knowledge.[1]

Nevertheless, as a result of these travellers' reports, the traditions of earlier times and the knowledge of the nearer East possessed by traders were supplemented and popularized. The journeys of the travellers of the later thirteenth and the fourteenth centuries were a veritable revelation to Europe of the condition of Tartary, Persia, India, China, and many intervening lands. Especially strong was the impression made by the reports about China and Japan. The land of the Seres, lying on the border of the eastern ocean, had indeed been known to the ancients, and mentioned by tradition

[1] *Travels of Sir John Mandeville* (ed. of 1900).

as the source from which came certain well-known products; but under the name of Cathay, which Marco Polo and his contemporaries gave to it, it attained a new and strong hold on men's imaginations. Its myriad population, its hundreds of cities, its vast wealth, its advanced civilization, its rivers, bridges, and ships, its manufactures and active trade, the fact that it was the easternmost country of Asia, washed by the waters of the external ocean —all made Cathay a land of intense interest to the rising curiosity of thirteenth-century Europe.[1]

Similarly the great island of Cipangu, or Japan, lying a thousand miles farther to the eastward, though never actually visited by Marco Polo, and described by him with a vague and extravagant touch, was of equally keen interest to his readers, as were the "twelve thousand seven hundred islands" at which he calculates the great archipelagoes which lie in the Indian Ocean and the Pacific.

It was his accounts of "the province of Mangi," "the cities of Zaiton and Quinsay," "the Great Khan," "the island of Cipangu," and of their vast wealth and active trade that took special hold on the mind of Columbus. His copy of Marco Polo may still be seen, its margins filled with annotations on such passages, made by the great navigator;[2] and it was to these that his mind reverted when he

---

[1] Pigeonneau, *Histoire du Commerce de la France*, II., 12, etc.
[2] Vignaud, *Toscanelli and Columbus*, 95.

had discovered in the West Indies, as he believed, the outlying parts of the Khan's dominions.[1]

To the westward also ancient knowledge was re-acquired and made clearer. The "Fortunate Isles" were rediscovered and identified as the Canaries by the Italian Lancelot Malocello in 1270,[2] then forgotten and rediscovered in 1341[3] by some Portuguese ships, manned by Genoese, Florentines, Castilians, and Portuguese. In 1291 Tedisio Doria and Ugolino Vivaldi, Genoese citizens, equipped two galleys and sailed out through the Straits of Gibraltar and then to the southward, with the object of reaching the ports of India, but were never heard of again.[4] Both the Madeira Islands and the Azores became known as early as 1330, though perhaps only in a shadowy way, and were visited from time to time later in the fourteenth century, before they were regularly occupied in the fifteenth.[5]

Through the thirteenth and fourteenth centuries, therefore, thanks for the most part to Italian travellers, substantial gains were made in exactitude and clearness of knowledge of the Old World. Though the bounds of geographical knowledge were not carried much farther, and less than one-fourth of

[1] *Columbus's Journal*, October 21, 23, 24, 26, 30, November 1, etc.

[2] Beazley, Hakluyt Soc., *Publications*, 1899, lxi., lxxviii.

[3] *Ibid.*, lxxx.; Peschel, *Zeitalter der Entdeckungen*, 37.

[4] Peschel, *Zeitalter der Entdeckungen*, 36.

[5] Nordenskiold, *Periplus*, 111–115; Major, *Prince Henry the Navigator*, chaps. v., viii., xiv.

the surface of the globe was as yet known to Europeans, within these bounds knowledge became far more clear.

Ignorance and superstition were still abundant; a mythical kingdom of Prester John was believed by one geographer to exist in Africa, by another to be situated in India, and by still another to be in China; the Atlantic was still dreaded by some as the dark, unknown limit of the world; ignorant men may still have believed that the sea boiled at the equator, and that men with dogs' heads and other monsters had each its own part of the earth; but Italians of any education, especially those acquainted with the writings of their countrymen, must have been quite free from such mediæval notions. By the year 1400 scientific information, critical habits of thought, and an interest in all forms of knowledge had reached in Italy a high degree of development and were fast spreading through Europe.

The theory that the earth was round was familiar to the Greeks and Romans, and was supported in the Middle Ages by the great authority of Aristotle.[1] The only difficulties lying in the way of an acceptance of this view through the mediæval period were, in the first place, the mental effort required to conceive the earth as round when its visual appearance is flat; and, secondly, the opposition of churchmen, who interpreted certain texts in the Bible in such a way as to forbid the conception of the earth as a

[1] Aristotle, *De Cælo*, II., 14.

sphere. Yet neither of these influences was strong enough to prevail over the opinions of the majority of learned men. To them the earth was round, as it was to Aristotle, Ptolemy, and other ancients.[1] The ball which the Eastern emperors carried as an emblem of the world-wide extent of their rule, and which was borrowed from them by various mediæval potentates, had probably not lost its meaning. Dante, in the *Divina Commedia*, not only plans his Inferno on the supposition of a spherical earth, but takes for granted the same conception on the part of his readers.[2]

The conception of the sphericity of the earth was really a matter of mental training. In the fifteenth century those who had gained this knowledge were fewer than in modern times, but the class who did so believe were no less sure of it. Astronomers, philosophers, men of general learning, and even navigators and pilots were quite familiar with the idea and quite in the habit of thinking of the earth as a sphere. In all probability Columbus represented the beliefs of his class, as well as his own, when he said, "I have always read that the world, comprising the land and the water, is spherical, as is testified by the investigations of Ptolemy and others, who have proved it by the eclipses of the moon and other observations made from east to west, as well as by the elevation of the pole from north to

---

[1] Ruge, *Zeitalter der Entdeckungen*.
[2] *Inferno*, canto 34, lines 100–108.

south." [1]   Opposition to voyages westward was based rather on the probability of the enormous size of the earth and on the supposed difficulty of sailing up the slope of the sphere than it was upon any serious doubt of its sphericity.

The habitable world was quite a different conception.   It consisted of Europe, Asia, and Africa, these three continents forming a continuous stretch of land lying on the surface of the spherical earth, the rest of its surface being presumably covered with water.   There was more or less speculation about the existence of other habitable lands on the earth than those which were known, but the interest in this possibility was languid at best, and it was denied by learned churchmen on biblical grounds.

The map-makers of that period continued, like those of the earlier Middle Ages, to base their work on mere half-mythical traditions, unrelieved and uncorrected by the results of actual discoveries. Their maps are still much like picture-books, filled with biblical and literary lore, indicating but a slight attempt to incorporate exact measurements and outlines.   A development more revolutionary than the mere gradual increase of knowledge was necessary to break the bonds of academic tradition. [2]

Just at the beginning of the fourteenth century,

---

[1] Hakluyt Soc., *Publications, Hist. of Columbus—Third Voyage*, II., 129.

[2] Santarem, *Essai sur l'Histoire de la Cosmographie*, I., 75, 167, 178.

however, a new line was struck out in map-making by the construction and steady development of sailing charts, or "portolani." These humble attempts at geographical representation were intended as practical aids to navigation for Mediterranean mariners, and were based on practical observation. During the fourteenth and early fifteenth centuries they reached a wonderful degreee of accuracy. The coasts, bays, islands, and promontories of the Mediterranean were plotted out in them and drawn with striking correctness. Some four hundred such sketch-maps remain to us, drawn by Italians from the fourteenth to the sixteenth centuries, besides nearly a hundred made in other countries.[1] They did not undertake to give the internal features of the countries whose coast-lines they depicted, and as their main purpose was to aid Mediterranean trade, they did not extend so far beyond its shore as the erudition of the age would have made possible.

The best of the world maps of the fifteenth century were based on these Italian portolani rather than on mediæval maps, and at the same time added such enlarged information as became common in the Italy of the fifteenth century.[2]

Thus, at the very beginning of the fifteenth century European explorers had the benefit of the traditional ancient geography, of the new exactness of knowledge drawn from the observations of recent

---

[1] Beazley, in Hakluyt Soc., *Publications.* 1899, cxx.
[2] *Ibid.*, cxxi., etc.

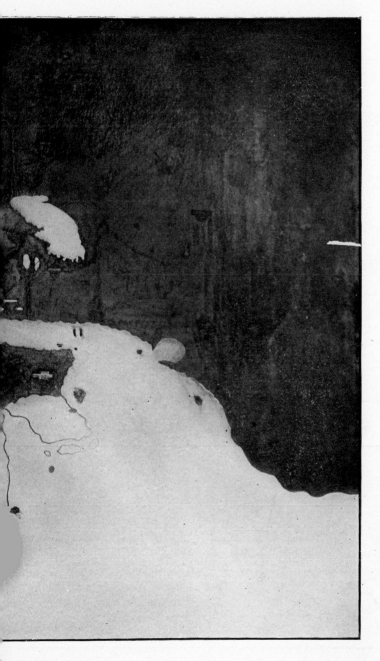

travellers, of the accurate but limited portolani of the Italian navigators, and finally of the more pretentious, if vague and often misleading, world maps of learned geographers. If a sailor wished to navigate the Mediterranean and its adjacent waters, if he planned to sail up the coast of Europe to the British Isles and on into the Baltic, or to pass down the Atlantic coast of Africa to Cape Nun, he might rely on the maps and charts which the Italian geographers could furnish him. Or if he launched his galleys on the Red Sea he might use their guidance down the east coast of Africa to the equator. He would also find tolerably accurate descriptions of all the southern coasts of Asia. In the interior a traveller by land could know beforehand the main features of the countries he might traverse. Beyond these limits, either by sea or by land, geographical knowledge must be sought by discovery or followed along the lines of dim report. If European sailors should follow the coast of Africa below the twenty-seventh parallel of north latitude, or of Europe above the sixtieth, or if they should direct their course into the western ocean beyond the Azores, they would be sailing into the unknown, and whatever they should find would be fresh acquisition.

The two instruments which were the most requisite for distant voyaging, the compass and the astrolabe (the predecessor of the quadrant), were already, in 1400, known and used by Mediterranean navigators. The property of turning towards the north, possessed by a magnetized needle, was certainly known as early as the close of the twelfth century; and even its use by sailors to find their directions when the sun and stars were obscured. More than one mediæval writer describes the process by which a needle is rubbed on a piece of magnetic iron, then laid on a straw or attached to a piece of cork, and floated on water till its point turns towards the north star.[1]   But its properties savored of magic; the earlier sailors, who hugged the shore, scarcely needed it, and it came into general use as slowly and imperceptibly as most of the other great inventions of the world.

The introduction of the compass into general use is, by tradition, ascribed to the Italian city of Amalfi, and it is easy to believe that the enterprising sailors of this commercial republic brought it into established recognition.   By the early years of the fifteenth century the compass was provided with the card, marked with the directions, placed in the compass-box, and made a well-known part of the equipment of the navigator.[2]   The mariner could now tell his directions wherever he might be, and the spider-web net-work of "compass-roses" on many of the early maps shows how anxious the map-maker

[1] Alexander Neckham, *De Utensilibus; De Natura Rerum*, book II., chap. xcviii.; Guyot de Provins, *La Bible;* Jacques de Vitry, *Historia Orientalis;* Brunetto Latini, *Epistolæ*, who mentions Roger Bacon as showing him a magnet at Oxford in 1258.   Quoted in Beazley, Hakluyt Soc., *Publications*, 1899, cxliv., etc.   [2] Azurara, *Discovery of Guinea*, chap. ix.

was to provide lines along which the navigator might lay his course according to his compass. The makers of the better class of portolani evidently had the use of the compass in drawing their charts.[1]

The changed position of the heavenly bodies as the early traveller passed northward or southward struck him with especial force. Marco Polo, describing the island of Sumatra, says, "But let me tell you one marvellous thing, and that is the fact that this island lies so far to the south that the north star, little or much, is never to be seen."[2] He also notes on his journey northward through India, when he sees it again, "two cubits above the water." When Cadamosto, the Venetian, saw the pole-star at "the third of a lance's length above the edge of the waves," he recorded it as one of the most striking phenomena of his journey towards the equator.

Two instruments were known by which the elevation above the horizon of the pole-star, or any other heavenly body could be measured. The older of these was the "cross-staff," or St. James's staff, a simple rod marked into degrees, at the end of which the eye was placed and along which a measured cross-piece was pushed, till one of its ends hid a point on the horizon and the other the sun or star whose height was being measured. The astrolabe

[1] Santarem, *Essai sur l'Histoire de la Cosmographie*, I., 280–305.　[2] *Marco Polo* (Yule's ed.), book III., chap. ix.

was a somewhat more elaborate instrument, consisting of a brass circle marked with degrees, against which two movable bars were fastened, each provided at the ends with a sight or projecting piece pierced by a hole. This was hung by a ring from a peg in the mast or from the hand, so that gravity would make one of its bars horizontal. Then the other bar was sighted to point towards some heavenly body. Chaucer, in 1400, gave to his "litel Lowis my sone" an astrolabe calculated "after the latitude of Oxenford," and wrote a charming treatise to explain to him in English its use, "for Latin ne canstow yit but smal, my lyte sone." In this treatise he described to him, among other things, "diverse tables of longitudes and latitudes of sterres." [1]

By means of either of these instruments latitude could be measured or calculated. Longitude was a more difficult problem; it involved the calculation of the difference of time as well as measurements of elevation of the heavenly bodies. The calculations necessary to discover actual locations from an observation were too long and complicated to be made on each occasion; and "ephemerides," or calculated tables of elevations of planets and of differences of time, were required. Just when the earliest of such tables were constructed and when chronometers came into use is obscure, but they

[1] Chaucer, *A Treatise on the Astrolabe*, Prologue; Skeat, *The Student's Chaucer*, 396.

were in existence in at least a rudimentary form early in the fifteenth century.[1]

The condition of Europe early in the fifteenth century as compared with its condition early in the thirteenth shows a great advance in those lines which made extensive exploration possible, and this advance was chiefly due to Italians. Increased knowledge, improved equipment, instruments of astronomical observation, navigating charts, and a race of educated navigators, made a part of the European background of American history as truly as did the incentive to exploration afforded by the search for new routes to the East. Of course much progress remained to be accomplished in the making of maps and globes, in the improvement of instruments, and in the calculation of tables during the period of discovery. The awakened scientific interest which had already shown itself as part of the Renaissance found scope in the practical requirements of distant voyages. While men were discovering new continents and seas, they were at the same time solving many problems of geographical science and perfecting the equipment by which further advance was made practicable.

[1] Humboldt, *Examen Critique*, I., 274.

CHAPTER IV

PIONEER WORK OF PORTUGAL

(1400-1527)

THE great period of explorations, of which the discovery of America was a part, lay between the years 1485 and 1520, between the discovery of the Cape of Good Hope by Diaz and the circumnavigation of the globe by the ships of Magellan. Long before this period of fruition, however, there was a significant movement of discovery, and an important acquisition of knowledge, experience, and boldness in exploration. This early dawn, preparatory to the later day, consisted in a series of discoveries on the west coast of Africa, due to the energy of the Portuguese and to the enlightenment of their great Prince Henry.

Portugal was especially fitted to be the pioneer in modern maritime exploration. Without geographical or racial separation from the rest of the Iberian peninsula, the national distinctness of Portugal was largely a matter of sentiment gathering around the sovereign. The nationality of Portugal had been created in the first place by the policy of its rulers, and preserved by them until the growth of separate material interests, a national language and literature, and traditions of glorious achievements confirmed the separateness of the Portuguese nationality from that of Spain.

The desire to hold aloof from other Spanish countries turned the attention of the king of Portugal to more distant alliances, and the open western seaboard naturally suggested that these should be with maritime states. In 1294 a treaty of commerce was signed with England. A century later, 1386, a much closer alliance with that country was formed and a new treaty signed at Windsor.[1] This was followed in the next year by a marriage between the king of Portugal and Philippa, daughter of the English John of Gaunt and first cousin of King Richard. This "Treaty of Windsor" was renewed again and again by succeeding English and Portuguese sovereigns, and remained the foundation of their relationship until it was superseded long afterwards by still closer treaty arrangements. With Flanders, Portugal had frequent peaceful intercourse, both in trade and in diplomacy. A Venetian fleet also called from time to time at the harbor of Lisbon on the way to and from England and Flanders, and thus brought Portugal into contact with the great Italian republic, and may have aroused an interest in the far Eastern trade products of which loaded the galleys.

The contract before referred to by which Emanuel

[1] Rymer, *Fœdera*, II., 667, VII., 515–523.

Pesagno was made hereditary lord high admiral, in 1317, continued to be fulfilled by the descendants of the first great admiral through the whole fourteenth and fifteenth centuries, and kept up a constant connection with Genoa.[1] Thus the associations of Portugal were with a line of seaboard states extending from England to Italy. After 1263 the maritime interests of the Portuguese kings became more distinct by their conquest from the Moors of the kingdom of Algarves, giving them a southern as well as a western sea-coast.[2]

It was at Sagres, on Cape St. Vincent, which juts out into the open Atlantic Ocean on the extreme southwest of this province, that Henry, the fifth son of John II. of Portugal, established his dwelling-place in 1419, and created a centre of maritime interest and a base of exploring effort which was of worldwide influence. Henry was duke of Viseu, lord of Cavailham, viceroy of Algarves, and grand master of the Order of Christ. He had no wife or children; his private estate was, therefore, available for the expenses of exploring voyages; and projects of geographical discovery became his chief occupation. Whatever other duties or services were required of him on account of his membership in the royal family, he always returned to Sagres and to his exploring expeditions. He possessed also the

[1] M. G. Canale, *Storia del Commercio, Viaggi, &c., degl' Italiani,* book II., chap. x., etc., quoted by Payne, *New World,* 96.
[2] Stephens, *Hist. of Portugal,* 81.

interest and support of his father and brother, who successively occupied the throne. After his death his work was carried on by his nephew, King Alfonso V. The work of Henry was, therefore, substantially the concern of the whole royal family of Portugal for three generations.[1]

Prince Henry "the Navigator," as he has come to be called, gathered around him a body of men trained as sailors; he learned the use of charts and instruments, taught these arts to his captains, and ultimately made the neighboring port of Lagos the most famous point in the world for the departure and return of exploring expeditions.[2] During forty years expedition after expedition was equipped almost yearly and sent down along the west coast of Africa, in the effort to solve its mystery and, if possible, to sail around its southern extremity.

In the process of exploration Prince Henry was governed by some of the strongest of human impulses. The crusading spirit was hot within him, and he hoped to continue in Africa the old struggle of the Portuguese Christians against the Moorish infidels. Gentler missionary ideals caused him to plan to spread Christianity into new lands, and to make connection with Prester John, the Christian ruler of the India which lay to the eastward of Africa.[3]

---

[1] Major, *Prince Henry the Navigator*, chaps. iv., vi., xiii., xviii.
[2] Nordenskiold, *Periplus*, 121 A. For discussion of divergent views of Prince Henry's "school of navigation," see Beazley, in Hakluyt Soc., *Publications*, 1899, cvi.–cxii.
[3] Azurara, *Discovery of Guinea*, chaps. vii., xvi.

His interest in trade was equally strong; he was familiar with the internal trade of Africa, and he lost no opportunity of developing traffic along the sea-coast.[1]

Yet it was the instinct of the explorer that inspired Prince Henry with the steady devotion to his life work. The fine curiosity which placed geographical discovery above all material gain, and rewarded his captains, not in proportion to what they had accomplished, but in proportion to the efforts they had made to carry the boundaries of knowledge farther, kept him and them intent on the work of exploration.[2] Henry possessed, at the beginning of his explorations, little more than the traditional geographical conceptions of the later Middle Ages. Besides some twelve or fourteen extant fourteenth-century maps drawn by Italian draughtsmen, which were probably all known to Henry, his brother Pedro gave him one which has since disappeared, which had been constructed at Venice, and which "had all the parts of the world and earth described."[3] He was probably also familiar with the classical tales of the circumnavigation of Africa.

Besides this he had some important personal knowledge. During a Portuguese invasion of the Barbary states of Africa in 1415, in which Prince Henry served with his father and brothers, and

---

[1] Azurara, *Discovery of Guinea*, chap. vii.
[2] Bourne, " Prince Henry the Navigator," in *Essays in Historical Criticism*, 173–189.   [3] Major, *Prince Henry*, 62.

later when he was himself in command, he found that there were caravan routes whose termini were at Ceuta and other Mediterranean towns. From the Sahara and the Soudan, across the desert, came caravans to the Mediterranean coast bringing gold, wine, and slaves, and news of trading routes far to the southward.

Moreover, these routes extended to rivers and sea-coasts unknown to Europeans, which must, nevertheless, be connected with the open Atlantic Ocean, and might well be on the southern shore of that continent. "He got news of the passage of merchants from the coast of Tunis to Timbuctoo and to Cantor on the Gambia, which inspired him to seek those lands by way of the sea." [1] "The tawny Moors, his prisoners, told him of certain tall palms growing at the mouth of the Senegal or western Nile, by which he was able to guide the caravels which he sent out to find that river." [2]

The first decade of Henry's efforts, from 1420 to 1430, resulted in little in the way of new discovery. The Madeira and Azores islands were rediscovered and their full exploration and permanent colonization begun. Every year saw one or more caravels sent from Lagos southward to follow the coast of the main-land; but they skirted no shores that were not desert, and turned back baffled by their own fears. Cape Boyador long remained a barrier whose imagi-

[1] Diego Gomez, quoted in Beazley, *Introduction to Azurara's Chronicle* (Hakluyt Soc., *Publications*, 1899).   [2] *Ibid.*

nary dangers of reef and shoal served as an excuse for the still more unreal horrors of the "Sea of Darkness."

The next decade saw better results. In 1434 Gil Eannes, one of the boldest of the captains who were growing up in Prince Henry's service, when he reached Boyador, sailed far out to sea, doubled the cape, and, returning to the coast, landed and gathered "St. Mary's roses," and took them home to the prince as a memento of the "farthest South."[1] The greatest barrier had been passed, that of superstitious dread, and almost every voyage now brought its result of progress farther southward. Soon the boundaries of Islam were passed, for natives were found on the coast who were not Mohammedans.

The third decade saw still further advance. In 1441 Nuno Tristam discovered Cape Blanco, the "White Cape," glistening with the white sand of the Sahara. In 1445 Dinis Diaz, of Lisbon, sailed at last beyond the desert and reached Cape Verd, the "Green Cape,"[2] fifteen hundred miles down the African coast, and as far from Gibraltar south as Constantinople was east. By this time the captains of Prince Henry had reached the fertile and populous shores where the western Soudan borders on the Atlantic Ocean, and a new obstacle to further exploration revealed itself in the attraction and the profit of the slave-trade.

[1] Azurara, *Discovery of Guinea*, chap. ix.
[2] *Ibid.*, chap. xxxi.

The first " Moors " or negroes were some ten or twelve captured and brought home in the year 1441 by Antam Gonçalvez, to satisfy the curiosity of the prince and to obtain information useful for the further prosecution of the voyages. Others were soon brought for other purposes. Of the two hundred and thirty-five Moors who made up the first full cargo of human freight, the prince gave away the fifty-six which fell to his share as one-fifth, although it is recorded with the somewhat grotesque piety of the fifteenth century that "he reflected with great pleasure on the salvation of their souls that before were lost." [1]

There is no reason to believe that Henry planned or wished the development of a trade in slaves; [2] but labor was scarce on the great estates of southern Portugal, slaves were in demand, and very different desires from those of the prince might be gratified by capturing and bringing to the slave-market of Lagos the unfortunate natives of the newly discovered coasts. Hence one expedition after another, sent out for purposes of discovery, returned, bringing tales of failure to reach farther points on the coast, but laden with human booty to be sold. Private adventurers sought and obtained the prince's permission to send out caravels, and these also

---

[1] Azurara, *Discovery of Guinea*, chap. xxv.
[2] The statement to the contrary in the *Cambridge Modern Hist.*, I., 10, is not deducible from any contemporary evidence.

brought home cargoes of slaves. Only the most vigorous pressure, exercised on the choicest spirits among the Portuguese captains, served now to carry discoveries farther.

Nevertheless, a basis of interest in distant voyages had been found which had not existed before; and the further exploration of the African coast was certain, even in default of the personal enlightenment and enthusiasm of the Navigator. The expeditions sent by the prince and private voyages made familiar to the mariners of Portugal two thousand miles of coast instead of six hundred as of old. Guinea was eventually reached.

In 1455 the Venetian Cadamosto entered into Henry's service; and, followed closely by Diego Gomez, discovered the Cape Verd Islands and passed so far around the shoulder of northwestern Africa as not only to reach the ends of the caravan routes from Morocco, and to open up trade in gold, ivory, and the products of the Guinea coast, but to suggest that there was open sea now all the way eastward to India. The temporary disappointment of finding that this was not true was left to the successors of Prince Henry, for his death occurred in 1460. But the work was still carried on by his nephew, Alfonso V., and by the next king of Portugal, John II.

A series of bold pilots now passed beyond the whole Guinea coast, crossed the equator, and made their way down almost two thousand miles

more of the African coast. The belief became as-
sured that "ships which sailed down the coast of
Guinea might be sure to reach the end of the land by
persisting to the south"; and stone pillars six feet
high were ordered to be erected at landing-places to
indicate possession and mark the stages of the route
to the Indies.

Finally, in 1486, Bartholomew Diaz, the third
member of his family to take part in the discoveries of Prince Henry, with two vessels sailed the
remaining distance on the coast, and passed so far
to the eastward that his sailors mutinied and refused to go farther. Diaz then suddenly realized
that, notwithstanding the necessity for his return,
he had at last found the passage - way to India
dreamed of through so many ages and sought for
at such heavy cost.

A period of still greater discoveries was already
at hand. "It was in Portugal," says Ferdinand Columbus, "that the admiral began to surmise that if
men could sail so far south, one might also sail west
and find lands in that direction." The Portuguese
were so wedded to the search for the southeast route,
and it was so nearly achieved at this time, that their
interest was but languid in the plans for a search to
the westward. Another people therefore took it up,
and soon the exploration of the New World was in
full tide, and the period of pioneer effort passed into
the era of great accomplishment.

Meanwhile Portugal saw the fruition of Prince

Henry's work in the circumnavigation of Africa. Ten years later than the exploit of Diaz, in 1496, a fleet sailed from Lisbon under Vasco da Gama which was destined to round the Cape, make its way up the east coast of Africa till familiar parts of the Indian Ocean were reached; then to sail across to India, cast anchor, and secure cargo in Calicut and many other ancient ports; and to return thence safely to its port of departure.[1]   The Portuguese search for a new route to the lands of Eastern products was thus successful; and once found, this path became familiar.   The fleet of Cabral in 1500 immediately followed that of Da Gama, and, driven to the westward as it sailed to the south, discovered Brazil, as a casual incident of its successful voyage to India.   Thus, if the voyage of Columbus had never been undertaken, America would have been found within less than a decade.

Albuquerque followed around the southeast passage in 1503; a permanent traffic between Portugal and India was established, and thereafter yearly fleets of merchant and war vessels rounded the Cape. Soon most of the points of vantage of the Indies were in Portuguese control—Ormuz, Diu, Goa, Ceylon, Malacca—and the enterprising little western state had trade settlements in Burma, China, and Japan.[2]   The private path of the Portuguese ul-

[1] *The First Voyage of Vasco da Gama*, in Hakluyt Soc., *Publications*, 1898.
[2] Hunter, *Hist. of British India*, I., 110–133.

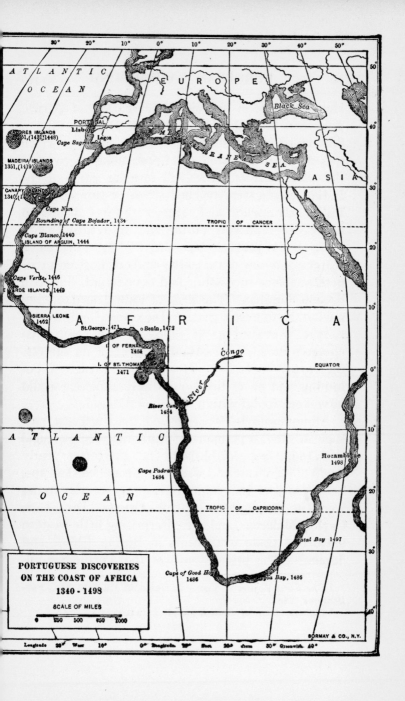

PORTUGUESE DISCOVERIES
ON THE COAST OF AFRICA
1340 - 1498

SCALE OF MILES

timately became the public highway of the nations. Spain, Holland, England, and France sent fleets around the Cape of Good Hope, and made use of the route to the East which the Portuguese had discovered.

The actual progress of scientific knowledge and practical equipment for navigation made at Sagres, Lagos, Lisbon, and on the seas, during the voyages sent out by Prince Henry and his immediate successors, is unfortunately not accurately known; but some glimpses of it may be obtained. "In his wish to gain a prosperous result of his efforts," says an almost contemporary historian, "the Prince devoted great industry and thought to the matter, and at great expense procured the aid of one Master Jacome from Majorca, a man skilled in the art of navigation and in the making of maps and instruments, and who was sent for, with certain of the Arab and Jewish mathematicians, to instruct the Portuguese." [1]

When trained Italian navigators applied to Henry, as was the case with the Venetian Cadamosto, they were readily taken into his service, and he sent word by them that he would heartily welcome any other such volunteers. When the prince's work fell into the hands of his nephew, King John, the latter appointed the German Behaim, of Nuremberg, who lived in Lisbon from 1480 to 1484, to be one of the

[1] De Barros, *Decadas da Asia*, quoted in Beazley, *Henry the Navigator*, 161.

four members of his "Junto de Mathematicos." It was Behaim who introduced to the Portuguese the improved ephemerides calculated by the German Regiomontanus, and printed at Nuremberg in 1474. He also improved the astrolabe and the staff, drew charts and made globes, and accompanied one of the West-African expeditions in 1489.[1]

Diego Gomez, one of Henry's captains, remarks, in describing his voyage of 1460, "I had a quadrant with me and wrote on the table of it the altitude of the arctic pole, and I found it better than the chart; for though you see your course of sailing on the chart well enough, yet if once you get wrong it is hard by map alone to work back into the right course."[2] Azurara also contrasts the incorrect charts with which Henry's sailors were provided before their explorations with those corrected by the later observations.[3] His navigators, therefore, used the compass, the quadrant, and carefully constructed charts; but their advances in the use of this equipment are not recorded.

The first portolano to note the discoveries on the coast of Africa made by the Portuguese was that of Gabriele de Valsecca, of Majorca (1434–1439). A map drawn by Andrea Bianco, of Venice, at London in 1448, seems to have been intended especially to indicate them, as it gives twenty-seven new names

---

[1] Major, *Prince Henry the Navigator*, 326–328.
[2] Quoted, in Beazley, *Henry the Navigator*, 297, 298.
[3] Azurara, *Discovery of Guinea*, chap. lxxvi.

along the coast to the south of Cape Boyador.   But
the map which was distinctively the outcome of the
new discoveries was the so-called "Camaldolese map
of Fra Mauro," drawn by Mauro, Bianco, and other
draughtsmen during the year 1457, in the convent
of Murano in Venice.   King Alfonso of Portugal
himself paid the expenses of its construction, and
sent charts showing the recent discoveries.   It included all the new knowledge obtained up to that
time by Prince Henry's explorers.   It is the first
large map drawn with the exactness and the reliance
on observed facts of the portolano, notwithstanding
the fact that it included a larger part of the earth's
surface in its field than any earlier map.   Though
disappointing in some respects, it stands in the forefront of improved modern maps, and not unworthily
represents the advance made in the knowledge of
the world's surface as a result of the Portuguese
efforts up to that time.

The scientific importance of the discoveries of
the Portuguese and the intellectual alertness of
the Italians are alike illustrated by an incident that
occurred at the court of Ferdinand and Isabella in
1491.   Columbus having explained to the sovereigns his scheme for a western voyage to reach the
Indies, most of the Spanish prelates who were present declared his ideas heretical, supporting themselves upon the authority of St. Augustine and
Nicholas de Lyra.   Alessandro Geraldini, an Italian,
preceptor of the royal children, who was standing be-

hind Cardinal Mendoza at the time, "represented to him that Nicholas de Lyra and St. Augustine had been, without doubt, excellent theologians but only mediocre geographers, since the Portuguese had reached a point of the other hemisphere where they had ceased to see the pole-star and discovered another star at the opposite pole, and that they had even found all the countries situated under the torrid zone fully peopled." [1]

In ship-building Henry and his navigators made positive progress. The Venetian Cadamosto testifies that "his caravels did much excel all other sailing ships afloat." Many varieties of vessels are mentioned in the records of Prince Henry's time— the barca, barinel, caravel, nau, fusta; the galley, galiot, galeass, and galleon; the brigantine and carrack. Of all these the caravel became the favorite for the long, exploring voyages. It was usually from sixty to one hundred feet long and eighteen to twenty-five feet broad, and of about two hundred tons burden. It had three masts with lateen sails stretched on the oblique yards which were swung from the masthead, and was steered, at least partly, by the turning of these great, swinging sails. [2] John II. encouraged the immigration of English and Danish ship-builders and carried improvements still further.

---

[1] Mariéjol, *L'Espagne sous Ferdinand et Isabelle*, 96.
[2] *Revista Portuguesa Colonial* (May 20, 1898), 32–52, quoted in Beazley, *Introduction to Azurara's Chronicle* (Hakluyt Soc., *Publications*, 1899, p. cxii).

The greatest service to navigation done by Prince Henry and his successors was that of providing a school of sea-training. Not only were the whole group of early Portuguese explorers, Henry's own captains, "brought up from boyhood in the household of the Infant," [1] but there was scarcely a name great in navigation in the succeeding period which had not in some way been connected with these voyages. Diaz, Da Gama, Albuquerque, Da Cunha, Cabral, and the other captains who made the Portuguese empire in the East; Magellan, who found still another way to India by the southwest; Estevam Gomez, who sailed to the arctic seas; Bartholomew and Christopher Columbus,—were all taught or practised in that school. Columbus lived in Lisbon from 1470 to 1484, married there the daughter of Bartholomew Perestrello, the discoverer and captain-general under Prince Henry of Porto Santo in the Madeiras; and, besides his voyages on the Mediterranean and to England and Iceland, went repeatedly to the coast of Guinea and lived for some years in the Madeiras. Between 1477 and 1484 he was regularly engaged in the maritime service of the Portuguese crown.

Besides these great names, many navigators who had only local repute or have remained nameless were Portuguese in birth and training, and belonged to the same maritime school. In 1502, close upon the English grants of exploring and trading rights to the

[1] Azurara, *Discovery of Guinea*, chap. xiii.

Cabots, came a similar concession to "Hugh Elliott and Thomas Ashehurst, merchants of Bristol, and to John Gunsalus and Francis Fernandez, Esq., subjects of the king of Portugal."[1] The expedition of the French captain De Gonneville to Brazil, in 1503, was guided by two Portuguese pilots;[2] and twenty of the sailors on Magellan's Spanish fleet of 1519, besides the commander, were Portuguese.[3] Three vessels from Dieppe, under Portuguese pilotage, in 1527, rounded the Cape of Good Hope and visited Madagascar, Sumatra, and the coast of India.[4]

Actual skill in navigating vessels was increased and developed to a high degree in the struggle with the adverse maritime conditions on the coast of Africa. The violent and disturbing currents, the terrible surf of the beaches, the cyclones of the Guinea coast, the trade-winds, which were always head-winds to the mariners returning from the southwest, the uncharted reefs and bars, all favored a school of seamanship which trained the Portuguese and Italian sailors to meet far worse difficulties than those likely to confront them in the later and more distant voyages to the westward.

Other experiences of the Portuguese were later utilized by the Spaniards in their American colonies. The slave-trade was a sombre precedent, followed

---

[1] Rymer, *Fœdera*.   [2] Pigeonneau, *Hist. du Commerce*, II., 50.
[3] Navarrete, *Coleccion*, II., 12.
[4] De Barros, *Decadas da Asia* (Madrid ed., 1615), 42 decade, book V., chap. vi., 296.

only too readily; the system of grants of newly discovered territory to captains or contractors who
would continue its discovery or conquest, exploit its
resources, and pay to the crown a large share of its
products was followed, somewhat intermittently, in
the West Indies and Central and South America.[1]

One of the permanent lessons of the Portuguese
explorations was the need for and effectiveness of
royal or quasi-royal patronage.   Italian expeditions
bore no fruit and could bear none, for this requirement of patronage was but ill-afforded by her merchant cities or even by her merchant princes.   It
was impossible for Venice or Genoa to take a part
in the new discoveries and follow the new lines of
trade, not only because of their unfavorable geographical position, not only because they were then
engaged in a desperate military and economic struggle to retain their old Levantine trade conquests
and connections, not only because their wealth and
prosperity were deeply smitten by their mutual
struggles and their common losses from the repeated
blows of the Ottoman conquest, but because Italy
had no royal family to take under its patronage distant discovery, conquest, trade, and colonization.
Italy furnished most of the knowledge, the skill, and
the individual enterprise that made the great period
of explorations; but Portugal, under the leadership
of her great prince, was its true pioneer.

[1] Bourne, *Spain in America*, chap. xiv.

CHAPTER V

THE SPANISH MONARCHY IN THE AGE OF COLUMBUS

(1474–1525)

THE limits of Portuguese discovery and dominion were soon reached; and as the fifteenth century advanced, Spain emerged not only as one of the great powers of Europe but as the first exploring, conquering, and colonizing nation of America. A century before any other European state obtained a permanent foothold in the New World, Spain began the creation of a great colonial empire there, which was soon occupied by her settlers, administered by a department of her government, converted by her missionaries, and made famous throughout Europe for the wealth which it brought to the mother-country. Such a work at such a time could only be accomplished by a vigorous and rising nation, and, in fact, Spanish advancement in Europe during this period corresponded closely with her achievements in America. There are few recorded instances of a development so rapid and a transformation so complete as that which took place in Spain under Ferdinand and Isabella, between 1474 and 1516.

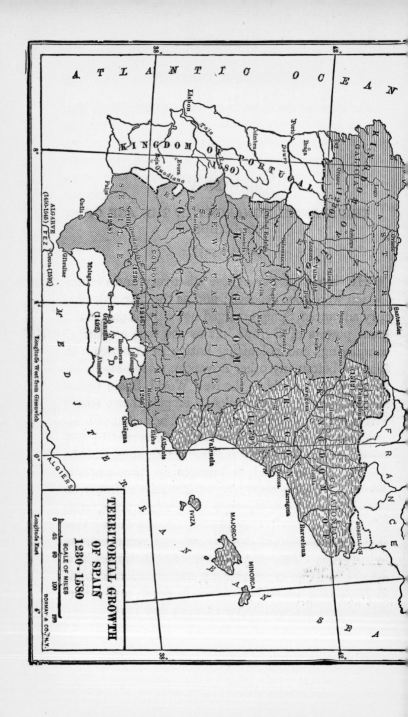

TERRITORIAL GROWTH
OF SPAIN
1230 - 1580

SCALE OF MILES

0   45   80   100   150

BORMAY & CO., N.Y.

Longitude West from Greenwich

Longitude East

For a career destined to be scarcely inferior to that
of any of the great empires of history, Spain had at
the beginning of this period an inadequate and undeveloped political organization. Even that royal
power which was the condition precedent to distant
conquest and colonial organization was new. Spanish national unity, royal absolutism, and religious
uniformity, which were famous throughout Europe
in the sixteenth century, were all of recent growth;
the centralized control over all parts of her widely
scattered colonies which Spain, above all colonizing
countries, exercised, was a power attained and a
policy adopted only at the moment of the acquisition
of those colonies.

When, in 1474, Isabella inherited the crown of
Castile, and, in 1479, her husband, Ferdinand, became king of Aragon, they united, by close personal
and political bonds, what had formerly been near a
score of domains, variously joined or detached.

The king of Aragon had already incorporated
into a personal union three separate countries—the
kingdom of Aragon, the kingdom of Valencia, and
the ancient principality of Catalonia, each with its
own body of representatives, its own law, its pecul-
liar customs, and its separate administrative system. Castile was in name a political unity, having
one monarch and one body of estates. Nevertheless, its provinces represented well-marked ancient
divisions. Leon had once been a separate kingdom,
and was still coupled with Castile itself in the full

title of that monarchy; while Galicia, Asturias, and the three Basque provinces were inhabited by peoples of different political history, of different stock, and living under different customs. Navarre, Granada, and Portugal, although within the Iberian peninsula, were, at the accession of Ferdinand and Isabella, still independent; though the first was destined to be united to Aragon, the second to Castile, and even the third was to be amalgamated for eighty critical years with the greater monarchy. Thus Spain was a congeries of states, joined by the marriage bond of the two rulers of its principal divisions, but by no means yet a single monarchy or a united nation. It was the work of the Catholic sovereigns to carry this unification far towards completion by following common aims, by achieving success in many fields of common national interest, and by imposing the common royal power upon all divergent and warring classes and interests in the various Spanish states.

The personality of Ferdinand and Isabella was the first great factor in the strengthening of the monarchy; for they were both individuals of authority, energy, and ability.[1] Their union was the next element; for the royal power of the united monarchies could be used to break down opposition in either. Great achievements in Spain and in Europe increased their authority and power by the prestige of success. Finally, the discoveries, con-

[1] Bergenroth, *Cal. Letters and State Papers, Spain,* I., 34, etc.

quests, and colonization of America gave a unique position to the rulers of these distant possessions. Not only did the products of the American mines and American commercial taxation furnish a material basis of strength and influence; not only did a great commercial marine and a great navy grow up around the needs of intercourse with the colonies; but the romantic interest of the discoveries, the wild adventures, and the wonderful success of the conquistadores, and the extent of the colonies, filled the imagination and gave an ideal greatness to the monarchs in whose name these conquests were made, and by whom the New World was ruled.

There was need for all the authority of the new sovereigns at the time of their accession in 1474. Under the weak rule of Isabella's brother, Castile had become a prey to disorder amounting almost to anarchy; in Galicia brigandage was so common as to be unresisted, except by townsmen staying within their walls; in Andalusia private warfare among the great noble houses had let loose all the forces of disorder and violence; Isabella's claim to the crown was disputed and her rival upheld by foreign support.[1] The united sovereigns met these difficulties with vigor, and the first two years of Isabella's rule in Castile gave repeated instances of victorious warfare, of successful assertion of authority, and of harsh justice. The turbulent districts were reduced to order and the foreign invader expelled.

[1] Maurenbrecher, *Studien und Skizzen*, 45, 46.

The disorder in Andalusia seemed to demand personal action. In 1477, therefore, the two sovereigns made a formal entry into Seville, and the queen asserted her royal power in a way that could not be misunderstood. In true patriarchal fashion she established her tribunal in the Alcazar, sitting in a chair on an elevated platform surrounded by her council and officers, in all solemnity and according to traditional forms, listening to the complaints of high and low, rich and poor, and granting summary justice to all who claimed it, irrespective of rank or means. Her decrees were carried out, ill-doers forced to make amends, and turbulent nobles reduced to promising to keep the peace. The visit of Isabella to Seville may well be taken as the beginning of the work of the new monarchy in Spain.[1]

The next step towards an enforcement of royal authority taken by the new monarchs involved the acknowledgment of an institution seemingly independent of the monarchy. Spanish cities and communes had at various times formed hermandads, leagues or brotherhoods, to enforce order, to support themselves against great nobles, or to strengthen themselves for the carrying out of some object of common policy. Instances could be found in which their combined strength had been used against the king himself or his officials. On the other hand, their united power had been used efficaciously to form a sort of rural police, each city undertaking

[1] Perez, *Los Reyes Catolicos in Sevilla*, 1477–1478, p. 13.

the protection of certain roads and stretches of country.[1]

Two influential ministers, with the approval of Ferdinand and Isabella, in 1476, obtained the agreement of the Cortes of Castile and of a junta of the towns for the formation of a santa hermandad, or "holy brotherhood," for three years, for which rules were drawn up, submitted to the monarchs, and finally promulgated. The nobles gave a reluctant assent to the requirements of these rules, so far as they affected their estates and vassals. Altogether two thousand horsemen were to be equipped, each horseman supported by a body of one hundred households. These were grouped into companies under eight captains and placed in detachments at certain distances along all the roads. Besides the armed soldiers of the brotherhood, a whole system of alcaldes was organized with exclusive jurisdiction over certain kinds of offences. A common treasury existed for the support of expenses.

When any theft, assault, arson, or rape was discovered or complained of, immediately the bells were rung, and the nearest detachment of soldiers of the brotherhood started on a pursuit which was carried to the boundaries of the next district, where its detachment took up the pursuit, and so on until the culprit was seized or the boundaries of the kingdom reached. No town, house, or castle could

[1] Antequera, *Hist. de la Legislacion Española*, 194–197.

refuse the right of search. When arrested, a decision of the nearest alcalde was given within five days. If convicted, the culprit had hand or foot cut off or was put to death. The favorite mode of execution in earlier times had been to bind the offender to a stake, and shoot him with arrows "till he died naturally"; but Isabella required that he should be hanged first, and that only then might his body be used as a target and a warning for others. The rapidity of pursuit and the certainty of capture of offenders, the promptitude of justice, and the barbarism of the punishments made a strong impression; and the combination of popular vengeance with official sanction made the hermandad an effective form of national police. It was introduced into Aragon in 1488.

Although this system seemed to emanate from the people, the general control over it was preserved by Ferdinand and Isabella by placing in influential positions in its administration trusted ministers of their own, and by joining themselves in its organization. When its work of insuring order was measurably accomplished and the people began to complain of its expense, the sovereigns were able to transfer the military force into a contingent for the Moorish war, and the treasury into an addition to the commissariat for the same purpose. In 1498 it was reduced to the proportions of a petty and inexpensive local police. It had proved itself, as utilized by these strong monarchs, a means of ob-

taining order and recruiting an army without cost
to the royal treasury.

The vigor of the royal administration, however,
expressed itself rather in the development of purely
royal organs than in those which were so largely
popular as the hermandad. A group of royal councils became, under Ferdinand and Isabella, the most
powerful instruments of the royal will, the most
effective means for obtaining additional power and
beating down all opposition. Early in the reign,
the old royal council, which traditionally consisted
of twelve members, including representatives of
each of the three orders of the state, was reconsti-
tuted so as to consist of one ecclesiastic, three nobles,
and eight or nine letrados, or lawyers.[1] The last
class, who made up its majority, were men learned
in the Roman law, and therefore devoted to the
idea of absolute monarchy; without connection
with the church or the nobility, and therefore interested in the strengthening of the kingship against
both; shrewd, trained, capable, and hard working.

From this time forward the council, in constant
attendance on the king, well organized, provided
with a corps of clerks and officers, and holding
daily sessions, became the serviceable and effective
auxiliary of royal power. It had duties of consulta-
tion, advice, and in some cases decision, on matters
of internal and external policy, of legislation and
administration; and, in fact, of action in the whole

[1] *Cortes de los Antiguos Reinos*, 112, etc.

sphere of the affairs of state. In time the council was gradually subdivided into three bodies: the Council of Justice, the Council of State, and the Council of the Finances, whose functions were indicated by their titles. The first of these was, in a certain sense, the direct representative of the old single royal council, and was frequently known as the Council of Castile. Its president was always considered the highest personage in the kingdom, next the king; its members were of that class of letrados whom the king could most securely rely on, and to it fell the duty of enforcing the royal supremacy as against all ancient claims, privileges, and liberties.

In addition to these outgrowths from the primitive council of the king, new councils were created from time to time, analogous in powers, but holding oversight over special spheres of national interest. Some of these were temporary, others permanent. Among them were the Council of the Hermandad, which lasted only for the twenty-two years of the existence of that institution; the Council of the Suprema, or of the Inquisition; the Council of the Military Orders, the Council of the Indies, and the Council of Aragon.[1] These great administrative boards were a characteristic part of the Spanish system of government, a natural outgrowth of its wide-spread fields of action.

The Council of the Indies was constituted in 1511,

[1] Antequera, *Hist. de la Legislacion Española,* 347, 348.

under the presidency of Juan de Fonseca, arch-
deacon of Seville, and was exactly analogous to the
other councils. It accompanied the king, and had
under him all ultimate control in policy, in jurisdiction, and in legislation over the Spanish possessions in America and in the East. Its members
were habitually drawn from those men who had
had experience as public servants in the West Indies
or in the Philippines. The more direct oversight
of individual voyages to the Indies, the regulation
of details of colonial affairs, and a large sphere of
general activity were possessed by the powerful Casa
de Contractacion at Seville. A Bureau of Pilots
also existed, whose office it was to collect nautical
information, provide charts, and give assistance to
Spanish navigators. But both of these offices were
under the control of the Council of the Indies.[1]

All these councils were stronger in discussion than
in execution; their archives came to include a vast
mass of records and special reports on subjects fall-
ing within their respective fields, and their procedure
favored penetrating investigation and full debate.
But decision was hard to come at, and the con-
sciousness that final decision after all rested with the
king paralyzed effectiveness. The custom of sub-
mitting all questions of policy to investigation by
the appropriate council became invariable in later
Spanish history, and it resulted in cumbrous in-

[1] J. de Veitia Linage, *The Spanish Rule of Trade to the West
Indies*, trans. by Captain J. Stevens, book I., chap. iii.

effectiveness. Interminable inquiry and discussion
ended frequently only in suspension of judgment or
a divided report. Points of policy of imminent
importance had to await a dilatory investigation and
equivocal conclusions. This impotence of the central
organs of government did not come in the time of
Ferdinand and Isabella and their immediate successors, and the growing inefficiency of the councils
was long overcome by the resolution of the monarchs. Nevertheless the system was part of the
price paid for centralized government, acting independently of local initiative or independence.

The preponderance of power that was being obtained by the sovereigns in the affairs of central
government by means of the royal councils was
gained in the local affairs of provinces, towns,
and communes, by the appointment of corregidores.
Such officials were appointed from time to time
by earlier sovereigns to represent them in various
towns, but the system had never been extended
widely. In 1480 the king and queen sent one or
more corregidores into every self - governing town
and city in Castile where such officials did not exist
already.[1] They were to act alongside of the older
local regidores and alcaldes as special representatives of the crown, defending its rights and claims,
and fulfilling its duties of general oversight and
protection. As a matter of fact, the great work
they accomplished was the enforcement of royal

[1] Pulgar, *Cronica de los Reyes*, II., chap. xcv.

supremacy over local privileges. Little by little
they extended their powers and encroached upon the
old local self - government, bringing to bear all the
weight of the central government upon local conditions.[1] The steady pressure of the corregidores
was supplemented by the periodical visits of the
pesquidores, veidores, or inspectors, whose duty it
was from time to time to visit the various locali-
ties, examining into the conduct of the corregidores and other officials, listening to complaints
against them, reporting on the revenues, condition of the roads, and other local conditions and
needs.

Councils, corregidores, inspectors, and various
other instruments of royal power fast sapped the
strength of older institutions and gave authority
and efficiency to the royal government; but they
were expensive and the crown was poor. Moreover, these institutions were only the permanent
elements in a policy which had a thousand temporary occasions of expense. Not even Ferdinand
and Isabella could carry out so vigorous a régime
unless provided with larger revenues. They determined, therefore, to emancipate the crown from
its poverty. A few years after their accession they
felt themselves strong enough, supported by the
representatives of the towns, in the Cortes of Toledo,
to convoke the great nobles and churchmen of the
kingdom and demand from them an investigation

[1] Mariéjol, *L'Espagne sous Ferdinand et Isabelle*, 172–174.

into the conditions under which the ancient domains of the crown had been alienated.[1] The Cardinal Pedro de Mendoza and the queen's confessor, Ferdinand de Talavera, were appointed to judge of the propriety of the gifts of former sovereigns. They did their work so adequately that pension after pension, estate after estate, endowment after endowment, were resumed by the crown. These resumptions were principally to the loss of the great noble families which had enriched themselves at the expense of the crown. None, it is true, were impoverished thereby, but a more normal relation of comparative income between sovereign and subject was established in the process.[2]

Another and more permanent addition to the royal income was made by the absorption into the crown of the grand masterships of the three military orders which existed in Castile, the Knights of Santiago, of Calatrava, and of Alcantara. In the course of three centuries of conquest from the Moslems these orders had added estate to estate, territory to territory, town to town, benefice to benefice, till their possessions extended widely through Spain, their income perhaps equalled that of the king, and their rule as landlords extended over almost a million people, or one-third the population of Castile.[3]

[1] Pulgar, *Cronica de los Reyes*, II., chap. xcv.; Calmeiro, Introduction to *Cortes de los Antiguos Reinos*, II., 63, 64.
[2] Mariéjol, *L'Espagne sous Ferdinand et Isabelle*, vi., 24.
[3] Vicente de la Fuente, *Hist. Generale de España*, V., 79.

At the head of each of these orders was a grand master, whose rich income, military following, and prestige made him one of the greatest nobles in Europe. There was reason in the claim that these grand masterships were antagonistic to royalty. Those who held them were the most turbulent nobles of Spain, and in earlier times had been the leaders in many a revolt against the crown. Their military system was co-ordinate with, and sometimes in conflict with, that of the king; their estates surrounded royal fortresses and sometimes excluded royal forces from frontier districts.

In 1487 when the grand mastership of the order of Calatrava became vacant, Ferdinand presented himself in the chapter of the commanders of the order, exhibited a papal bull giving him the administration of the order, and forced the assembly to elect him grand master. In 1494, with less formality, the grand master of Alcantara was induced to resign to the king his office, receiving, in recompense, the dignity of archbishop of Seville. Two years later, when the grand master of the order of Santiago died, Ferdinand had himself elected without difficulty.[1] Some time after this Isabella issued a pragmatic decree, declaring that the grand masterships of the orders should always be annexed to the crown. These dignities were of great value; not only did they bring in a princely income, but they practically extended the estates and patronage

[1] Maurenbrecher, *Studien und Skizzen*, 54.

of the crown by all the broad lands, cities, and villages, the offices, honors, and benefices with which the piety and chivalry of three centuries had endowed the orders.

When once such foundations had been laid, the crown extended rapidly its aggressions upon the old powers, privileges, and customs of classes and local bodies. To the nobility were interdicted the possession of fortified castles, the practice of private warfare, the use of artillery, the duel,[1] the use of quasi-royal formulas in their documents,[2] and other proud old feudal customs. No slight influence was exercised upon the nobility by the increasing ceremony, size, and expenditure of the court, to which they came to be attached in positions of nominal service and honorable dependence, a position altogether favorable to the supremacy of the monarchs and unfavorable to the independence of the nobility.

Side by side with the consolidation of royal power went the creation of the territorial unity of the Spanish peninsula. The greatest step was the conquest of Granada. Rich, warlike, and proud, this ancient Moorish state resisted the persistent attacks of the Catholic sovereigns for eleven years, from 1481 to 1492.[3] At least once Ferdinand wearied of the struggle and the expense, and longed to turn

---

[1] Mariéjol, *L'Espagne sous Ferdinand et Isabelle*, 35.

[2] *Cortes de los Antiguos Reinos*, IV., 191, 192.

[3] Prescott, *Ferdinand and Isabella*, chap. ix.

the efforts of the united Castilian and Aragonese arms eastward, where the natural ambitions of his own kingdom drew him towards France, Italy, and the islands of the Mediterranean.[1] Isabella's determination, however, never wavered, and in 1492 Granada opened her gates to her conquerors, the Moorish dynasty disappeared from Spain, and their mountains and plains were added to the kingdom of Castile.

In the very next year Ferdinand reunited to his dominions, by amicable treaty with the king of France, the two northern provinces of Catalonia, Cerdagne and Roussillon—which had been detached for thirty years. There remained Portugal and Navarre. The first of these independent kingdoms had already attained a degree of national independence, power, and wealth which prevented its absorption, though it was in the days of Spain's greatest power to be dragged for eighty years in her train. Navarre, balanced on the Pyrenees, had long been drawn alternately to France and to Aragon. In the closing years of the fifteenth and the opening years of the sixteenth century, neutrality became impossible; and in 1512 a powerful Spanish army under the duke of Alva marched into Navarre; its castles and towns capitulated, the latter under a promise of the maintenance of their privileges; the king retreated to the trans - Pyrenean part of his kingdom, and Ferdinand added to his other titles that of king

[1] Mariéjol, *L'Espagne sous Ferdinand et Isabelle*, 63.

of Navarre.[1] By the time of the death of Ferdinand, the unity of the peninsula, except for Portugal, was complete. The immediate successors of the Catholic sovereigns wore the crowns of all the countries that ever have made part of Spain.

Just as Spain became territorially one, she was made homogeneous in race and religion so as ultimately to become a land of one race and one faith. The Jew and the Moor were both destined to disappear; every element alien in blood and every element unorthodox in religion to be driven out of the land. This complete purity of blood and unity of belief were only attained long afterwards, in a period when Spain had little else than her orthodoxy to pride herself upon, but they were well begun in the time of the Catholic sovereigns.

The Jews were the first to meet with serious persecution. They were very numerous: in one town, Ciudad Real, an assessment at one time showed 8828 heads of families, or other adult males of the Jewish race.[2] They were famous as physicians and merchants, and, as in other lands, were often money-lenders. From time to time waves of religious antagonism swept over the country, and under the terrible pressure of slaughter and imminent danger, great numbers of Jews were baptized and became conversos, or "New Christians." These converts, freed from the dis-

---

[1] Boissonade, *Réunion de la Navarre à la Castille*.
[2] Lea, *The Moriscos of Spain*, 383.

abilities of their religion and gifted with superior
natural abilities, rapidly attained to high positions
in church and state.   Intermarriages between the
New Christians and those of Castilian blood were frequent, and many families of great eminence had
Jewish blood in their veins.

The conversos were under constant suspicion of
being Christians only formally; it was believed that
in their hearts they retained their ancient faith
and secretly performed its rites; they were credited
with antagonism to Christianity and suspected of
practising sorcery to destroy the "Old Christians."
There was some basis for the first, at least, of these
suspicions.   Many doubtless failed to abandon completely their ancestral ceremonies; and not only
they but even some Old Christians felt the attraction
of their mysterious and ancient traditions.[1]   The
practice of Jewish rites, known as "Judaizing,"
under the wide relationships and high connections
of the conversos, long went on unchecked.   In 1475
the pope conferred on his legate in Castile full in-
quisitorial powers to prosecute and punish "Judaizing" Christians; but the mandate was not carried out.[2]

In 1480, however, the Catholic sovereigns re-
quested from the pope authorization for the appointment by themselves of inquisitors to root out
this heresy.   A bull for the purpose was granted

---

[1] Mariéjol, *L'Espagne sous Ferdinand et Isabelle*, 44.
[2] Lea, in *Am. Hist. Rev.*, October, 1895, p. 48.

them, and on September 27, 1480, the Spanish Inquisition was established at Seville. In January, 1481, it began its work, and branches were gradually established in other centres till it had extended its tribunals to cover all Castile. Its work proved heavy; in its first eight years the tribunal of Seville alone put to death seven hundred persons and condemned five thousand more to severe penalties.[1] One of the great councils of the realm was formed to direct its operations, at the head of which was the inquisitor-general. The third in the line of inquisitors-general extended the Inquisition to America.

The authority of the Inquisition extended only over baptized persons; and, therefore, Jews who had never given up their religion, although under many disabilities, were not subject to its jurisdiction; but immunity to unconverted Jews could not consistently be continued during a harsh persecution of Judaizing Christians, and from the commencement of the work of the Inquisition pressure was brought to bear by clergy and populace upon the sovereigns to force all Jews either to be baptized or to emigrate.[2] The policy of enforced conversion or expulsion was steadily advocated by the inquisitors; since, if the Jews were baptized they would come under the jurisdiction of the Inquisition; if they left the country, Spain would be free from the reproach of harboring heretics.

[1] Bernaldez, *Hist. de los Reyes*, chap. xliv., quoted by Mariéjol, *L'Espagne*, 46. [2] Lea, *Religious History of Spain*, 437.

Isabella seems to have hesitated to carry out this policy, as well she might. But the tide of popular hatred rose higher and higher, driven on by the famous case of *El Santo Niño de la Guardia*, the reputed murder of a Christian child by Jews to obtain its heart for purposes of sorcery.[1] Finally, by the edict of March 31, 1492, all Jews were expelled from Spain, as they had been from England as early as 1290, and successively from many other states of Europe at intervening periods.[2] The same year that saw the discovery of America and the capture of Granada saw the expulsion of some one hundred thousand Jews and the enforced baptism of the fifty thousand that remained.[3] One great and costly step had been made in the direction of unity of race and religion in Spain.

The Moors in Spain were still more numerous than the Jews, though more concentrated. Through the later mediæval centuries, in the process of reconquest, Moorish populations which made formal surrender were preserved as subjects of the Christian kings; while those that were taken prisoners in battle were retained as slaves. Both classes, protected by the laws in their religion and their property,[4] frequently still practised their Mohammedan

---

[1] Lea, *Religious History of Spain*, 437–468.

[2] Amador de los Rios, *Los Judios de España y Portugal*, III., 603.

[3] Isidore Loeb, in *Revue des Études Juives*, 1887, p. 182, quoted in Lea, *The Moriscos of Spain*, 16.

[4] *Las Siete Partidas*, pt. i., tit. v., ley 23, etc., quoted in Lea, *The Moriscos of Spain*, 2.

faith. Practically the whole rural population of the kingdom of Valencia was Moorish, and in the cities of the southern provinces of Castile they made a considerable part of the population. In the century and a half of peace just preceding the war with Granada they increased steadily in numbers and in economic value to Spain.

The conquest of Granada, in 1492, brought the population of that country under the rule of Ferdinand and Isabella. The old body of Moorish subjects of Aragon and Castile, now reinforced by all the teeming population of the south, made an element of the population of united Spain of infinite promise. They were skilful, industrious, temperate, and moral; their agriculture and manufactures were far more advanced than those of the Christians; and they were more laborious, thrifty, and peaceable. They might be relied upon to furnish through taxation a steady and abundant income to the crown, and through their labor to make the landed estates of the nobles profitable.

Though treaty guarantees and the permanent material interests of the new sovereigns alike favored the protection and pacification of the Moorish inhabitants of Granada, other motives antagonized this policy. Religious enthusiasm and racial antipathy, as well as immediate greed, urged a disregard of the terms of capitulation, or, at least, such an interpretation of them as would drive the Moors either to conversion or exile. The latitudinarian-

ism of earlier centuries had disappeared. The whole
spirit of the time was now averse to tolerance or
anything approaching local, national, or religious
independence. At first, under Talavera, a sincere,
earnest, and partially successful effort was made to
convert the Moors individually to Christianity; but
soon a demand arose and became ever more urgent
that the Moors, like the Jews, should be given the
simple and immediate alternative of baptism or
exile. In 1500 this policy was adopted in Granada;
in 1502, by royal edict signed by Isabella, it was applied to all the dominions of the Castilian crown;
and in 1525 it was promulgated in Aragon, Valencia,
and Catalonia. As a result many of the Moors emigrated to Africa; the rest became Moriscos — that
is to say, Christians in religion, although Moors in
blood. Thus religious uniformity was attained in
Spain. In theory, at least, every inhabitant of the
united kingdom was a Catholic Christian. But the
enforced Christianity required of the Moriscos produced only an outward and imperfect conformity,
and the problem of this alien element remained long
unsolved to plague the Spanish monarchs, and to
bring untold misery on the Moriscos themselves.[1]

Thus the fragmentary and embryonic group of
Iberian nations of the fifteenth century grew into
the powerful Spanish monarchy of the sixteenth.
A single centralized government was created, and
the divided currents of national life were gathered by

[1] Lea, *The Moriscos of Spain*, chaps. v.-xi.

it into one great stream. Notwithstanding many survivals of mediæval conditions and later reversions to the earlier type, internal warfare and domestic disorder disappeared from the peninsula, and divergence of foreign policy no longer weakened its influence in Europe. The absolute monarchy was founded, and whatever there was of ability, enterprise, and wealth in Spain came under its control. The sovereign was in a position to give patronage to voyages of adventure, to legislate for distant dominions, and to make the most remote Spanish possessions contributory to the general objects of Spanish policy.

Spain stood out as one of the greatest states in Europe. With her close approximation to a united nationality, her all-powerful monarchy, her highly elaborate bureaucracy, her increasing body of law, soon to be codified into a great whole, her nascent literature, her military gifts and resources, the wealth and romance of the Indies, she stood on the threshold of the sixteenth century with imposing power and dignity. The part she played during that century was a conspicuous one. Her generals and her troops became the most famous and the most successful in Europe. Her diplomatic representatives were able to take the highest tone and to win most successes among European states, in the international intrigues of the sixteenth and early seventeenth centuries. She was rich enough to pension or bribe the ministers and courtiers of half the courts of Europe, and even to dazzle the eyes and impose upon the judgment of such a sovereign as James I. of England. Her literature and her art flourished with her political greatness, and she had all the external appearance of a great, cultured, and flourishing nation.

We know now, as was recognized by some observers even then, that Spain was a hollow shell. After the reign of Charles V. population stood stationary, or declined, and wealth decreased. Philip II. enforced orthodoxy, excluded all non-Catholic literature, and summoned home all Spanish students in foreign universities, thus dooming Spain to intellectual stagnation. She exhausted her resources in unwise or hopeless foreign struggles, like the war of conquest of Italy and the effort to reconquer the Netherlands; she wasted her peculiar opportunities by driving from her borders the enterprising Jews and industrious Moriscos, and by allowing commerce and finance to fall into the hands of foreigners. But most of these errors were, at the death of Ferdinand, in 1516, still in the future; and the Spanish monarchy and nation had much of the reality as well as the appearance of greatness.

CHAPTER VI

POLITICAL INSTITUTIONS OF CENTRAL EUROPE
(1400–1650)

AMERICA'S political and social institutions are unquestionably founded upon those of England, and these will be described in their proper place in this volume. But the institutions of three other European nations were for considerable periods dominant in certain parts of the New World, and have left an impress that is even yet far from being effaced. They are those of Spain, France, and Holland.

Since the Indies were, in theory, an outlying part of the kingdom of Castile, they naturally reflected the recently achieved absolutism of the Spanish monarchy. This absolutism in Castile extended over all fields—legislation, judicial action, and administrative control. Although the most formal and permanent statutes were drawn up by the king with the consent of the cortes, or even at its request, yet the custom of issuing pragmatica, or ordinances enacted by royal authority, grew until their provisions filled a large sphere. They were promulgated on all sorts of subjects, and became, immediately on their issue, authoritative rules of action. The whole subsequent legislation for the American colonies, springing as it did from the mere will of the sovereign, was an outcome of this custom.

The king was the fountain of justice, in whose name or by whose grant all temporal jurisdiction was exercised. In no country of Europe was this principle more clearly acknowledged than in Spain. Immediately attending upon him was an audiencia, or group of judicial officers whose duty it was to carry out these functions in the most immediate cases. The audiencia was a high court of law and equity, deciding both civil and criminal cases; and, as is always the case in early stages of government, exercising much administrative and financial control through the forms of judicial action. The insufficiency for these ends of a peripatetic body bound to follow the king in all his movements was early recognized, and the royal audiencia was made stationary at Valladolid. Later a second such court was established, first at Ciudad Real, then, after the conquest, at Granada. Ultimately others were organized in Galicia, Seville, Madrid, Burgos, and several additional centres. The system was early transported and extensively developed in the American possessions, where twelve independent audiencias existed. There, as at home, this court system gradually superseded the more individual and military rule of the adelantado, which had been characteristic of the early conquest period.[1]

[1] **Moses**, *Spanish Rule in America*, 66, etc.

The adelantado was the representative of the administrative powers of the crown. Five such officials in the fifteenth century governed respectively the provinces of Castile, Leon, Galicia, Andalusia, and Murcia; another was appointed over Granada when it was conquered; and still another administered the temporal affairs of the vast estates of the archbishopric of Toledo. Their duties were partly military, partly civil, and under them were subordinate royal officers with a great variety of titles such as sarjento mayor, alferez real, alcalde. The title of adelantado was naturally given to Columbus, Pizarro, and several of the other early conquistadores as the nearest equivalent to their position as civil and military governors of the wide-spreading, newly conquered lands of America.[1]

The supremacy of the crown extended to the church as well as to the state. Spain, in the Middle Ages and far into modern times, presented the anomaly of a nation and government most ardently devoted to orthodox Christianity and to the church, and yet jealous and impatient of the powers of the Pope. In 1482 Isabella protested against the use of a papal provision for the appointment of a foreign cardinal to a Castilian bishopric, and claimed a right to be consulted in all ecclesiastical appointments. A serious contest ensued, the ultimate result of which was that the queen obtained a clear right of appointment, which, in the reign of

[1] Moses, *Spanish Rule in America*, 68, 69, 112.

Charles V., was formally recognized as such by the pope.[1]

This position of the monarchs at home made easy and natural the adoption of their position of supreme patrons of the church in Spanish America. In the colonies conquered, settled, and Christianized under their influence they had a completeness of control, not only over appointments, but over the establishment of new church centres and the disposition of the titles to ecclesiastical property generally, which was quite unknown anywhere in Europe.

The supremacy of the crown in Spain is evidenced in no way more markedly than by its entire freedom from dependence on the military and landed classes of the country. Yet the nobility were numerous, rich, and distinguished. In the sixteenth century there were twelve dukes, thirteen marquises, and thirty-six counts in Castile, some of whom had princely estates and power. The heads of such families as that of Mendoza or Guzman or Lara or Haro or Medina Celi were among the greatest men in Europe. Yet the highest of these nobles was still at an immeasurable distance below the king. The resumption of royal estates, the seizure of the grand masterships, the enforcement and extension of all the latent powers of the monarchy had freed the Spanish kings from all danger of control by the great nobility.

[1] Vicente de la Fuente, *Hist. Generale de España*, V., 150, quoted in Mariéjol, *L'Espagne sous Ferdinand et Isabelle*, 28.

The chief characteristic of the Castilian nobility, however, was not its wealth, but its numbers. Next in rank to the great nobles, or ricos hombres, were the caballeros, the knights, and below them was a vast number of hidalgos, mere gentlemen. In Castile all were accounted gentlemen who were sons of gentlemen, legitimate or illegitimate; all those who took up their residence in a city newly conquered from the Moors, providing themselves with horse and arms without engaging in trade; those who lived without trade in certain provinces and cities which had that privilege. Whether rich or poor, those who belonged to the noble class had many privileges: they paid none of the general taxes; they were free from imprisonment for debt; they had the preference in appointments to office in state and church; they had precedence on all public occasions; and, except in case of treason or heresy, they had the privilege in case of execution of being decapitated instead of hanged.[1]

These hidalgos and caballeros, many of them poor, living on inadequate estates, in service to other nobles or in irregular ways in the towns, furnished promising material for volunteer forces in war, for distant conquest, and for an expanding government service; but they were weak elements of economic progress. The conquistadores of Spanish America, the soldiers in Italy and the Netherlands, and the drones of Spain were all to be found among the

[1] Mariéjol, *L'Espagne sous Ferdinand et Isabelle*, 278–284.

teeming lower Spanish nobility and gentry. They
made admirable soldiers. With all their pride and
all their indolence, Spanish gentlemen were not too
proud to fight, even in the ranks and afoot; or too
lazy to endure effort and privation when they were
for a military end. The Spaniards as a race were
then, as now, abstemious, and could make long
marches on a slender commissariat. Many of them
were used to the extremes of heat and cold of the
mountainous regions of their native country, and
were fitted for the most trying of long campaigns.
All the material was ready to the hand of the king
for use in his European campaigns, or to be let loose
for adventure in America. With this acknowledged position of legislative, judicial, administrative, and ecclesiastical supremacy at home; with the
headship of a numerous, loyal, and warlike nobility;
with the possession of a numerous trained official
class, it was easy for the Spanish monarchs to impose a centralized and homogeneous system of
despotic government upon the distant and wide-
spread colonies of America.

The assertion of the absolute authority of the
king over the Indies was never neglected or allowed
to lapse. The adventurers who discovered and ex-
plored the West Indies, Central and South America,
Mexico, and much of what is now territory of the
United States; the captains who conquered these
lands; the governors who organized and ruled them;
the colonists who occupied them—all drew their per-

mission so to act from the king, or if they went beyond their commissions quickly legitimated their actions by an appeal to him for an act of indemnity and a more adequate commission. Foreigners were by the edict of the king excluded from the Spanish possessions, or permitted a narrow field of action there; the policy of the colonies in matters of trade, relations with the natives, religion, and finance was dictated by the king. Upon the advice of his Council of the Indies he issued a continuous series of rules and ordinances, and finally drew up for the American possessions the "New Laws."

Yet supreme over her colonies as was the absolute monarchy of Spain, a false idea of their condition would be obtained if it were forgotten that the monarchy was only one of the national institutions. Other political habits of the people were firmly established as well as that of subserviency to the crown. Spain was the classic land of participation of all classes in government through the cortes; almost as old as the monarchy were the fueros, or franchises and charters; protected by these fueros, the cities and towns had become numerous, powerful, and almost self-governing; and even rural communities had in many cases a complicated and semi-independent system of control of their own affairs.

The cortes may be neglected here, since no such representative body ever arose in the colonies; but the same is not true of local self-governing municipalities. Not only were they characteristic of

Spain, but analogous institutions were established as a Spanish population grew up and was organized in the Indies, where there was a strong tendency to revert to practical self-government and thus to defeat the centralizing policy of the monarchy.

Several hundred cities, towns, and rural communities in Spain held fueros granted to them by the king, a great noble, or some ecclesiastical body. These charters in many cases dated from the eleventh or twelfth century and conceded the most extensive rights and privileges. Under them townsmen could surround themselves with a wall, organize a military force, elect their own magistrates, judge their own inhabitants, collect their own taxes, pay only a fixed sum to the crown, and in other ways live almost as a separate political body under the general protection only of the king.[1]

Notwithstanding many differences among the towns in size, character, and political privileges, among those of Castile there was a certain similarity of organization which may be described as follows, and may be looked upon as the type on which all municipalities in Spanish America were originally constructed.[2]

The citizens who possessed full political rights were known in the most general sense as vecinos; when acting as electors they were spoken of as forming the concejo, cabildo, or council. The actual

[1] Antequera, *Hist. de la Legislacion Española*, 128–139.
[2] Bourne, *Spain in America*, chap. xv.

body which met and directed municipal affairs was the ayuntamiento, made up of the more important magistrates and officials, of whom there was usually a considerable number and variety. The alcaldes exercised judicial functions, both civil and criminal; the regidores had charge of the administrative work of the community; the corregidores of its oversight in the interest of the king; the alguazil mayor commanded the military forces; the mayor domo had the oversight of the town property. In some towns one or more of the alcaldes had the title of alcalde mayor, and held a presiding function. There were various lower officials, such as alarifes, rayones, and others in great variety.[1] The town officials were in some cases appointed by the king, in others elected by the vecinos, in still others divided between royal and local appointment. They were usually drawn from the body of the citizens, but in some cases from gentlemen or even noblemen who had houses in the town or simply owned property there.

This municipal organization and certain other ancient institutions tended to reappear in the colonies, and thus to modify and limit that absolutism of the central government which was without doubt the leading characteristic of the Spanish colonial system. The provincial interests of the colonists also opposed the monarchy. The great distance of the colonies from Spain, the rigidity of official custom, the difference between the interests of the colonists

[1] Antequera, *Hist. de la Legislacion Española*, App. ix., 542.

and the desires of the government, and the lack of vigor at home combined to prevent a really effective control of the colonies. "*Obedezcase, pero no se cumpla*" (Let it be obeyed, but not enforced) was a saying sufficiently descriptive of the attitude of the colonies towards unpopular decrees from home.

The servitude of men of dependent races, which became such a fundamental characteristic of Spanish America, is an instance of this incompleteness of control by the central government. Slavery was a product of American conditions and was not general in the mother-country. A small number of Moorish slaves captured in war and of negroes imported through Portugal were scattered through Spain, but they did not form a class, and were protected rather than depressed by the law.[1]

Slavery in America was always distasteful to the home government, and only reluctantly permitted because of the apparent necessities of the case and in the hope of ameliorating the lot of the Indians. The whole plan of the asiento was based on the principle of regulating and limiting slavery. The shameful extermination of the native races of the West Indies is a long, sad history of kindly intentions and wise regulations on the part of the home government, made nugatory by the determined self-interest and heartless cruelty of the colonists.[2] The

---

[1] Lea, *The Moriscos of Spain*, 2.
[2] Lea, "The Indian Policy of Spain" (in *Yale Review*, August, 1899); Bourne, *Spain in America*, chap. xviii.

fervor of Las Casas could readily obtain from the Spanish monarchs proclamations declaring the freedom of the Indians and even definite statutes providing for their good treatment; but neither his fervor nor the monarch's power could secure the enforcement of the laws or save the miserable natives.[1]

In theory the Spanish sovereigns ruled the Indies with an autocratic sway. In practice the colonies were governed by a bureaucracy or, more commonly, allowed to drift. Yet by the forms of Spanish rule they were deprived of all wholesome local freedom, of all power of independent action, and of all deliberate choice of their own policy. They did not, therefore, develop during their colonial period a robust provincial life and character; and only late and with great difficulty did they struggle into independence and obtain self-government.[2]

The institutions of France which were transferred to the New World or which exercised a direct influence on its political development belong to a period a century or a century and a half later than those of Spain which have just been described. Yet during that period there had been no essential alteration in the general direction of political development in France, and the system which Canada reflected in the seventeenth century was a more elaborate rather than a different system from that of

[1] Lea, "The Indian Policy of Spain" (*Yale Review*, August, 1899), 132, 135, 138, 141, 143, etc.
[2] Paxson, *The Independence of the South-American Republics*, chap. i.

the sixteenth.   This development had, indeed, been in progress since the Hundred Years' War, and consisted in the steady rise of the power of the centralized monarchy.   In Spain we have seen a sudden growth of absolutism and centralization within one reign.   In France the foundation of the absolute monarchy was laid earlier, it was constructed more uniformly, and the resulting edifice was more firm and symmetrical.

The extension of the royal household, the subdivision of the royal councils, the creation of the parlements,[1] the appointment of governors of provinces, bailiffs, and intendants, and the establishment of a complicated hierarchy of financial and judicial officers and official bodies,[2] were processes which arose from the fundamental conditions of France and from the genius of her government.   In this development there were periods of rapid growth, as that of Francis I.; of temporary reaction, as that of the religious wars.   Of the periods of the former class none was more important and definitive than that which was in progress during the years in which Canada was struggling into existence—that is to say, the reigns of Henry IV. and Louis XIII., from 1589 to 1643.   By the latter date, that of the accession of Louis XIV., the work was accomplished.

France was, in theory and in practice, a despotism.   It was so in theory, for Louis himself could

---

[1] Lavisse, *Histoire de France*, V., pt. i., 8
[2] *Ibid.*, V., 247.

declare, "All power, all authority, are in the hand of the king, and there can be none other in the kingdom than those which be established there." The epigram attributed to that monarch, "L'état, c'est moi," was not an exaggerated description of the royal functions, according to the views of the king and of his most thoughtful ministers. "The ruler ought not to render accounts to any one of what he ordains. . . . No one can say to him, 'Why do you do thus?'" said Bossuet. In his copy-book as a child Louis XIV. was taught to write, "To kings homage is due; they do what they please." In practice the absolute power was no less a reality, since by royal decree the king not only made war and peace, determined upon foreign and internal policy, established religion, and codified law, but also disposed of the property of his subjects through arbitrary taxation. A systematic scheme of government, in which all lines should converge upward to the sovereign, could be drawn more justly for France in the seventeenth century than for any political structure since the Notitia Dignitatum was drawn up for the later Roman Empire.

The royal government was as simple territorially as it was in functions. It extended over all the territory of France and of the French possessions beyond the seas. Instead of a collection of provinces, of some of which the king was direct ruler, of others only feudal lord, as had been his position in the fourteenth century, he was now king equally over every one of his subjects in every part of his dominions. The administration of this territory had been transferred from its feudal lords to the king by the appointment in the fifteenth century of governors of the provinces, whose position was almost that of viceroys.

An even more effective instrument of royal control was afterwards created in the form of the intendants. Dating in their beginning from the middle of the sixteenth century, reintroduced by Henry IV. in his reconstruction of France after the religious wars,[1] these officials were settled upon by Richelieu in the period between 1624 and 1641 as the principal agents and representatives of royal power. Eventually each province had its intendant alongside of the governor, and these thirty-four officials exercised the real government over France. They were drawn not from the great nobility, as were the governors, but from the petty nobility or purely official class; they had no local connections or interests apart from the crown which they served; they could be removed at will; they exercised powers only by consent and direction of the crown; they were, therefore, absolutely dependent. On the other hand, they were habitually invested with powers of almost unbounded extent. They could withdraw cases from the ordinary judges and hear and decide them themselves; they recruited and organized the army; they had oversight of the

[1] Rambaud, *Hist. de la Civilisation Française*, I., 537.

churches, the schools, roads, canals, agriculture, trade, and industries; they must see that peace was kept; and they must watch over and report on the actions of all other royal officials in the province, including the governor. It was the intendant who made the despotic government of the king a reality. John Law declared, in a letter to D'Argenson, that "this kingdom of France is governed by thirty intendants."

This despotism undoubtedly made France great, but it cost a terrible price. Like all supreme powers, it was jealous, and suffered no other public institutions to exist alongside of it. In competition with its power all older bodies became weak. The Estates General did not meet again after 1614; the parlements humbled themselves; provincial, municipal, and communal governments dropped into obscurity; the individual man, unless he was a functionary, lost all habit of political initiative, independence, or criticism. The mighty machine of the government was too vast, too complicated, and too distant for the common man to do aught but submit himself to it and lose much of his individual force thereby.

Enforced orthodoxy in religion was a natural outcome of the unity and symmetry of government; hence, notwithstanding the large number of Huguenots, the economic value of the Protestant element in the population, and the tolerance which might be expected from so enlightened a government, the

Edict of Nantes was repealed in 1685, and, theoretically at least, all the population of France and of the French possessions were after this time orthodox Catholic Christians, thus again obtaining uniformity, but at the price of almost irreparable loss of population and of activity of mind.

Yet alongside this supreme despotic government had been preserved certain relics of feudalism. The sovereigns and great ministers who had humbled the aristocracy did not wish to humiliate it. While depriving the nobles of all political power they had carefully preserved to them their social privileges. This was done partly by giving them a favored position in the administration of the great machine of centralized royal government, partly by allowing the continuance of old feudal privileges. To the nobles were reserved all the higher positions in the army, navy, civil service, administration of the provinces, and in the church;[1] and the government of French possessions beyond the seas was in almost all cases given to noblemen.

Of the feudal privileges of the nobility a number were profitable in money or gratifying to pride. Every landed noble had some degree of jurisdiction, frequently that of "high, mean, and petty justice" —that is to say, the right of trying and settling a large variety of judicial matters among his tenants; his right of punishment extending in some cases even to the infliction of the death penalty. He had

[1] Rambaud, *Hist. de la Civilisation Française*, II., 75–78.

the right to receive certain payments upon every sale or lease of the lands of any inhabitant of his fief; he received fees upon sales of cattle, grain, wine, meat, and other articles within the limits of his lands; he alone had the privilege of hunting and fishing or of collecting a fee for granting the privilege to others; and he alone could keep a dove-cote or a rabbit-warren; he had the banalités—*i.e.*, the right of requiring all tenants on his estates to grind their grain at his mill and to bake at his oven; he had corvées—the right to a certain amount of unpaid labor from his tenants; his land was exempt from the taille, the most burdensome of taxes; and he had many other and diverse seigneurial rights, often, indeed, more vexatious to the tenant than they were profitable to the seigneur.[1] These rights of land-holders were survivals from an earlier period; but they were survivals which still had great value and considerable vitality. Although permitted to exist by the absolute monarchy, they were in reality antagonistic to it in spirit, and might at any time, and actually did, become a serious disadvantage to it. Among the more primitive surroundings of Canada these privileges of a landed aristocracy obtained new life and vigor, and feudalism played a conspicuous if not a leading part in the troubled history of that colony.[2]

Of the political institutions of Holland not so

---

[1] Rambaud, *Hist. de la Civilisation Française*, II., 84–90.
[2] Parkman, *The Old Régime in Canada*, chaps. xii.-xv.

much need be said, for New Netherland was a commercial not a political creation, the factory of a trading company, not a self - governing colony. Yet, under the general control of the West India Company, municipal institutions were established at Manhattan, and in the form of the patroonships feudal powers were granted to large landholders along the Hudson and Long Island Sound; and in both these cases the models were drawn in large part from the home land.

The United Netherlands was a confederation of seven provinces, Holland being far the most influential. But Holland itself, as was true of the others, was in many respects a confederation of municipalities. The peculiar history of the country had been such that from a comparatively early period the towns and cities had obtained charters from their overlord, the count of Holland, or from lesser noblemen, granting them the most extensive rights and privileges. These rights had continued to be extended till the power of the count within the towns was narrowly restricted. His representative was the schout, but that official exercised rather a prosecuting and executing than an independent power, bringing offenders before a town court,[1] and carrying out its judgments.

The schepens who made up this court, with two or more burgomasters and a certain number of prominent citizens, organized as a council or vroed-

---

[1] Davies, *History of Holland*, I., 77.

schap, carried on the affairs of the city, making its laws, exercising its jurisdiction, and administering its finances in almost entire independence of the central government.[1] The representatives of the larger towns, along with the deputies of the nobles, also made up the states of Holland, any one city having the right of veto in any proposed national action.[2]

Outside of the towns the open country was either domains of the count, or fiefs held from him by church corporations or nobles. On the latter many old feudal powers survived through the sixteenth century. The nobles exercised always low and sometimes high jurisdiction, they taxed their own tenants, they carried on private war with other nobles, and they enjoyed an exemption from the payment of taxes. The feudal conditions in these rural domains and the highly developed internal organization of the cities seem at first glance diametrically opposed; but, after all, their relation to the central government was much the same, the city being treated as a fief held by its council;[3] and as a matter of fact it was these two institutions which were introduced into New Netherland.[4]

[1] Fruin, *Geschiedniss der Staatsinstellingen in Nederland*, 68, 69.   [2] Davies, *History of Holland*, I., 85.
[3] Jameson, in *Magazine of Am. Hist.*, VIII., chap. i., 316.
[4] O'Callaghan, *Documentary History of New York*, I., 385–394.

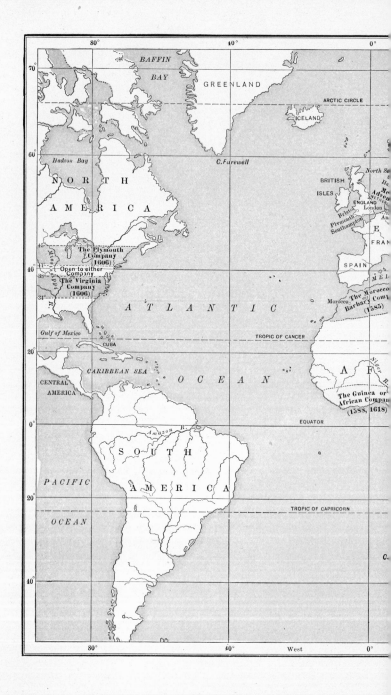

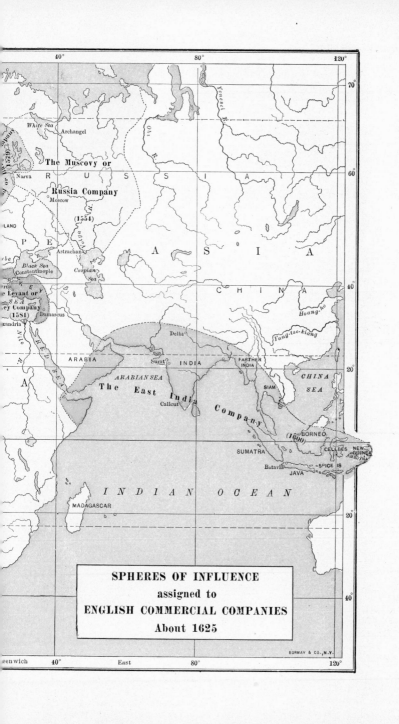

SPHERES OF INFLUENCE
assigned to
ENGLISH COMMERCIAL COMPANIES
About 1625

CHAPTER VII

THE SYSTEM OF CHARTERED COMMERCIAL COMPANIES

(1550–1700)

THE priority of Portugal and Spain in distant adventure did not secure them from the competition of the other nations of Europe, whose awakening activity, ambition, and enterprise perceived clearly the advantages of the New World and of the new routes to the south and east. Almost within the first decade of the sixteenth century an Englishman cries out: "The Indies are discovered and vast treasures brought from thence every day. Let us, therefore, bend our endeavors thitherwards, and if the Spaniards or Portuguese suffer us not to join with them, there will be yet region enough for all to enjoy."[1] Soon England, France, and the Netherlands were sending exploring and trading expeditions abroad, and somewhat later they all aimed at colonial empires comparable with that of Spain. These colonial settlements were chiefly made for commercial profit and depended

[1] Lord Herbert (1511), quoted in Macpherson, *Annals of Commerce*, II., 39.

closely on a new and peculiar type of commercial organization, the well-known chartered companies. It was these companies which established the greater number of American colonies, and the ideals, regulations, and administrative methods of corporate trading were interwoven into their political fabric.

Revolutions in commerce have been as frequent, as complete, and, in the long run, as influential as have been revolutions in political government. Europe in the fifteenth century had a clearly marked and well-established method of international commerce; yet before the sixteenth century was over a fundamentally different system grew up, which was destined not only to characterize trade during the next two hundred years, but, as has been said, to exercise a deep influence on the settlement and government of colonies in general and on the policy of their home governments.

A complete contrast exists between international trade in 1400 and 1600. The type of commerce characteristic of the earlier period was carried on by individual merchants; that belonging to the later period by joint-stock companies. Under the former, merchants depended on municipal support and encouragement; under the latter they acted under charters received from national governments. The individual merchants of the earlier period had only trading privileges; the organized companies of the later time had political powers also. In the fifteenth century the merchants from any one city or group of cities occupied a building, a quarter, or fondaco, in each of the foreign cities with which they traded; in the seventeenth they more usually possessed independent colonies or fortified establishments of their own on the coasts of foreign countries. In the earlier period trading operations were restricted to Europe; in the later they extended over the whole world.

The essential elements of the organization of trade at the period chosen for this description are its individual character, its restriction to well-marked European limits, and its foundation upon concessions obtained by town governments.

At the beginning of the fifteenth century there were five principal groups of trading cities, whose merchants carried on probably nine-tenths of the commerce of Europe. These groups were situated: (1) in northern Italy; (2) in southern France and Catalonia; (3) in southern Germany; (4) in northern France and Flanders; (5) in northern Germany. Two of them were in the south of Europe, and found their most considerable function in transmitting goods between the Levant and Europe; the Hanse towns of northern Germany, at the other extremity of Europe, carried the productions of the Baltic lands to the centre and south; the Flemish and south German groups, intermediate between the two, exchanged among themselves and transmitted goods from one part of Europe to another. There were, of course, vast differences of organization among the trading towns. Venice and Cologne, Barcelona and Augsburg, Bruges and Lübeck were too far separated in distance, nationality, the nature of their trade, and the degree of their development to have the same institutions. And yet there were many similarities.

The city authorities obtained for their citizens the privileges of buying and selling within certain districts and under certain restrictions, and very frequently of having their own warehouses, dwelling houses, and selling - places. Examples are to be found in the fondachi of Venice, Genoa, and other Italian, French, and Catalan cities, established in the Greek and Mohammedan districts of the eastern Mediterranean, on the basis of grants given by the rulers of those lands and cities. Just as character-istic examples can be found in western Europe; in London the "Steelyard" was a group of warehouses, offices, dwellings, and court-yards owned jointly by the towns of the Hanseatic League, and occupied by merchants from those towns who came to England to trade under the concessions granted them by the English government.[1] The south Germans had their fondaco dei Tedeschi in Venice, and the north Germans their "St. Peter's Yard" in Novgorod. The Venetian merchants trading to the city of Bruges usually met for mercantile purposes in the house of a Flemish family named Van de Burse, a

[1] Lappenberg, *Geschichte des Hansischen Stahlhofes zu London*.

name which is said to have given the word "bourse" to the languages of modern Europe.[1]

The union among the merchants of any one city or league was one for joint trading privileges only, not for corporate investment or syndicated business. Each merchant or firm traded separately and independently, simply using the warehouse and office facilities secured by the efforts of the home government, and enjoying the permission to trade, exemption from duties, and whatever other privileges might have been obtained for its merchants by the same power. The necessity for obtaining such concessions arose from the habit of looking at all international intercourse as to a certain degree abnormal, and of disliking and ill-treating foreigners. Hence the Germans in London, the Venetians in Alexandria, the Genoese in Constantinople, for instance, needed to have permission respectively from the English, the Mameluke, and the Greek governments to carry on their trade. Although they found it highly desirable for many reasons to hold a local settlement of their own in those cities, such a possession was not a necessary accompaniment of the individual and municipally regulated commerce of the thirteenth, fourteenth, and fifteenth centuries. Where but a few traders made their way to any one market, and that only irregularly, they lodged with natives, sold their goods in the open market-place, organized no permanent

[1] Mayr, in Helmolt, *History of the World*, VII., 81.

establishment, and had no consulate.   On the other
hand, where trade was extensive and constant, the
settlement was like a part of the home land located
in the midst of a foreign population.

As the fifteenth century progressed many influences combined to bring about a change in this system.   The most important one of these influences
was the growth of centralized states in the north,
centre, and west of Europe.   As Russia, Denmark,
Sweden, England, Burgundy, and France became
strong, the self-governing cities within these countries necessarily became politically weak; and the
trading arrangements they had made among themselves became insecure.   Strong nationalities were
impatient of the claims of privilege made by foreigners settled or habitually trading in their cities;
the interests of their own international policy often
indicated the desirability of either favoring or opposing bodies of merchants, which in the time of their
weakness the governments had treated with exactly
the opposite policy; finally, the desire of their own
citizens for the advantages of their own foreign
trade often commended itself to the rulers as an
object of settled policy.[1]   In other words, national
interests and municipal interests were often opposed
to one another.

Internal difficulties in many cities and internal
dissensions in the leagues of cities helped to weaken
the towns as guarantors of the trade of their citizens.

[1] Schanz, *Englische Handelspolitik*.

As a result of these political influences, before the fifteenth century was over the distribution of commerce was much changed and municipal control was distinctly weakened. The Italian and the German cities became less active and wealthy, while London, Lisbon, Antwerp, and many other centres grew richer. Individual cities and even leagues of cities ceased to be able to negotiate with other municipalities or with potentates to obtain trading privileges for their citizens, since such matters were now provided for by commercial treaties formed by national governments. One of the main characteristics of earlier commerce, its dependence on city governments, thus passed away.

Then came the opening up of direct commerce by sea with the East Indies, the discovery of America, and the awakening of ambition, enterprise, and effort on the part of new nations to make still further explorations and to develop new lines of commerce. The old organization of commerce was profoundly altered when its centre of gravity was shifted westward to the Atlantic seaboard, and Europe got its Oriental products for the most part by an ocean route. Cities which had for ages had the advantage of a good situation were now unfavorably placed. Venice, Augsburg, Cologne, and a hundred other towns which had been on the main highways of trade were now on its byways. Many of these towns made strenuous, and in some cases and for a time successful, efforts to conform to the new conditions.[1] Vigorous industry, trade, and commerce continued to exist in many of the old centres, and some of the most famous "merchant princes" of history, such as the Fuggers and the Medici, built up their fortunes in the old commercial cities in the fifteenth and sixteenth centuries. Nevertheless, these were the exception rather than the rule; and such successes were due to financial rather than commercial operations. In a general sense the old commerce of Europe, so far as it followed its accustomed lines, suffered a grievous decline.

More important than the decay of the old method was the growth of the new. A vast mass of new trade came into existence; spices and other Oriental products, now that they were imported by the Portuguese and afterwards by Spanish, Dutch, French, and English, by direct routes and by water carriage, were greatly cheapened in price, and thus made attainable by many more people and much more extensively consumed. The early explorers of America failed to find either the route to the East or the Eastern goods which they sought, but they found other articles for which a demand in Europe either already existed or was ultimately created. Sea-fish abounded on the northeastern coasts of America to a degree that partially made up their loss to the disappointed seekers for a northwest passage. Whale oil and whalebone were obtained in the same waters. Dye-woods, timber, and ship stores were found on

[1] Mayr, in Helmolt, *History of the World*, VII., 64–66.

the coasts farther south.   Furs became one of the
most valued and most permanent imports from
America.   Gradually, as habits in Europe changed,
other products came to be of enormous production
and value.   Sugar stands in the first rank of these
later products; tobacco, cocoa, and many others
followed close upon it.   As colonists from Europe became established in the New World they
must be provided with European and Asiatic
goods, and this gave additional material for commerce.

Besides creating an increased commerce with the
East and a new commerce with the West, the awakened spirit of enterprise and the new discoveries
widened the radius of trade of each nation.   Men
learned to be bold, and the merchants of each European country carried their national commerce over
all parts of Europe and far beyond its limits to the
newly discovered lands.   English, Dutch, French,
and Danish merchants met in the ports of the White
Sea and in those of the Mediterranean, and com-
peted with one another for the commerce of the East
and the New World.   Trading to a distance was the
chief commercial phenomenon of the sixteenth century, and was more influential than any other one
factor in the transformation of commerce then in
progress.   Distant trading proved to have different
requirements from anything that had gone before:
it needed the political backing of some strong national government; it needed, or was considered to need,

a monopoly of trade; and it needed the capital of many men.

These requirements were not felt in Portugal and Spain as they were in the other countries of Europe, because each of those countries had control of an extensive and lucrative field of commerce, and because in them government itself took the direction of all distant trading. The Portuguese monopoly of the trade with the coast of India and with the Spice Islands was practically complete. Through most of the sixteenth century her ships alone rounded the Cape of Good Hope; her only rivals in trade in the East were the Arabs, who had been there long before her, and their traffic was restricted to a continually diminishing field.

Until Portugal was united with Spain in 1580, and after that until Holland broke in on the Portuguese-Spanish monopoly of the East Indies in 1595, her control of Eastern commerce was as nearly perfect as could be wished.[1] Government regulation of this commerce extended almost to the entire exclusion of individual enterprise. The fleets which sailed to the East Indies were determined upon, fitted out, and officered by the government, just as those of Venice were.[2] The Portuguese annual fleet sent to the Indies counted sometimes as many as twenty vessels. In the one hundred and fifteen

---

[1] Cunningham, *Western Civilization*, II., 183–190.
[2] Saalfeld, *Geschichte des Portugessche Kolonialwesens*, 138, etc., quoted in Cunningham, II., 187.

years between 1497 and 1612 eight hundred and
six ships were sent from Portugal to India,[1] all
equipped for the voyage and fitted out by the government with cannon and provided with armed
forces.

The management of the fleet was in the hands of
the government office known as the Casa da India.
The merchants who shipped goods in these vessels
and brought cargoes home in them were, it is true,
independent traders, carrying on their business as a
matter of private enterprise;[2] but they were subject to government regulations at every turn and
supported by government at every step.   At first
foreign merchants were admitted to the Eastern
trade under these conditions, but subsequently it
was restricted to Portuguese, and ultimately became
a government monopoly.   Under this system Lisbon
became one of the greatest commercial cities of the
world.   Venetian, Florentine, German, Spanish,
French, Dutch, and Hanse merchants took up their
residence in Lisbon, purchased East Indian goods
from the merchants who imported them, and dealt
in other imports and exports resulting from this
activity of trade.[3]

In Spain the government regulation of commerce
was scarcely less close.   All goods which were sent
from Spain to America must be shipped from the one

[1] Hunter, *Hist. of British India*, I., 165.
[2] Cunningham, *Western Civilization*, II., 187.
[3] Mayr, in *Helmolt, History of the World*, VII., 70.

port of Seville, and they must be landed at either one or other of wo American ports—Vera Cruz, in Mexico, or Portobello, on the Isthmus of Panama. Two fleets were sent from Seville each year, one for each of these destinations. All arrangements for these fleets, all licenses for those who shipped goods in them, and all jurisdiction over offences committed upon them were in the hands of the government establishment of the Casa de Contractacion at Seville.[1] No intruders were allowed in the Spanish colonies; the only persons who could take part in the trade were merchants of Seville, native or foreign, who were specially licensed by the government. Monopoly as well as government support was thus secured to the distant traders between Spain and her colonies in the West and in the East Indies.

For two hundred years this system of government fleets in Portugal and Spain was kept almost intact. Since the government provided merchants with military defence and economic regulation, since it minimized competition among them and guaranteed to them a monopoly of commerce in the regions with which they traded, there was small need of organization or of a union of forces among them. Consequently commercial companies are almost unknown in Portuguese and Spanish history.[2]

In Spain and Portugal government control of

---

[1] Veitia Linage, *Spanish Rule of Trade to the West Indies*, book I., chap. iii.

[2] Moses, *Spanish Rule in America*, 166–171.

trade was at a maximum. In the other countries of Europe, notwithstanding occasional plans for such control, as in the Netherlands in 1608,[1] the part which government took in commercial matters was much less, the part taken by private merchants was far greater. In fact, many of the earliest trading ventures were of an almost purely individual character. The patent given by Henry VII. to the Cabots in 1497, similar letters granted in 1502 to certain merchants of Bristol,[2] a grant to Robert Thorne in 1527, the long series of authorized expeditions from 1575 to 1632 in search of the northwest passage, the charters given to Humphrey Gilbert in 1578 and to Sir Walter Raleigh in 1584, and many other patents made out in the sixteenth century to prospective colony builders, all were granted to individuals or to groups of loosely organized adventurers.[3]

In contrast both with government - controlled commerce and with purely private trading and enterprise, the chartered companies of England, Holland, France, Sweden, and Denmark arose. They were by no means self-controlled and independent companies; they were dependent on their governments for many rights and privileges and for constant support, protection, and subsidy. On the other hand, the governments expected them not only to develop a profitable trade but to furnish certain

[1] Jameson, *Usselinx*, 43. [2] Rymer, *Fœdera* (2d ed.), XIII., 37.
[3] Brown, *Genesis of the United States*, I., 1–28.

advantages to the nation, such as the creation of colonies, the increase of shipping, the provision of materials for use in the navy, the humiliation of political rivals, the preservation of a favorable balance of trade, and ultimately the payment of imposts and the loan of funds. They stood, therefore, midway between unregulated individual trading, in which the government took no especial interest, and that complete government organization and control of trade which has been described as characterizing the policy of Portugal and Spain.

Some fifty or sixty such companies, nearly contemporaneous, and on the same broad lines of organization, are recorded as having been chartered by the five governments mentioned above, a few in the second half of the sixteenth century, the great proportion within the seventeenth century.[1] Of course, some of these companies were still-born, never having gone beyond the charter received from the government; some existed only for a few years; and some were simply reorganizations. The formation of these companies marks a distinct stage of commercial development, and furnishes a valuable clew to the foundation and early government of European colonies in America.

England, Holland, France, Sweden, and Denmark, as well as Scotland and Prussia, each had an " East

[1] Some are enumerated in Cawston and Keane, *Early English Chartered Companies;* a still larger number in Bonnassieux, *Les Grandes Compagnies du Commerce.*

India Company"; Holland, France, Sweden, and Denmark each had a "West India Company"; England, Holland, and France each had a "Levant" or "Turkey Company"; England and France each had an "African Company"; and a date might readily be found in the seventeenth century when all these were in existence at the same time. The following list of such companies shows their number and simultaneity. The list cannot claim to be exhaustive or absolutely accurate, for the history of many such organizations is extremely obscure, the dates of their foundations questionable, and some companies chartered at the time were, perhaps, not commercial in their nature.

1554. (English) Russia or Muscovy Company.
1576. (English) Cathay Company (first).
1579. (English) Baltic or Eastland Company.
1581. (English) Turkey or Levant Company.
1585. (English) Morocco or Barbary Company.
1588. (English) African Company (first).
1594. (Dutch) Company for Distant Lands.
1596. (Dutch) Greenland Company.
1597–1599. (Dutch) East India Companies (early).
1598–1599. (French) Canadian Companies (early).
1600. (English) East India Company.
1602. (Dutch) East India Company.
1602. (French) Company of New France.
1604. (French) North African Company (first).
1604. (French) East India Company (first).

1606. (English) London and Plymouth Companies.
1609. (English) Guiana Company.
1610. (English) Newfoundland Company.
1611. (French) East India Company (second).
1612. (English) Bermuda Company.
1614. (Dutch) Company of the North, or Greenland Company.
1615. (French) East India Company (third).
1616. (Danish) East India Company (first).
1618. (English) African Company (second).
1619. (Danish) Iceland Company (first).
1620. (English) New England Company.
1620. (French) Montmorency Company.
1621. (Dutch) West India Company.
1624. (Swedish) Company for Asia, Africa, America, and Magellania.
1626. (French) Company of Senegal (first).
1626. (French) Company of Morbihan (first).
1626. (French) Company of Saint Christopher (first).
1626. (Swedish) South Sea Company.
1626. (Swedish) East India Company.
1628. (French) Company of One Hundred Associates of New France.
1628. (French) North African Company (second).
1629. (English) Company of Massachusetts Bay.
1629. (Dutch) Levant Company (first).
1631. (English) African Company (third).
1633. (French) West Africa Company (first).
1634. (Dutch) Surinam Company.

1634. (Danish) East India Company (second).

1635. (English) China or Cathay Company.

1635. (French) Company of West India Islands.

1640. (French) Company of East Africa.

1643. (French) Company of North Cape of South America.

1644. (French) Company of St. Jean de Luz.

1644. (French) Baltic Company.

1647. (Danish) Iceland Company (second).

1650. (Dutch) Levant Company (second).

1651. (French) Cayenne Company.

1655. (French) West Africa Company (second).

1660. (French) China Company.

1662. (English) African Company (fourth).

1664. (French) East India Company (last).

1664. (French) West India Company (last).

1664. (English) Canary Company.

1669. (French) Northern Company (last).

1670. (French) Levant Company.

1670. (English) Hudson Bay Company.

1671. (Danish) West India Company.

1671. (French) Bordeaux-Canada Company.

1672. (English) African Company (last).

1673. (French) Senegal Company (last).

1683. (French) Acadia Company.

1684. (French) Louisiana Company.

1684. (French) Guinea Company.

1686. (Danish) East India Company (last).

1697. (French) China Company (last).

1698. (French) Santo Domingo Company.

When the English commercial companies were to
be chartered, it was not necessary to invent an entirely new type of organization.   A model already
existed ready to hand in the Society of Merchants
Adventurers, of which the origin goes back certainly to the fifteenth century, perhaps still earlier.[1]   The sphere of trade of this body of export-
ing merchants extended along the coasts of France,
the Netherlands, and Germany, opposite England,
and some distance into the interior.[2]   It is true
that the Merchants Adventurers had many mediæval
features which assimilated them more to the old
merchant and craft guilds than to the more modern
type of chartered commercial companies which were
about to come into existence.   They had, like the
craft guilds, a system of apprenticeship and different
degrees of advancement in their membership.[3]

The members were all controlled by a "stint,"
according to which an apprentice in the last year
of his term might ship one hundred pieces of cloth
in the year; while a full freeman in the society could
ship from four hundred to one thousand pieces a
year, according to the length of time he had been
a member.[4]   They were under strict regulations
against forestalling and undue competition.   They

[1] Lingelbach, *Brief Hist. of the Merchant Adventurers*, xxi.–xxv.
[2] *Ibid.*, xxvii.
[3] Lingelbach, *Internal Organization of the Merchant Adventurers*,
8–18.
[4] Lingelbach, *Laws and Ordinances of the Merchant Adventurers*,
67–74.

could display and sell their cloth only upon Mondays, Wednesdays, and Fridays, and "No person shall stand watchinge at the corners or ends of streetes, or at other mens' Packhouses or at the house or place where anie clothe merchant or draper ys lodged, nor seeinge anie such in the street shall run or follow after hym with Intent to Entyce or lead hym to his packhouse, upon pain of fyve pounds ster." [1]

In many respects, on the other hand, the Merchants Adventurers were quite similar to the later chartered companies, whose period of existence their own overlapped. In fact, considering the early date of their origin, the tardy development of English economic life, and the obstacles to trading in a foreign country even so near as the continental seaboard, the conditions which confronted them were much the same as those which the later companies had to meet, and they met them in much the same way. They obtained a charter of incorporation from the king; they possessed a monopoly of trade in a certain territory, as against other men of their own nation; they had a common treasury for joint expenses; and they acted as, and were even called, "the English nation," in the foreign country which was their abiding-place. [2]

The Merchants Adventurers, therefore, might be

[1] Lingelbach, *Laws and Ordinances of the Merchant Adventurers*, 89, 91.
[2] Lingelbach, *Internal Organization*, 29–34; *Laws and Ordinances*, passim; and *Charters of 1462 and 1564*.

looked upon as a late surviving mediæval merchant
guild, modified in form by the necessity of adapting
itself to trading in a foreign country; or it might
be considered as the earliest of the modern chartered
commercial companies, still retaining in the seventeenth century some of its mediæval features.
Viewed in either aspect, the Merchants Adventurers
were a living model for the organization of the new
type of companies, and the powers and form of government of the latter show a similarity to the older
company which is certainly not accidental.

The five or six English companies whose dates
of foundation lie within the sixteenth century all
yield in importance, interest, and later influence to
the East India Company, which was destined to an
almost imperial existence of two centuries and a
half, and which may well serve as the representative of the English chartered companies.   Its origin
was closely connected with the international relations of the last decades of the sixteenth century.

The availability of the port of Lisbon as the western distributing centre for Eastern goods ceased in
1580, when Portugal became a part of the dominions
of the king of Spain.   As war already existed between Spain and the Netherlands, and was soon to
break out between Spain and England, commerce was
much disturbed; and after a few years of troubled
intercourse that port was closed to the merchants
of Holland and England.   The union of the crowns
of Spain and Portugal at this time had much the

same effect on the supply of Eastern goods to these two Protestant seaboard states that the conquests of the Turks in the eastern Mediterranean had had for the Italian cities a century before.

It was not likely that the two most vigorous, free, and commercially enterprising states of Europe would allow themselves long to be excluded from the most attractive and lucrative trade in the world. After England, in her resistance to the Armada in 1588, applied the touchstone to the naval prestige of Spain and showed its hollowness, her merchants and mariners took heart and pressed directly to the East. In 1591 an English squadron of three ships, under Captains Raymond and Lancaster, with the queen's leave, sailed down the western coast of Africa, rounded the Cape of Good Hope, followed the east coast to Zanzibar, and then passed across to Cape Comorin, Ceylon, and the Malay peninsula. They had mixed fortune, but one vessel returned home laden with pepper, obtained for the most part from the hold of a Portuguese prize. In 1595 the first direct Dutch voyage was made along much the same route. Other English and Dutch voyages followed; and in 1600 and 1602, respectively, the English and Dutch East India companies were chartered. The following analysis of the charter of the former of these companies will give the main characteristics of the new commercial system: [1]

1. The charter, granted by Queen Elizabeth on

[1] *Charters Granted to the East India Company*, 3-26.

December 31, 1600, was addressed by name to the earl of Cumberland and two hundred and fifteen knights and merchants, whom it created a corporation and a body politic under the name of " The Governor and Company of Merchants of London Trading to the East Indies."

2. The territory to which they were given privileges of trade consisted of all continents and islands lying between the Cape of Good Hope and the Straits of Magellan—that is to say, the east coast of Africa, the southern shore of Asia, the islands of the Indian Ocean, and the west coast of America; so long as they made no attempt to trade with any port at the time of the charter in the possession of any prince in league with Elizabeth, who should protest against such trade.

3. The corporation was for all time; but the privileges of trade under the charter were granted for fifteen years, with a promise, if they should seem profitable to the crown and the realm, to extend them for fifteen years more; and with a reservation, on the other hand, of the power to terminate them on two years' notice.

4. The powers of the company were those of an ordinary corporation and body politic. The members of the company and their employees possessed a complete monopoly of trade in the regions described, so far as English subjects were concerned, having, moreover, the right to grant licenses to non-members to trade within their limits.

5. They could buy land without limitation in amount, and as a matter of fact the company gained its first foothold in each of its stations in the East by buying a small piece of land from the native government.

6. The company could send out yearly "six good ships and six pinnaces with five hundred mariners, unless the royal navy goes forth," and these ships should not be seized even in times of special naval restraint, unless the queen's need was extreme and was announced to the company three months before the ships were impressed.

7. They had the right, in assemblies of the company held in any part of the queen's dominions or outside of them, to make all reasonable laws for their government not in opposition to the laws of England, and they could punish by fine and imprisonment all offenders against these laws.

8. Nothing is said in the original charter of the powers of offence and defence, alliance and military organization; but these were probably taken for granted, as they were so generally used by merchants and navigators at the time, and were, as a matter of fact, exercised without limitation by the company from its first voyage.

9. Especial privileges and exemptions were granted to the company by freeing its members from the payment of customs for the first four voyages, by giving them from six to twelve months' postponement of the payment of subsequent import duties,

and by allowing them re-export of Indian goods free from customs duties. The laws against the export of bullion were also suspended in their favor to the extent of allowing them to send out on each voyage £30,000 in coin.

10. The organization of this company was comparatively simple, consisting of a governor, deputy governor, and twenty-four members of a directing board, "to be called committees," [1] all to be elected annually in a general assembly or court of the company. The governor and committees must all take the oath of allegiance to the English sovereign.

The East India Company remained for some years a somewhat variable body, as each voyage was made on the basis of a separate investment, by different stockholders, and in varying amounts. But in 1609 the charter was renewed, and in 1612 a longer joint-stock investment fixed the membership more definitely. By this time the company had become, in fact, as permitted by its charter, a closely organized corporation, with well-understood and clearly defined rights and powers, and it was soon started on its career of trade, settlement, conquest, and domination.[2] A new type of commercial organization had become clearly dominant.

[1] The word "committee" at that time was used for a single person, as in the case of "trustee," "nominee," "employee," and similar terms.

[2] Hunter, *Hist. of British India*, I., 270–305.

CHAPTER VIII

TYPICAL AMERICAN COLONIZING COMPANIES
(1600–1628)

AN exactly typical chartered commercial company, which combined all the characteristics
of such companies, of course did not exist. The
countries with which they expected to trade ranged
all the way from India to Canada; the political services which their governments imposed upon them
varied from the production of tar, pitch, and tur-
pentine to the weakening of naval rivals; while the
personal qualities of the founders of the companies
and the sovereigns or ministers who gave the charters differed widely. Moreover, the later development of many of these companies had but little
to do with the settlement of America. Nevertheless, three companies may be chosen which exerted
a deep influence on American colonization, and which,
with the English East India Company described in
the last chapter, are fairly typical of the general
system. These are the English Virginia Company,
the Dutch West India Company, and the French
Company of New France.

The charter of 1606 granted to the London and

Plymouth companies was of an incomplete and transitional character;[1] the second Virginia charter,[2] however, which was granted at the request of the company, May 23, 1609, created a corporate trading and colonizing company closely analogous to the East India Company, as will appear from the following analysis:

1. The company was chartered under the name, "The Treasurer and Company of Adventurers and Planters of the City of London for the First Colony in Virginia." It was fully incorporated, with a seal and all legal corporate powers and liabilities. In the charter itself were named some twenty-one peers, ninety-six knights, eighty-six of the lesser gentry, a large number of citizens, merchants, sea-captains, and others, and fifty-six of the London companies— in all, seven hundred and fifteen persons and organizations. They included a large proportion of the enlightenment, enterprise, and wealth of the capital, and, indeed, of all England. The grant was made to the company in perpetuity, although, as will be seen, some of its special exemptions and privileges were for a shorter term only.

2. The region to which the grant applied was the

---

[1] H. L. Osgood, " The Colonial Corporation " (*Political Science Quarterly*, XI., 264–268). This charter is printed in Stith, *Hist. of Virginia*, App. I.; in Brown, *Genesis of the United States*, and elsewhere.

[2] Printed in full in Stith, *Hist. of Virginia*, App. II., and, with a few omissions, in Brown, *Genesis of the United States*, I., 208–237.

territory stretching four hundred miles along the coast, north and south from Chesapeake Bay, and "up into the land from sea to sea westward and northward."

The possession of the soil was given to the company by the most complete title known to the English law, but with the requirement that it be distributed by the company to those who should have contributed money, services, or their presence to the colony.

3. Its commercial powers extended to the exploitation of all the resources of the country, including mines, fisheries, and forests, as well as agricultural products; and to the requirement that all Englishmen not members of the company should pay a subsidy of five per cent. of the value of all goods brought into or taken out of the company's territory, and all foreigners ten per cent. of the value of the goods. The company might send to Virginia all shipping, weapons, victuals, articles of trade, and other equipment that might be necessary, and also all such colonists as should be willing to go.

4. Powers of government in its territory were granted to the company with considerable completeness, the charter declaring that it might make all orders, laws, directions, and other provisions fit and necessary for the government of the colony, and that the governor and other officers might, "within the said precincts of Virginia or in the way by sea thither and from thence, have full and absolute

power and authority to correct, punish, pardon, govern, and rule" all the inhabitants of the colony, in accordance with its laws already made.

As to offensive and defensive powers, it had the right to repel or expel by military force all persons attempting to force their way into its territories and all persons attempting any hurt or annoyance to the colony. The governor might exercise martial law in the colony, and was provided with the general military powers of a lord-lieutenant of one of the English counties. Thus the company and its colony were organized not exactly as an *imperium in imperio*, but at least as an outlying *imperium*.

5. As for special subsidies and privileges, the government of King James was scarcely in a position to make money contributions for such an enterprise, or to give to it ships such as the continental governments might give to their companies; but for seven years the company was allowed to take out all that was necessary for the support, equipment, and defence of its colonists, and for trade with the natives, free of all tax or duty; and for twenty years it should be free from customs on goods imported into Virginia, and should forever pay only five per cent. import duty on goods brought from Virginia to England. Among privileges of less material value, but long after remembered for other reasons, the charter promised to the company that all the king's subjects whom it should take to inhabit the colony, with their children and their posterity, should have

and enjoy all liberties, franchises, and immunities of free-born Englishmen and natural subjects of the king just as if they had remained or been born in England itself.

6. The duties to be performed by the company as respects the government were very few. In recognition of the socage tenure on which the land was held, a payment of one-tenth of all gold and silver was required; and the members of the council of the company were required to take an oath of allegiance to the king in the name of the company. The main requirement from the company was colonization. It was fully anticipated, and in the preamble expressed, that the process of taking out settlers should be a continuous one; and a failure to transport colonists by the company's efforts would certainly have been a failure to fulfil the conditions of its charter.

7. Although there was no requirement of absolute conformity with the established church of England, yet on the ground of the desire to carry only true religion to the natives it was made the duty of the officials of the company to tender the oath of supremacy to every prospective colonist before he sailed, and thus to insure the Protestantism of the settlers.

8. The form of government of the company in England received much attention in the charter, as well it might, after the failure of the arrangements of the former charter. The membership, quarterly

assemblies of the general body of the members, more frequent meetings of a governing council of fifty-three officers, and their duties, were all minutely formulated; and the supremacy of this council, so consonant with the ideas of King James, and so opposed to the needs and the tendencies of the times, was carefully but, as it proved, unsuccessfully provided for.[1]

The charter of the Dutch West India Company was granted by "The High and Mighty Lords, the Lords States-General of the United Netherlands," June 3, 1621. It had already been under discussion in the various representative bodies of the Netherlands for fifteen years, and had been a fixed idea in the brain of its projector, William Usselinx, for at least fourteen years before that,[2] advocated in a dozen pamphlets and a hundred memorials and communications, written and oral, to the States-General; and it had the advantage of the state's experience with the Dutch East India Company. The shape given to the West India Company in its charter was not, therefore, merely an outcome of the plans of an individual, but a resultant also of the influence of the earlier commercial companies, of the political conditions of the time, and of the ambitions, economic and political, of the influential merchant-rulers of the Netherlands.[3]

---

[1] Osgood, "The Colonial Corporation" (*Political Science Quarterly*, XI., 269–273).   [2] Jameson, *Usselinx*, 21, 28, 70.
[3] *Ibid.*, 2–4.

1. The company was given for twenty-four years, during which no stockholders could withdraw and no new subscriptions would be received, the monopoly of the Dutch trade on the west coast of Africa, from Cape Verd to the Cape of Good Hope; in all the islands lying in the Atlantic Ocean; on the east coast of America from Newfoundland to the Straits of Magellan; and even beyond the straits on its west coast, and in the southern lands which at that time were still believed to stretch from Cape Horn across the South Pacific to New Guinea. All the non-European regions of the globe were thus divided by the States-General, with even greater boldness than by Pope Alexander, between the East and West India Dutch chartered companies.

2. Its commercial privileges included a general monopoly and extended to all forms of advancement of trade.

3. As to colonization, the charter provided that the company " may advance the peopling of fruitful and unsettled parts." Usselinx, the original author and the persistent advocate of the plan, would gladly have made more adequate provision for the establishment of colonies, the stimulation of agriculture and mining, good government in these colonies, their religious life, and the conversion of the natives. He had a picture in his mind of a great commercial dominion, settled from Holland and other countries, forming a market for European manufactures, and producing colonial goods for the use of the Nether-

lands.[1]   But the charter was granted in war time,
and by a body of aristocratic traders, who, as Bacon
says, "look ever to the present gain"; so that the
capture of Spanish plate-fleets and the sacking of
West Indian settlements are contemplated with as
much assurance and interest as are colonization and
more legitimate commerce.

4. In view of later disputes between England and
her colonies, it is worthy of note that even such an
enlightened advocate of a prosperous, self-governing
colonial empire as Usselinx should have insisted, in
1618, that the colonists were to pay taxes to the
home government, to trade with the Netherlands
only, and to have no manufactures that would com-
pete with those of the mother-country.[2]

5. The political or semi-public powers of the company, according to the charter, were very extensive:
it could form alliances and make war, so long as the
war was defensive or retaliatory, could build forts,
maintain troops, appoint officers, capture prizes,
and arrest offenders on the high seas.

6. By way of subsidy the company was given one
million florins, the use of sixteen government ships
and four yachts, and exemption from all tolls and
license dues on its ships.

7. The duties required of the company were an
oath of fidelity to Prince Maurice, the stadtholder,
and to the States-General, on the part of its officers;
the provision of a number of vessels equal at least

---

[1] Jameson, *Usselinx*, 43.   [2] *Ibid.*, 63.

to those provided by the government; the return of its ships whenever practicable to the ports from which they had set out; the preservation for military purposes of all prizes captured from enemies of the States-General; the periodical publishing of accounts; and the division, after six years, of all surplus over ten per cent. in such a way that, in addition to what the shareholders received, one-tenth should go to the States - General and one-thirtieth to Count Maurice.

The government of the Dutch West India Company was very complicated, reflecting the political arrangements of the Netherlands and the jealousies of a merchant aristocracy distributed in provinces and cities. There was a governor-in-chief of the company's colonial possessions, but his powers were dependent on a general board of nineteen directors, who were the supreme authority in the regulation of the company's affairs. Below this central body were five territorial chambers, with a combined membership of seventy-eight. The numbers, powers, and influence on the policy of the company of these chambers were in proportion to the wealth of the cities they represented and to the amount of the stock subscribed from these cities. The Amsterdam chamber, which was to subscribe one-half the capital stock, was far the most influential and had the largest number of directors; after it in order came the chambers of Zealand, of the cities on the Meuse, of the cities of North Holland, and of the cities of Friesland and Groningen. These local boards elected the general board, one-third of their number, chosen by lot, retiring each year.[1]

When Richelieu became prime-minister of France in 1624, one of the earliest definite lines of policy he initiated was the formation of privileged commercial companies.[2] He saw with great clearness and formulated in a state paper[3] the reasons for recognizing the superiority for distant commerce, under the conditions of that period, of chartered companies over individual traders. He was also much impressed with the power and success of the great East India companies of England and Holland. His first plan was a general French company of commerce, to include all the outlying sections of the world, and at least two such companies were chartered in succession. They came to nothing, and soon gave place to companies authorized each to carry on commerce with a specified part of America, Africa, Europe, or Asia.[4] The most important of these was the company of Canada, chartered in 1628 on the plans of Champlain, and intended to take the place of all earlier companies and individual grantees having privileges in that region. The chartered powers and privileges of this company may be analyzed as follows:

[1] Jameson, *Usselinx*, 33, 34.

[2] *Edict of Reformation of 1627*, art. 429; Isambert, *Recueil Général des Anciennes Lois Françaises*, XVI., 329.

[3] Michaud et Poujoulat, *Mémoires*, I., chap. xviii., 438.

[4] Pigeonneau, *Hist. du Commerce*, II., 426–431.

1. The region to which they extended was "the fort and settlement of Quebec, with all the country of New France, called Canada." [1] It was described as extending along the Atlantic coast from Florida to the arctic circle, and from Newfoundland westward to the sources of the farthest rivers which fell into the St. Lawrence or the "Fresh Sea."

2. The power of the company over the soil was complete. It was allowed to sell or dispose of it in such portions and on such terms as it should see fit, except that if it should grant great fiefs such as duchies or baronies, letters of confirmation to the grantees should be sought from the crown.

3. The continuance of the company in its full form with all powers and duties was to be for fifteen years, while for other purposes its life was to be perpetual.

4. Its commercial privileges extended during this term of fifteen years to the complete monopoly of all kinds of commerce by sea or land, all former grants being withdrawn; and the company was empowered to confiscate any French or other vessels coming to trade within its dominions. The value of Canada as a source of supply for furs was already known, and the fur trade was placed under the special control of the company forever. The whale and seal fisheries, on the other hand, were exempted from its control, even for the fifteen years, and left free to all Frenchmen.

[1] Isambert, *Recueil Général*, XVI., 216-222.

5. As a form of subsidy the king agreed to give the company two war-vessels of two hundred to three hundred tons, armed and equipped for a voyage; but they were to be victualled, supported, and, in case of loss, replaced by the company. He also presented them with certain cannon formerly the property of the East India Company. The nature of these gifts seems to intimate the possibility of warlike expeditions of the company against the king's enemies and its own, and prizes are referred to repeatedly as a possible source of income.

6. All goods of all kinds brought from New France were to be exempted for fifteen years from all duties and imposts; and all victuals, munitions of war, and all other necessaries exported from France to the colony should be likewise exempt. Other privileges were permission to nobles, clergymen, and officers to join the company without derogation from their rank, and an agreement to ennoble twelve prominent members of the company; full naturalization as French citizens of all colonists and converted natives; and the advancement of all artisans who should pursue their trades in the colony for six years, to full mastership in their respective occupations.

7. The duties the company was bound to fulfil in return for these concessions were primarily those of colonization. The company engaged to take over to New France two or three hundred colonists of both sexes within the year 1628, and altogether

four thousand within fifteen years; to lodge, feed, and provide them with the necessaries of life for three years after their emigration; and then to assign to them enough cleared land for their support and enough grain to sow it and to feed them till the first harvest. These provisions showed a clear insight into the difficulties of settlement of a new country, but they also imposed upon the company a crushing burden of expense which required true Gallic optimism to contemplate with any assurance of success.

8. Next to peopling of the colony came the conversion of the heathen. Indeed, this object, with proper piety, was placed in the forefront of the edict creating the company. In each settlement the company was bound to provide at least three priests and give them support for fifteen years, or else provide them with cleared land sufficient for their support. After the expiration of the fifteen years, and for further missionary efforts, the religious needs of the colony were commended to the charity and devotion of the company and the colonists.

9. It was required that all colonists should be natural-born Frenchmen and Catholics. The absolute orthodoxy of this colony from its inception was in striking contrast with the freedom from religious restriction of the colonies planned by Coligny before the civil wars had forced the government to introduce rigorous conformity.

10. The company's rights over the colony were

great: they could appoint officers of sovereign justice, who should be commissioned by the crown; and nominate military officials by sea and land over ships, troops, and fortresses, the king agreeing to appoint their nominees. They were empowered to build forts, forge cannon, make gunpowder, and do all things necessary for the security of the colony and its commerce.

11. The charter contained no provisions for the internal government of the company, simply recognizing the existing voluntary organization of one hundred associates, whom it describes as a "strong company for the establishment of a colony of native Frenchmen." As far as membership extends, they were allowed to join to themselves any additional number up to another hundred.

Thus was organized the company which, through the genius of Champlain and with much tribulation, laid the foundations of the colony of Canada.

Considering as types these four companies dating from 1600, 1609, 1621, and 1628, and representing England, Holland, and France, a comparison of their main characteristics leads to the following generalizations:

1. It is evident that there was in early modern times a movement for the organization and chartering of companies for distant commerce, closely dependent on their respective governments. These companies had their period of rise in the sixteenth century; a rapid and wide-spread development in

the seventeenth; and a subsequent decline and discredit in the eighteenth. The movement was European; every country whose situation or ambitions would at all admit of distant trading, and whose system of commerce was not, like that of Spain and Portugal, already stereotyped under government control, adopted approximately the same policy.

2. To each of these companies was secured by its charter the monopoly of trade in a particular region. Its members alone had power or right to carry on commerce with a specified people, over a specified extent of coasts or lands, and during a definite period of years. This monopoly might be only as against the fellow-countrymen of the members of the company; but an effort, generally successful, was made to exclude all other Europeans from each reserved field of commerce.

3. The companies were based on unions of the capital of many merchants or other adventurers. An official Dutch letter on the trade with America speaks of "knowing by experience that without the common assistance of a general company navigation and commerce could not be practised, maintained, and defended in the regions and quarters designated above, because of the great risks from corsairs, pirates, and other extortions which are met with upon such voyages." [1] The preliminary equipment of ships, the purchase of supplies and

[1] *Letters to the Dutch West India Company*, June 9, 1621.

merchandise, the acquisition of land, the building of forts and the supply of weapons and military material; the payment of a military force to protect their commerce against natives or interloping Europeans; the expenses, in many cases, of transporting and supporting colonists; and, finally, the long waiting before returns could be reasonably hoped for —some or all of these expenses were inseparable from the whole plan of establishing distant trade. It was no wonder that individual traders gave place to great unions of the merchants of London, Amsterdam, or Dieppe, who risked part of their means and united their resources to form companies to trade with the East and West Indies, Africa, and other outlying parts of the world.

4. Neither the possession of a monopoly nor the creation of a large, joint capital was considered enough to launch an enterprise of this kind. The grant of public or political powers by government was necessary to make its economic objects attainable, and these were given with a free hand. The companies very generally received, explicitly or by implication, rights of peace and war, of supreme justice, of administrative independence, and of legislation for their own territory, members, and servants. A chartered company was in many cases the holder from the crown of a wide fief in which it possessed more than feudal powers. As a matter of fact, the companies generally remained quite dependent on the home authorities, but this resulted

from the desire to save expense, from the supremacy of commercial ideals, or from patriotism, rather than from deficiencies in their charters.

5. In the grant of these extensive political powers the home governments had ulterior motives. The seventeenth century was a period of intense international rivalry, and the chartered commercial companies were pieces in the game. It was not mere profit in pounds, shillings, and pence which Elizabeth hoped to obtain from the voyages of the ships of the East India Company, but a weakening of the power and wealth and colonial dominion of Spain. Even in the more peaceful times of James, the Spaniards saw, and were justified in seeing, in the popular interest in Virginia another phase of the national hatred of Spain.[1] It was at the close of the twelve years' truce between the Netherlands and Spain, just when the war was being resumed, that the Dutch West India Company was formed, and its greatest activity was in a warlike rivalry with its great opponent in South America. "The reputation of this crown" was combined with "the glory of God" in the charter of the Canada Company; and most of the commercial and colonizing projects of France in the seventeenth as in the nineteenth century, had a large element of political pride behind them. Sometimes it was warlike conquest, sometimes the expulsion of a rival, sometimes the acquisition of a

---

[1] Letters from Zuñiga to Philip III., in Brown, *Genesis of the United States*, docs. xxviii.–xxxiii., etc.

new base of operations, sometimes the obtaining of a more favorable balance of trade, sometimes mere international rivalry; but whatever the other elements, there were always some political objects in addition to the hope of obtaining dividends from trade.

6. For the history of America, the most important characteristic common to the chartered companies of the seventeenth century is the territorial foothold they obtained in the regions where they possessed their monopolies. It might be only a few acres of ground used for a fort, storehouses, and dwellings, which was all the English East India Company possessed for the first century and a half of its existence; or it might be the almost limitless domains of the Canada or Virginia Company. There was no distinction between two kinds of companies, one for commerce, the other for colonization, but simply one of relative attention given to the two interests, according to the character of the regions for which the companies had obtained their concessions. All the companies expected to carry on commerce; all expected to plant some of their fellow-countrymen on the soil of the country with which they meant to trade. If the region of their activity was the ancient, wealthy, thickly settled, and firmly governed coast of India, the settlers were only a few servants of the company. If, on the other hand, the region for which the monopoly of the company was granted was a broad and temperate tract, occu-

pied by a sparse population of savages, and offering only such objects of trade or profit as could be collected slowly or wrested by European labor from the soil or the forest, the quickest way to a commercial profit was the establishment on the distant soil of a large body of colonists from the home land.

This necessity for colonization in order to carry out their other objects makes the chartered commercial companies of the seventeenth century fundamental factors in American history. The proprietary companies of Virginia, Massachusetts, New Netherland, Canada, and other colonies were primarily commercial bodies seeking dividends, and only secondarily colonization societies sending over settlers. This distinction, and the gradual predominance of the latter over the former, is the clew to much of the early history of settlement in America. The commercial object could only be carried out by employing the plan of colonization, but new motives were soon added. The patriotic and religious conditions of the times created an interest in the American settlements as places where men could begin life anew with new possibilities. Hence the company, the home government, dissatisfied religious bodies, and many individuals, looked to the settlements in America with other than a commercial interest. The policy of the companies was modified and eventually transformed by the influence of these non-commercial interests.

As financial enterprises, the chartered commercial

companies were subject to such great practical difficulties that few of them survived for any great
length of time or repaid their original investment
to the shareholders. Some were reorganized time
and again, each time on a more extensive scale, and
each time to suffer heavier losses.[1] They experienced much mismanagement and some peculation
and fraud on the part of their directors; in some
cases false dividends were declared for the purpose
of temporarily raising the value of the stock. Their
credit was bad, and they sometimes had to borrow
money at fifty and even seventy-five per cent. interest.[2]

They encountered other difficulties quite apart
from the incompetency or dishonesty of their directors. Parliaments and States - General were opposed to monopolistic and privileged companies, and
threw what obstacles they could in their way; and
political exigencies often forced even the sovereigns
who had given them their charters to disavow and
discourage them.[3] Their greatest difficulties, however, arose from the very nature of the problem
which they were trying to solve. Distant commerce
with barbarous races, amid jealous rivals, carried
on with insufficient capital; the persuasion of reluctant emigrants to establish themselves in the

[1] W. R. Scott, "The Royal African Company" (*Am. Hist. Review*, VIII., 2).

[2] Bonnassieux, *Les Grandes Compagnies de Commerce*, 494, etc.

[3] Letter of October 8, 1607, from Zuñiga to the king of Spain, in Brown, *Genesis of the United States*, I., 121.

wilderness at a time when the mother-country was not yet overcrowded; the long waiting for returns and the failure of one dream after another—it was these difficulties in the very work itself that led to the failure of most of the companies and the scanty success of the others.

Nevertheless, the companies played a very important part in the advancement of civilization during the period of their existence. They enriched Europe with many products of the New World and the more distant Old World, which could hardly have reached it, or reached it in such abundance, except for the organized voyages of the chartered companies. The formation of chartered companies relieved certain nations of their dependence upon other nations for some of the necessities and many of the luxuries of life. National independence was furthered, at the same time that foreign products were made much cheaper. Spices, sugar, coffee, tea, chocolate, tobacco, cotton, silk, drugs, and other articles were made accessible to all. New shipping was built by the companies and additional commercial intercourse created.[1] New territories were made valuable and new centres of activity created in old and stagnant as well as in new and undeveloped countries. Above all, the chartered companies were the actual instruments by which many colonies were founded, and a strong impress given to the institutions of these colonies through all their later history.

[1] Bonnassieux, *Les Grandes Compagnies de Commerce*, 514.

CHAPTER IX

THE PROTESTANT REFORMATION ON THE CONTINENT

(1500–1625)

IN analyzing the forces which affected the colonization of America, the depth of the impression made upon Europe by the Protestant Reformation can hardly be overestimated. Although the direct and immediate influence of this great movement upon the fortunes of America was great, its indirect and remote effects have been still more important. One of these effects was the creation of a religious motive for emigration which, in conjunction with other incentives, was one of the earliest and most constant causes for the peopling of America.

It is true that the desire for religious freedom was only one among many such impelling forces. The desire to better their fortunes was perhaps the most fundamental and enduring consideration that influenced emigrants. Many settlers came because at home they had failed or were burdened with debt, or had become involved in ill repute or crime, and hoped to make a new start in a new land. Many sought the New World as many still press to the frontier, from sheer restlessness and recklessness, from the love of adventure, the hope that luck will do better for them than labor. Many came as a result of urgent inducements offered by projectors of colonies or agents of shipmasters, as in the case of the early "company servants" or the later "redemptioners" or "indentured servants."

No inconsiderable number came because they were forced to come: the earlier planters of colonies and patentees of lands received permission to seize for their uses men and women of the lower classes, much as men were pressed into naval service; paupers were handed over to the colonizing companies to be shipped to their settlements; repeatedly the prisons were emptied to provide colonists, and commissions were appointed, as in England in 1633, "to reprieve able-bodied persons convicted of certain felonies, and to bestow them to be used in discoveries and other foreign employments."[1] Somewhat later, transportation to the colonies to labor for a fixed number of years became a familiar form of commutation of the death penalty, and after 1662 it was made the statutory penalty for certain offences.

Yet among this multiplicity of motives for emigration to the colonies religion held a peculiar place. Many men for whom the dominant inducement was a more material one were partly led by religious

---

[1] *Cal. of State Pap., Domestic*, 1631-1633, p. 547.

motives; many of the changes in Europe that un-settled men and made them more ready to leave their old homes were results of the Reformation. Religious motives were the earliest to send any really large body of settlers to the English colonies, and they remained for more than a century probably the most effective motives.

During the first twenty years of the settlement of Virginia, where the religious incentive was least strong, less than six thousand settlers came over; during the first twenty years of the settlement of New England, where it was strongest, there were more than twenty thousand. The later churchmen of Virginia and the Carolinas, the Catholics of Mary-land, the Quakers of Pennsylvania and New Jersey, and a great body of Presbyterians, Huguenots, Mennonites, Moravians, and adherents of other sects which were products of the Reformation, sought under the more liberal laws of the colonies the re-ligious liberty which they could not find at home.

The working of this influence in England will ap-pear in a later chapter on the religious history of that country during this period; its peculiar develop-ment in Germany seems to demand a further word of explanation here. Three forms of reformed doc-trine and organization — Lutheranism, Calvinism, and Zwinglianism—grew up on German soil in the years between 1517 and 1555, and obtained more or less extensive recognition and power from imperial, princely, or city authorities. Lutheranism, the

most moderate and widely accepted form of Protestantism, was officially established in most of the
central and northern and in some of the southern
states and cities; Calvinism, less widely extended
but more strictly organized, held a similar position
in the southwest; while the doctrines of Zwingli,
which had been adopted and were enforced in the
greater part of Switzerland, spread to a number of
those southern regions of Germany from which
Switzerland was as yet indistinctly separated.[1]

A vast number of earnest souls were not satisfied
with any of these forms of official religion, and even
in the earliest days of the Reformation, preachers
arose who went beyond the moderate reforms of
Luther, Zwingli, or Calvin, and whose teachings
gained a ready acceptance. In Saxony, in Hesse, in
South Germany, and in Moravia; in the cities of
Constance, Strasburg, Augsburg, and Nuremberg; in
the Netherlands and in Switzerland, there was much
preaching and formation of independent religious
communities quite apart from, and indeed in opposition to, the official Reformation.[2] These radical
preachers and their followers represented very different beliefs and practices. That which was common to them all was an acceptance of the Bible
literally interpreted as a guide both to doctrine and
to church organization. The effort to return to the

---

[1] Armstrong, *The Emperor Charles V.*, I., 228–231.
[2] Moeller, *Hist. of the Christian Church* (English trans.), III.,
36, 64, 88, 94.

apostolic organization of the church led them to
reject any but an unpaid ministry, and to insist that
none should be members of their congregations except such as were personally converted and who
conformed their lives to the teachings of the Bible.

Their idea was, therefore, the formation of little
companies separated from the surrounding people
of the world rather than the Lutheran or Zwinglian plan of a reorganization of the national church
on Protestant lines *en masse*. An austere piety,
the wearing of plain clothes, the avoidance of forms
of social respect, the refusal to take an oath or to
hold civil office, an assertion of the sinfulness of
paying or receiving tithes or interest, an approach
to communistic practice in matters of property—
some or all of these were widely disseminated among
the lower classes of the people to whom such teachings principally appealed.

The doctrine which came nearest to being a point
of uniformity and a possible bond of union among
these reformers was their objection to infant baptism.   To them baptism was the mark of a personally attained relation to Christ, and was, therefore,
meaningless when administered to an unconscious
infant.   Certain "prophets" who came to Wittenberg from Zwickau confronted Luther and Melanc-
thon with this principle as early as 1521; and radical
reformers proclaimed it in opposition to Zwingli at
Zurich in 1523.   Everywhere advocacy of an exact
adherence to the verbal teaching of Holy Writ and

a rejection of the claims of an established church, were accompanied by opposition to infant baptism. In 1525 for the first time the logical deduction from their premises was made; those baptized only in their infancy were asserted not to have been effectively baptized at all, and were rebaptized as a sign of their conversion.[1] From this time onward rebaptism, or, from the point of view of its advocates, the first valid baptism, became the test and mark of adoption into many communities of true believers. Those who practised this rite were, therefore, called "Anabaptists"—that is to say, those who baptized a second time—or, more frequently, merely "Baptists."

The rebaptism of a person who had been already once baptized was not only in the eyes of the established church an impiety, it was in the eyes of the established law a capital crime, and the history of Anabaptism in Germany is the history of a long martyrdom. In Catholic and Protestant countries alike these radicals were persecuted. From Strasburg and Nuremberg they were expelled, in Zurich their leaders were drowned, in Augsburg they were beheaded, in Austria, Wittenberg, Bavaria, and the Palatinate they were burned at the stake.

In 1534 their sect was brought into sudden and fatal prominence by the revolt in Münster and its vicinity. Here a body of adherents of radical religious doctrines added to their creed a tenet not

[1] Moeller, *Hist. of the Christian Church* (English trans.), III., 65.

common to the general body of Anabaptists—that is to say, the duty of taking up temporal arms to overthrow the existing powers and to introduce the New Jerusalem. The old episcopal city was seized by the Anabaptist leaders, bloody battles were fought, and after a six months' orgy of fanaticism, libertinism, and violence the rebels were defeated by the united troops of Catholic and Lutheran powers and a terrible vengeance taken.

Anabaptists everywhere, no matter how peaceable and moderate their principles, suffered under the imputation of holding such doctrines as had led to the terrible excesses at Münster, as they had long before been held to sympathize with the Peasants' Revolt; and their persecutions became correspondingly harsher. Nevertheless, they continued to form communities and to spread through Germany, the Netherlands, and Switzerland. The attractiveness of the teachings of wandering Anabaptist preachers long continued unabated, and their regularly organized congregations or communities, because of their thrift, honesty, and plainness of life, survived and flourished, wherever they could obtain even the barest and most temporary toleration.

They were necessarily a people without a national home. Seldom for a whole generation did any considerable body of Anabaptists or Pietists remain undisturbed in any one locality. Expelled by imperial edict from Bohemia, they made their way to Hungary and Transylvania; fined, imprisoned, and in danger of death in Protestant Switzerland, they migrated to the Tyrol, to the Palatinate, and to the south German cities, only soon to be visited there with still worse persecution. During the two great religious wars they suffered especial hardships, and in the midst of the Thirty Years' War they were rigorously expelled by the emperor from all his hereditary dominions, even from Moravia, where they had been allowed to exist for almost a century.[1]

Either from original differences of doctrine and personal influence, or from later divisions and re-organization, grew up those bodies which, although often, as has been seen, grouped under the general head of Anabaptists, have become known in Europe and America as Mennonites, Amish, and Dunkers; and each of these bodies has experienced various divisions. The Schwenkfelders, Boehmists, and other mystics or pietists, are habitually grouped with these sects, rather because of their similar historical origin and attitude to the established churches than of any identity of religious belief.

By the close of the seventeenth century the condition of these dissenters from the established churches had become more tolerable; but they were at best a remnant, narrowed in spirit by persecution, repeatedly separated from their earlier homes, still under the ban of ecclesiastical disapproval, and

[1] Moeller, *Hist. of the Christian Church* (English trans.), III., 437–442.

even where tolerated living under burdensome restrictions. The rising colonies of the New World, especially those which promised religious liberty, and above all that one of them whose Quaker founder held doctrines so like their own, must have exerted, notwithstanding their alien race and tongue, an almost irresistible attraction upon them. In view of the political and religious history of Germany in the sixteenth and seventeenth centuries, it is therefore no wonder that a vast number of Germans emigrated to America, and that in Pennsylvania were soon to be found numerous representatives of every religious sect that existed in the fatherland.

The religious divisions which sprang from the Protestant Reformation were not restricted to the Old World. In America, also, religion was a centrifugal influence, splitting up old colonies, and establishing new centres of population, which in turn attracted other groups of emigrants from Europe, and brought into existence still other types of government and society.[1] The results were shown in the characteristics of Rhode Island and Connecticut, of Germantown and Bethlehem, in some of the principal contrasts between New France and New England, and in many of the lesser diversities that have distinguished different sections of America in their subsequent history. Many influences combined to give form and character to each American settlement: its race

[1] Eggleston, *Beginners of a Nation*, 266–346.

elements, the commercial requirements of the controlling chartered company, the demands of the
home government, the theoretical ideas of the
founder, the habitudes of the colonists in the lands
from which they came. Among these influences,
as among the motives for emigration, the religious
experiences and desires of the settlers were a prime
factor.

The Reformation indirectly affected America by
wars which soon led to the rise of some nations, the
fall of others; they pitted Catholic states against
Protestant states, they weakened Germany, France,
and the southern Netherlands by a sanguinary civil
struggle, and were avoided in England only by
harsh persecution.

In the Iberian peninsula the progress of Protestantism was so slight and so quickly crushed out
that it played no part in the colonization of Portuguese or Spanish America. It is true that the somewhat outworn machinery of the Inquisition was re-
juvenated in the sixteenth century, so as to reach a
Protestant movement in Seville, the sailing-point for
the American fleets; and this was made an excuse for
the introduction of a stricter and more vigorous policy
of orthodox uniformity in Spain. The Inquisition
also found occupation in looking after heretic foreign merchants and sailors in Spanish seaports, and
Jews and Protestant Germans in the American colonies; but no Spaniards ever emigrated to America
to escape religious persecution.

As for France, the terrible religious wars of the sixteenth century weakened her projects of colonization, as they did all her other activities, and divided her people into two hostile parties, one of which must ultimately crush out the other. The short-lived colonies established in the middle years of the sixteenth century in Brazil and in Florida were due largely to the hope that they might be places of refuge for oppressed Huguenots. The first French colonies which had any successful outcome, however, were the creation of the other religious party; for Richelieu, when he took up the establishment of colonies in 1624, insisted on Catholic orthodoxy in the religion of the colonists. This precaution was doubtless due to the Huguenot efforts for independence and their treasonable negotiations in France. In founding distant colonies as extensions of the power of the home government, a minister could hardly permit the domination in the new colonies of a party with which he was in deadly conflict at home. Whatever his motive, orthodoxy was insisted on; and New France, like New Spain, became unbrokenly Catholic.

The English colonies, however, ultimately profited by what the French colonies had lost. After the revocation of the Edict of Nantes, in 1685, persecution sent a stream of Huguenots to the various English colonies of America, and added thereby a valuable and interesting strain to the richly mingled blood of the American race.

CHAPTER X

RELIGIOUS WARS IN THE NETHERLANDS AND GERMANY

(1520–1648)

THE revolt of the Netherlands, which created a new and vigorous European state in the sixteenth century, and a great commercial and colonizing world-power in the seventeenth, was as much a religious as a political movement. The centralizing, autocratic, and unconciliatory policy of Philip II. was probably enough in itself to have caused rebellion in the Netherlands; while the religious conflict was so bitter that it would almost certainly have caused a revolt, even if there had been no political friction. The revolt of 1568 and the war which lasted till 1609, as a matter of fact, turned on causes belonging equally to both fields.

When Charles V. visited the Netherlands in 1520, on his way to claim the imperial crown, the twenty-two provinces then gathered into his hands were all nominally Catholic; and the large majority of the population were sincerely attached to Rome. Yet reformed doctrines soon made their way into the country in several forms. In the southern and central states, Flanders, Brabant, Hainault, Holland, and Zealand, Calvinism entered from France; into Friesland and North Holland came many Mennonites; in some of the towns there were Anabaptists; in the great commercial cities, such as Antwerp and Amsterdam, Lutherans were numerous, some of them immigrants from Germany, some converted to that faith through the communications between lower Germany and the adjacent provinces of the Netherlands.[1] Even the Catholics of the Netherlands were not of a bigoted or militant type; heresy had been wide-spread there since the thirteenth century, and the inhabitants had not the horror of it that was felt in some more orthodox countries.[2]

Among the wealthy, turbulent, strong-minded, and patriotic Netherland burghers and peasantry Reformation doctrines and principles readily spread and gained acceptance; yet they were met by the most determined and harsh opposition from the government which now held the Netherlands in the hollow of its hand. In 1521 Charles V. issued from Worms an edict dooming to loss of property and death every Dutch, Flemish, or Walloon adherent of the teachings of Luther; and in 1523 two monks were burned at Brussels as first-fruits of the long and miserable harvest which was so abundantly reaped afterwards.

[1] Blok, *Hist. of the People of the Netherlands* (English trans.), III., 22.

[2] Motley, *Rise of the Dutch Republic*, I., Introd., xii.

A series of edicts known as the "Placards" was now issued by Charles, prohibiting private meetings for religious worship, reading of the Scripture by laymen, discussions on questions of faith, the destruction of religious emblems, the harboring of heretics, the possession of heretical books, and, in general, all heretic or non-Catholic opinions and practices. These edicts were enforced by all the power of the civil government, and by the activity of four inquisitors. The "Placards" reached their culmination in the edict of 1550, renewing and making more severe all punishments for religious offences. When Charles, in 1556, laid down the burden of government in favor of his son, the persecutions had numbered their hundreds, if not thousands, of victims; but heresy had spread only the more widely, and Protestantism in its various forms had become only the stronger.

Philip II. entered upon the struggle with heresy even more vigorously than his father. Even the Catholics of the Netherlands were opposed to the enforcement of the "Placards," while the heretics who were suffering and multiplying under it were looking forward almost desperately to some change that would make their position more tolerable. The States-General, the nearest approach to a national legislature that the Netherlands possessed, in 1559 pleaded for mildness. It was only the Spanish ruler who was determined to apply the heresy laws in all their vigor; and when he left the Netherlands and began to direct their administration from Spain, the religious question became more and more the great unifying element in national resistance to his policy.

William of Orange, in the council of state, took the lead in drawing up a petition to the king for the amelioration of the " Placards " and for the suspension of the decrees for an inflexible orthodoxy which had just been promulgated from Trent. He pointed out the necessity of recognizing the proximity and influence of Lutheran Germany upon the Netherlands, the actual extension of Protestantism in the provinces, and the degree to which the old church had lost its authority over the hearts of men. In words that rose in dignity and significance far above the ordinary contests of Catholics and Protestants, he declared: " I am Catholic, and will not deviate from religion; but I cannot approve the custom of kings to confine men's creed and religion within arbitrary limits." [1] Philip replied to this petition of the Catholic nobles of the Netherlands by the edict of Segovia, dated October 17, 1565, insisting more vehemently than ever before on the enforcement of the laws against heresy in all their severity, including what was practically the introduction of the Spanish Inquisition. On the other hand, the Reformation pressed on with rapid strides; vast crowds gathered outside of Tournai, Harlem, Antwerp, and other cities to listen to Calvinist preachers. Ten, twelve, and twenty thousand of the pop-

[1] Blok, *Hist. of the People of the Netherlands* (English trans.), III., 14.

ulace assembled at a time to sing psalms and hymns and to listen to the appeals of teachers eloquent and devout, but almost invariably heretical.

The inevitable crisis was now hastening on. The lesser nobles, including some Calvinists, soon formed the "Confederation," sent their petition to the king, and in 1567 broke out in fruitless rebellion. Almost at the same time the mob rose in the image-breaking riots which spread like wild-fire over all the provinces except the most southern. Then came Alva, with his unlimited powers, his veteran troops, his "Council of Blood," his more than ten thousand victims of political and religious persecution, and the awful severity and barbarity that have made his name a synonym of cruelty and heartless despotism. William of Orange brought an army into Brabant in 1568, and revolt was soon in full progress. Even under Charles V. there had been much emigration from the Netherlands to Germany and England, to escape religious persecution. Now the barbarities of Alva increased the number many-fold. It was estimated that there were at one time sixty thousand Dutch and Walloon refugees living in England. By 1568 the emigrants were said to number four hundred thousand.

As the revolt progressed and the various cities expelled the officers of the Spanish governor and put themselves under the banner of Orange, they became little oases of toleration. The instructions of William to his lieutenants in the north in 1572 or-

dered them "to restore fugitives and the banished
for conscience' sake—and to see that the Word of
God is preached, without, however, suffering any
hindrance to the Roman Church in the exercise of
its religion." [1]   By November, 1576, when the
treaty known as the Pacification of Ghent was made
between Holland and Zealand on the one hand and
the fifteen southern provinces on the other, liberalism
in religious views had progressed as far as the power
of the patriotic party extended; and all "Placards"
and edicts on the subject of religion were suspended
till a national assembly should take final action on
the subject.   At the same time it was provided that
there should be no action against the Catholic religion, outside the territory of Holland and Zealand. [2]

Soon the Flemish provinces, where Protestantism
had made least headway and where distrust of the
north was strong, were "pacified" by Don John of
Austria and Alexander of Parma.   The Union of
Arras, of January 6, 1579, became a centre of union
and reconciliation to Spain and Catholicism for the
fifteen southern provinces.   Just three weeks afterwards the Union of Utrecht was formed, which
united the seven northern provinces and became the
basis of the free republic of the United Netherlands:
each province was to make its own religious arrangements, though toleration was secured by the

[1] Motley, *Rise of the Dutch Republic*, pt. iii.
[2] Blok, *Hist. of the People of the Netherlands* (English trans.),
III., 105, 106.

provision that no one should be molested or questioned on the subject of divine worship.[1] Thus while the southern provinces set their feet in the path of a return to Roman Catholic uniformity, the northern provinces pledged themselves to toleration of Catholics and of all sects of Protestants alike.

Toleration is to the modern student the chief interest and glory of the foundation of the United Netherlands; but it was not toleration but Protestantism which then gave the young republic its peculiar strength, vigor, and enterprise. Even in the Pacification of Ghent and the Union of Utrecht, Holland and Zealand were recognized as Protestant states. As the bitter struggle progressed, their Protestantism became more pronounced and more militant. Exiled Calvinists from the south flocked to Amsterdam, Middleburg, Rotterdam, and other northern cities in great numbers, intensifying the Protestant character of these communities and enriching them with capital, business ability, and an astonishingly large proportion of gifted men.[2] The formal abjuration of Philip by the United Provinces in 1581, on grounds so largely religious, could not but bring into still greater prominence the Protestantism of the country which now claimed its independence. The long-continued warfare that followed the assassination of the beloved prince of Orange, the sieges, mutinies, and battles by land and

[1] Arts. 5, 9, 10, 11, 12, 13, quoted in Motley, pt. vi., chap. i.
[2] Jameson, *Usselinx*, 27.

sea, steadily deepened the religious and political hatred between the Netherlands and Spain.

By the year 1596 internal theological struggles between Remonstrants and Contra - Remonstrants approached the proportions of a civil war; and the victory gained by the latter party through the intervention of the stadtholder Maurice connected religion and politics, church and state, even more clearly, and made still more intense the fiery Protestantism of the Dutch government.[1] Strengthened by her efforts, hardened by her struggles, awakened to vigorous life by the exhilaration of the long and arduous conflict, the little Protestant state approached the end of the sixteenth century, enterprising in internal plans and eager for new fields of foreign commerce. The probability that commercial expansion would bring her into conflict with Spain added zest to the prospect and gave promise that in extending trade, conquering distant possessions, and establishing colonies, she would at the same time be weakening her bitterest enemy.

Hence the early Dutch expeditions to the Indies, the formation of the East and West India Companies, the establishment of the colonies in Brazil, Guiana, and North America, and of commercial factories in the East Indies, were all of them in a certain sense part of the religious and political struggle between the Netherlands and Spain. When the twelve years'

· Blok, *Hist. of the People of the Netherlands* (English trans.), II., 398–447.

truce was signed, in 1609, those provinces which had returned to the Spanish obedience were uniformly Catholic, but their prosperity and international significance had disappeared. The independent provinces, on the other hand, were, for all their toleration, almost uniformly Protestant, and they were already one of the great maritime and commercial powers of Europe.[1]

The United Netherlands speedily colonized New Amsterdam, Guiana, Cape Colony, Java, and other places, with a population persistent in Protestantism and in many race characteristics. Unfortunately for Holland the number of her emigrants was never great enough to enable her permanently to play a great part in the history of colonization. The Dutch are not an emigrating people. Yet those who did emigrate carried with them such an assertive character and so highly developed a group of institutions that they exercised a deep and permanent influence over communities like New York, in which they soon ceased to be the dominant element; while their institutions in Holland made such a strong impression upon English sojourners in their midst that some of their characteristics reappeared long afterwards in American colonies in which no Dutchman had ever settled.[2]

The Reformation, with the wars to which it gave rise, made Germany for a time the most conspicu-

---

[1] Blok, *Hist. of the People of the Netherlands* (English trans.), III., 326–334.   [2] Douglas Campbell, *Puritan in Holland.*

ous state in Europe, but its ultimate effect was to reduce that state to a degree of material poverty, political insignificance, and intellectual torpidity unknown before in her experience. Civil war was long delayed; the political necessities and the astute policy of Charles V., the conservative instincts and patriotic scruples of Luther, and the doubtful position of many of the German provinces and cities, long prevented any attempt by the emperor to enforce the orthodoxy required by the Diet of Worms, and induced the Lutherans to go more than halfway in accepting the policy of postponement.[1] Yet even this early period was troubled by successive minor outbreaks of violence. The "Knights' War" of 1523, the Peasants' Revolt of 1524 and 1525, the Zwinglian wars in Switzerland in 1531, and the Anabaptist outbreak at Münster in 1534 were all connected with the religious ferment of the times.

From 1530, when the League of Schmalkald was formed to unite the Protestant princes and cities, Germany really belonged to two camps, and civil war was only a question of time. The time came in 1546, the year of Luther's death, when Charles was at last free from foreign complications and could make the attempt to reintroduce conformity into Germany. The Schmalkaldic War, although marked by a series of imperial successes and temporarily closed by a triumphant truce in 1548, was

[1] Armstrong, *The Emperor Charles V.*, I., 201–203, 240–256, 319–327.

unstable as it seemed, remained the foundation of an outward if somewhat troubled religious peace for more than sixty years. Yet a renewal of the conflict was threatened from time to time, and in 1618 the terrible Thirty Years' War broke out. The earlier contests had been civil wars only; the renewed war was no longer merely a German struggle. In 1625 Christian IV., king of Denmark, entered the war as leader on the Protestant side, only to yield to the perseverance of Tilly, the general of the Catholic armies, and to the genius of Wallenstein, the representative of Emperor Ferdinand; and to retire in 1629, leaving north Germany more completely than before at the mercy of the emperor and of the Catholic party. Scarcely a year later Gustavus Adolphus, full of enthusiasm for the Protestant cause and provided with funds from France, brought his veteran regiments and his military ability from Sweden into Germany, and fought in consecutive years his three wonderful campaigns. After the death of the "Lion of the North," in 1632, the "Swedish period" endured still two years; and when, in 1634, Catholic and Protestant princes entered upon a truce they made terms upon an equality, though there was even yet but little promise of a permanent settlement.

Just before the fatal battle of Lützen, in the midst of military preparations, a decisive step was taken by Gustavus which ultimately led to the creation of one more American colony. Ever since the regeneration of Sweden under the kings of the house of Vasa, and still more markedly after the adoption of the Reformation, efforts had been made to extend Swedish relations with other countries.[1] Therefore when William Usselinx, who had been so influential in the establishment of the Dutch West India Company, left Holland in 1624, and presented himself to Gustavus Adolphus in Gothenburg, he received a ready welcome, and was engaged by the king to organize a similar company for Swedish trade with the distant parts of the world.[2] Sweden was poor, the king was much absorbed in his military operations, and the plans for a "General Commercial Company of the Kingdom of Sweden" dragged along slowly, only stirred into life from time to time when there was a prospect that a naval war might enable the company to add the profits of privateering to the ordinary reward of commerce. The untiring efforts of the promoter of the plan, however, and the sincere interest taken in it by the king, kept the proposal still in existence; and in his camp at Nuremberg, October, 1632, three weeks before his death, Gustavus gave his approval, though not his actual signature, to an extended and amplified charter of the Swedish West India Company.

Six months later, at Heilbronn, the charter was signed by Chancellor Oxenstjerna, creating it a company with powers of trade, settlement, and gov-

[1] Jameson, *Usselinx*, 95–97.   [2] *Ibid.*, 88–94.

ernment on the coasts of America, Africa, and Asia.[1]
There was after this time, as before, a close connection between the progress of the great war and
the fortunes of the Swedish colonizing company.
It was the exaltation produced by the prominent
part taken by the northern kingdom in that struggle that gave its rulers and merchants courage and
ambition for such distant enterprises. It was the
war that brought Sweden into close relations with
other and more advanced countries of Europe, especially with the Netherlands, which was already
playing a part in distant commerce and settlement.
It was a momentary renewal of her triumphs in
Germany and a temporary combination of Swedish
and Dutch capital that led to the sending out of
the *Kalmar Nyckel* and the *Gripen*, under the aus-
pices of the company, and the founding of New
Sweden on the Delaware in 1638.[2]

The peace of 1634 was of short duration, and the
"French period" ensued, when for twelve years
armies of Swedes, French, Spaniards, and Danes,
besides those of the German states themselves,
fought to and fro through the empire. Nor was it
till the definitive peace of Westphalia, in 1648, that
the war actually came to an end. Thus through a
whole generation Germany was torn by warfare,
humiliated by foreign interference, and confused by

---

[1] Jameson, *Usselinx*, 168.
[2] Odhner (trans. by G. B. Keen), in *Pa. Magazine of Hist.
and Biog.*, III., 269–284.

the introduction of new issues. One after another, foreign states were drawn into the struggle until a mere German civil war had developed into a general European conflict, in which foreigners were struggling for German territory. Catholics made alliances with Lutherans and with Calvinists, until what had begun as a religious struggle became a purely political contest among unpatriotic German princes and ambitious neighbors of Germany contending for power and prestige.

When, at the peace of 1648, political questions had been settled, territorial changes agreed upon, the Netherlands and Switzerland definitely separated from the empire, Alsace surrendered to France, and much of Pomerania to Sweden, the religious conflict was brought to an end as far as possible by returning to the old plan of the treaty of Augsburg, except that such toleration as was then granted to Catholics and Lutherans was now extended to Calvinists also. To these provisions some further extensions of religious liberty were added by securing guarantees of protection to subjects differing in their religion from their princes and by including in the highest imperial tribunal a certain number of Protestants.[1]

The material sufferings and losses of Germany during the war were almost beyond description.[2]

[1] Lamprecht, *Deutsche Geschichte*, V., sect ii., 764.

[2] Erdmannsdörffer, *Deutsche Geschichte*, 1648–1740, I., 100-115.

The armies, made up largely of soldiers ot different nationalities, without attachment to the countries through which they marched, without interest in the questions at issue, without a regular commissariat, often without pay, brutalized by long campaigning and repeated sacks of cities, followed by an immense rabble of non-combatant men, women, and children, were a barbarian horde, and ravaged the lands in which they were established like a fire or a pestilence. The tortures they inflicted upon the peasantry and the citizens, the robbery, the outrages, the wanton destruction, pressed close to the limits of human endurance, and seemed almost to threaten the extermination of the population. The prosperity of the cities was crushed by war contributions, even when they escaped being plundered like Magdeburg; and the debasement of the coinage practised by the emperor and the princes bore hardly upon all who bought or sold.[1] During the later campaigns of the war military operations in many regions became almost impracticable from the very impoverishment of the country; no sustenance existed for friend or for enemy; population in some parts was almost destroyed, and it was everywhere extensively displaced.[2] The conservatism, the settled rooting of the people in the soil, acquired and inherited property, moral and material fixity, were all alike disturbed.

[1] Gindeley, *History of the Thirty Years' War* (English trans.), ɪɪ., 390–395. [2] *Ibid.*, 398.

The half-century that followed 1648 did but little to restore prosperity or repose to Germany. The western provinces especially were the scene of frequently renewed warfare. The territorial ambitions of Louis XIV. were directed to the German lands which lay on the eastern border of France, and there was no strength in the empire to resist his aggressions or to make him fear either defeat or reprisals. Even the European coalitions which forced upon him successive treaties did not prevent renewed attacks or heal the scars of the repeated devastations of the lower and the upper Rhine country. The culmination of this period of suffering was the terrible ravaging of the Palatinate, in 1688, when the fertile region about Heidelberg, Mannheim, Speyer, and Worms was harried and burned and pillaged by the soldiers of Louis, with the same brutality and more destructiveness than the wild Swedish and mercenary armies of the Thirty Years' War had used.

A people with an experience such as that of the Germans in the seventeenth century was thenceforth easily drawn away from home. One generation of continuous warfare throughout all Germany, followed by another generation of intermittent invasion from France, and closed by a crisis of rapine and devastation, made hundreds of thousands of the German people homeless, despairing, and eager for escape. It was this situation of the people, combined with the religious condition

before described, that made Germany the best re-
cruiting-ground for American colonists to be found
in Europe. Before the close of the seventeenth
century a stream of emigration set from Germany
towards America which furnished to Pennsylvania
one-third of her pre-Revolutionary inhabitants, and
made a considerable part of the population of several
of the other colonies.

A second effect of the Thirty Years' War was the
practical dissolution of the empire and the loss by
the emperor of all centralized control over its policy. This was a cumulative result of the war rather
than a definite provision of the peace. The princes,
nobles, and cities had so frequently allied themselves with foreign states against the emperor and
against one another, their policy had been so constantly regulated by their own interests alone, in
entire disregard of those of the nation at large, and
the religious divisions had been settled on such a
sectional basis, that there was now no thought of
derogating from their independence for the sake of
the central power of Germany. By Article VIII. of
the treaty of peace all German states were definitely permitted to form independent alliances among
themselves and with foreign states, so long as these
were not directed against either the emperor or the
empire.[1] As a matter of fact, the bond of union
among the states of Germany had become so weak
as to be almost non-existent. The emperor was the

[1] Lamprecht, *Deutsche Geschichte*, V., § 2, pp. 765, 766.

actual ruler of the Hapsburg dominions and the nominal head of the empire; but Germany was a geographical rather than a national expression, and its head could play no part as a national ruler outside of his immediate hereditary dominions.

Germany had many interests in America. Martin Behaim, Regiomontanus, and other German scientists contributed largely to the development of the science of navigation during the period of discovery; Waldseemüller suggested the name that has been universally accepted for the New World; the numerous printing-presses of Germany did much to make known to Europe the history of the exploration and early conquests and the wonders of the Indies; under Charles V. the empire was brought closely into connection with Spain, the greatest colonizing power of the seventeenth century; her Fuggers, Welsers, and other capitalists provided much of the means for the early Spanish voyages, and for a time held extensive grants in Venezuela under the Spanish crown; and her teeming emigrants furnished a large part of the colonial population. Yet Germany as a nation has, of all the nations of Europe, exercised the least influence on the fortunes of America. Neither the emperor nor any German prince has ever exercised any direct or indirect power over any American territory. Many causes may have contributed to this failure, but the most effective was doubtless the Thirty Years' War. The religious disunion, the material impoverishment, and the political insignificance which this war caused, during the most important colonizing century, excluded Germany as a nation from a rôle among the European powers which have held control over parts of the New World.

CHAPTER XI

THE ENGLISH CHURCH AND THE CATHOLICS
(1534–1660)

ENGLAND passed through the crisis of the Reformation without a civil war, yet no country of Europe found greater difficulty in coming to a religious equilibrium after that change. Though actual rebellion was nipped in the bud wherever it appeared, as in the Pilgrimage of Grace of 1536 and in the Rising of the North of 1569, yet between those years, and long after the second rising, religious passions were embittered to the very verge of outbreak. In the early period of the Reformation changes were rapid and violent, and during more than a century and a half after Protestantism was established hostile legislation imposed heavy burdens upon all those who differed from the dominant party in religious faith.

When England became a colonizing country at the opening of the seventeenth century, the effect of the religious changes up to that time had been to produce four well-marked religious parties among her people—Churchmen, Catholics, Puritans, and Independents. First in order came the adherents of

the established church, a church which was in a very
real sense the creation of Queen Elizabeth and of
her times—for all that had gone before was unstable
and tentative, and might readily have been altered
by a ruler of different character or policy. When
Elizabeth ascended the throne in 1558 the great body
of the people of England, from a religious point of
view, was still a fluid mass, a sea accustomed to be
drawn, like the tide, by the planet that ruled the
sky, whether an Erastian Henry VIII., a Catholic
Mary, or a Protestant Protector Somerset.

Elizabeth declared at her accession that she would
not allow her people to swerve to the right hand or
the left from the religion established by law; and in
the main she succeeded in carrying out this policy.
The prayer-book, the articles of religion, the supremacy of the queen, the uniformity of service, the
practices and doctrines of the official English church
during the long reign of Elizabeth, meant something
very definite and made the established church an
objective reality. Of course she learned, as other
sovereigns have learned, that even the will of a
king may break against the rock of religious conviction; and large numbers of the people of England
during her reign remained, or became, dissatisfied
with the established church.

Nevertheless, when Elizabeth died Anglicanism
was the national church in a sense in which it had
not been before, and in exactly the same sense as
that in which the Roman Catholic church was the

church of Spain. A generation had grown up which had seen no other religious system in authority, whose beliefs and duties were taught them by its clergy, and whose sentiments and devotion naturally gathered around it as their object. This religious system, therefore, was strongly intrenched: it had all the authoritativeness of law, all the sanction of patriotic feeling in a period of intense patriotism, and the support of much sound learning; besides, the church was fast becoming hallowed by tradition and beautified to the imagination by sentiment. Yet for various reasons the Anglican church failed to obtain the allegiance of the whole English nation.

The second of the four great religious classes, the Catholics, held allegiance to a still older and more imposing organization. However clear the argument of English churchmen that the Anglican body was the church founded by the apostles and enduring continuously in England through all the intervening centuries, the "old church" was still to many the church of which the pope was the earthly head. From the time that Henry VIII. attacked the supremacy of the pope and many of the characteristic doctrines and practices of the mediæval church, a party separate from the national church came into being, which clung faithfully to that system.

The existence of the English Roman Catholics as a separate body from the established English

church may be considered to date from the res-
ignation of Sir Thomas More from the chancellor-
ship in 1532. During the remainder of Henry's
reign their position was equivocal and dangerous,
a number of conspicuous Catholics accepting martyrdom under the laws against treason, when brought to
the test of the acceptance or rejection of the king's
claim to the headship of the English church. Under
the enlightened rule of Somerset they were not
persecuted; but under his successor, and under the
personal rule of Edward VI., they fared much
worse.[1] The time of consolation came under Queen
Mary, when for a space of five years (1553-1558)
the English church and English Catholicism again
became identical.

Elizabeth on her accession had no antagonism to
the Roman Catholics as such. Neither in doctrine
nor in ceremonial was there any essential breach
between Elizabeth and the Catholic church; and for
a moment the world watched to see what her decision would be.[2] Yet the nature of her position
dictated to her a return to the ecclesiastical position
of her father, and an acquiescence in the main results
of the Protestant development under Edward VI.
She accepted the requirements of the policy readily
enough, and by the Acts of Supremacy and Uniform-

[1] Pollard, *England Under Protector Somerset*, 110-120, 258-
264, 322.
[2] Maitland, "Defender of the Faith" (*Eng. Hist. Review*, XV.,
120).

ity of 1559[1] the English Catholics again became a proscribed body, living in disobedience to the law, subject to severe pains and penalties for any speech or action against the established church, and even for the negative offence of absence from its religious services.

The disabilities of the Catholics according to the laws passed at the opening of the reign of Elizabeth were as follows: 1. No Catholic could hold any office or employment under the crown, or any ecclesiastical office in England, or receive any university degree: for all such persons were required to take an oath renouncing the authority of the pope, and acknowledging the headship of the queen in ecclesiastical matters.[2] 2. No Catholic could attend mass: the service of the prayer-book being required at all meetings for worship in England.[3] 3. No Catholic could remain away from the regular services of the established church: as the law required that "all and every person and persons inhabiting within the realm or any other the queen's majesty's dominions shall diligently and faithfully, having no lawful or reasonable excuse to be absent, endeavor themselves to resort to their parish church or chapel accustomed . . . upon every Sunday and other days ordained and used to be kept as holy days, and then and there to abide orderly and soberly during the time of the common prayer, preachings, or other service of

---

[1] 1 Eliz., chaps. i., ii.   [2] *Ibid.*, chap. ii., §§ 19–25.
[3] *Ibid.*, chap. ii., §§ 3–8.

God there to be used and ministered."[1] 4. No Catholic could speak, write, or circulate any arguments or appeals in favor of the ecclesiastical claims of the Catholic church or in derogation of the royal supremacy or of the prayer-book.

The penalties for violation of these laws varied from a fine of one shilling for absence from church on a Sunday or holy day to the terrible customary punishment for treason in the case of repeated conviction for supporting the claims of the pope. These fundamental disabilities remained in existence during the whole of the sixteenth and seventeenth centuries. They were added to from time to time as the religious conflict in England, and in Europe at large, became more embittered; although, on the other hand, there were occasional periods when the exigencies of policy or the sympathies of the sovereign temporarily suspended their enforcement. They remained the fundamental law long after the Act of Toleration of 1689 made easy the burdens of other Nonconformists, and until the gradual progress of enlightenment in the eighteenth century led to a willing neglect to enforce them; and they disappeared only in 1829.

The tendency during the reign of Elizabeth was constantly towards an increase in the severity of the laws against "popish recusants," as those who refused to conform to the established church were called, and to greater rigor in their application. At

---

[1] 1 Eliz., chap. ii., § 14.

four successive periods during that reign additions were made to the disabilities and sufferings imposed by law upon Roman Catholics.

1. An act of 1563 extended the lines of restriction so that the oath of supremacy must be taken by a much greater number of officials—by all schoolmasters, lawyers, and petty officers of court, and by all members of the House of Commons; and so that the first refusal of any person to take it, as well as the first occasion on which any one should in writing or speech support the claims of the pope, should be punished by confiscation and outlawry, the second offence by the penalties of treason.[1]

2. The difficulties of the Catholics were increased by the coming, in 1568, of Mary Queen of Scots to England, where she became a permanent centre of Catholic disaffection and hopes; by the Rebellion of the North in 1569; and by the papal bull of deposition of the queen in 1570. The laws at once reflected the anger and alarm of Parliament and ministers, and their care "for the surety and preservation of the queen's most royal person, in whom consisteth all the happiness and comfort of the whole state and subjects of the realm."[2]   From 1571 to 1575 four new treason laws,[3] directed against sympathizers with Mary and bringers of bulls from Rome, recall the savage legislation of Henry VIII. under somewhat similar circumstances.

[1] 5 Eliz., chap. i.   [2] 13 Eliz., chap. i., § 1.
[3] *Ibid.*, chaps. i., ii.; 14 Eliz., chaps. i., ii.

3. A third series of additions to the anti-Catholic
code was called out by the efforts of the Jesuits, from
1579 onward, to reconquer the heretical nations and
especially England, for the church.   Hence, in 1581,
the mere attempt to convert any subject of the
queen to Roman Catholicism, as well as the acceptance of such reconciliation with the church, was
made treason; the saying or hearing of the mass
was forbidden under penalty of heavy fine and long
imprisonment; recusants who were absent from
church a month at a time were fined £20 a month
for the length of time for which they stayed
away;[1] and by a later law the crown was allowed,
in case of recusancy, instead of the fine, to seize
two-thirds of the property of the offender.[2]

Certain offences which Catholics might be especially expected to commit, such as "by setting or
erecting any figure or by casting of nativities or by
calculations or by any prophesying, witchcraft,
conjuration, or other like unlawful means whatso-
ever, seek to know, and shall set forth by express
words, deeds, or writings how long her majesty shall
live, or who shall reign king or queen of this realm
of England after her highness's decease," were made
punishable by death and confiscation of goods.   In
1585 all Jesuits and Catholic priests trained abroad
were banished on pain of death, and all English
subjects studying abroad in one of those Jesuit
schools, which had already become famous as the

[1] 23 Eliz., chap. i.   [2] *Ibid.*, chap. ii.

best schools in Christendom, were required to return to England immediately and take the oath of supremacy or suffer the penalties of treason.

4. Within the next few years came the execution of Mary, the war with Spain, the defeat of the Armada, and the definite passing of the crisis of Elizabeth's reign. Nevertheless, the year 1593 was marked by an "act against popish recusants," which required all English Catholics to remain within five miles of their homes, and provided for a still closer search for Jesuits and priests.[1]

Thus an augmenting body of oppressive law, in addition to their fundamental disabilities, burdened the English Catholics at the accession of James I. in 1603. That event they may well have looked forward to and welcomed with joy. James was the son of Mary of Scotland, for whom many of them had made such deep personal sacrifices and on whose account all had been made to suffer. He was known to be a man of moderate spirit, easy good-nature, and philosophic breadth of mind. Circumstances, by relieving England from the fear of invasion from Spain, and by establishing the Protestant succession, might be considered to have left the way open for the admission of a more generous and tolerant treatment of the Catholic minority. The king controlled the enforcement or the non-enforcement of the law; his word could put the machinery of the courts, high and low, into motion for purposes of per-

[1] 35 Eliz., chap. ii.

secution; or, on the other hand, could open the prison doors to those already incarcerated, and restrain the indictment of those amenable to the law. James might fairly be expected to have the will, as he undoubtedly had the power, to treat the Catholics with greater leniency.

On the other hand, parliamentary and popular antagonism to the Roman Catholics had to be contended with. Notwithstanding the legal supremacy and complete predominance of the Anglican church, there was still a wide-spread fear of the "usurped power and jurisdiction of the bishop of Rome"; and much patriotic hatred of the Catholic enemies of England and of their sympathizers within the realm. This national sentiment was strongly reinforced by the fanatical Puritan fervor of opposition to "the devilish positions and doctrines whereon popery is built and taught." The Gunpowder Plot of 1605, in which Catesby, Guy Fawkes, and other Catholic conspirators showed themselves ready to sacrifice the king, his family, his ministers, and members of Parliament, filled James for a while with fears for his own safety. If James, therefore, should favor the Catholics he must do so in opposition to the overwhelming public opinion of the people of England and to his own timidity. What would be his policy? Would the persecuted minority be taken under the protection of the crown? Or would their position remain as it had been for half a century, or even be made worse?

Upon the answer to this question depended the happiness or unhappiness of the Catholics in England and the likelihood or unlikelihood that many of them would emigrate. Should their position become intolerable, those who could would either take refuge in one of the Catholic states of the continent or find an asylum in those boundless lands claimed by England across the sea. The minds of men through all Europe were turning towards America, not only as a sphere for trade and a base for the fighting out of Old World quarrels,[1] but as a place of settlement for men who could not conform to their Old-World religious surroundings.

Before the reign of James was over Sir George Calvert obtained a charter for Avalon, in Newfoundland, the ambiguity of whose terms made it possible to take Catholic priests and settlers there; and in 1632 he received in exchange for this a charter for Maryland, under which Catholics held all official positions and Jesuit missionaries carried on their work. The British island of Montserrat, in the West Indies, appears to have been settled in 1634 by Catholic refugees from Virginia;[2] and there were other floating proposals to colonize English and Irish Catholics in America.[3] It was evidently quite within the bounds of possibility that Catholic

[1] Zuñiga to the king of Spain, December 24, 1606, and September 22, 1607, in Brown, *Genesis of the United States*, I., 88–90, 116–118.

[2] Eggleston, *Beginners of a Nation*, 261, *n.* 9.

[3] *Cal. of State Pap.*, 1628, p. 95.

colonies should be established in those "other your highness's dominions," from which the House of Commons in 1623 especially petitioned that Romanists should be excluded.[1]

As a matter of fact, the policy of James and of his son and successor Charles towards the Catholics had little consistency, and shows an alternation of leniency and increased severity, reflecting the varying inclinations of the king and the changing exigencies of external and internal politics. During the first two years of his reign James lightened their burdens, in accordance with the promises of his first speech in Parliament, "so much as time, occasion, or law should permit." [2] The Gunpowder Plot then thoroughly frightened and angered the king and justified the House of Commons in its protests against leniency to the Catholics. In 1606 two long detailed statutes[3] were enacted, carrying much further in principle the persecuting provisions of the law under Elizabeth, increasing the burdens upon the conscience, the purse, and the liberty of Catholics, and specifying the most minute arrangements for the enforcement of the law and the discovery of those who were secretly Romanists.

Before many years a change came, due principally to the interest of James in the scheme of obtaining a Spanish bride for his son, and to his in-

---

[1] Rushworth, *Historical Collections*, I., 141.
[2] Prothero, *Statutes and Constitutional Documents*, 284.
[3] 3 and 4 James I., chaps. iv., v.

creasing subserviency to Gondomar, the shrewd Spanish minister. The king of Spain would not listen to any negotiations for the hand of his sister, unless the persecution of his co-religionists in England was stopped; and James, in order to carry out his foreign policy, blinded by his admiration for the Spaniard, and always prone to follow the line of least resistance, promised what he certainly could not perform, the parliamentary repeal of the anti-Catholic laws.

Nevertheless, he performed what he could, and ordered the suspension of their enforcement. In 1622 the lord keeper of the privy seal wrote to the judges that "it is his majesty's pleasure that they make no niceness or difficulty to extend the princely favor to all such as they shall find prisoners in the jails of their circuits for any church recusancy or refusing the oath of supremacy or dispensing of popish books, or any other point of recusancy that shall concern religion only and not matters of state."[1] A vast number of Catholics were, in this year, released on bail or freed completely from prosecution. When the Spanish marriage negotiations failed, just before the close of the reign of James, Parliament again petitioned the king to enforce the old penal laws, at last with success; and a momentary wave of severity towards the Catholics spread over England.

Spain was not the only Catholic country with

[1] Rushworth, *Historical Collections*, I., 63.

which England was in negotiation. The marriage of Charles with Henrietta Maria of France followed close upon his accession to the throne. The conditions of the marriage treaty called for greater leniency to the Catholics, and the influence of the queen secured it, though not in the degree promised. Yet on the whole the attitude of the crown and of the judges during the period from 1625 to 1640 was favorable to the Catholics; and although Laud was not plotting to hand over the English church to Rome, as was the popular belief, he was too sympathetic with the spirit of Roman Catholicism to put into force the savage laws against it which were upon the statute-book.

In 1640 Laud fell, the hand of the king was removed from the helm, and the domination of the Long Parliament and the protectorate for the next twenty years meant the bitter persecution of the Catholics; while the Restoration, in 1660, saw a partial toleration of them, preparatory to the Declaration of Indulgence and the active efforts of James II. in their favor twenty-five years later.

Through all this succession of alternately rigorous and lenient applications of the harsh laws of the statute-book, as a matter of fact few Catholics left England, and no American colony remained for any considerable length of time a Catholic community. The reasons for this result are not hard to find. In the first place, it may well be questioned whether the position of the Catholics in England was ever so bad as one would expect to find it from reading the laws and parliamentary proceedings. In all Tudor and Stuart legislation there was a wide chasm between the passage of the law and its enforcement; the statute-book is loaded with laws that were never carried out, or were put into force only to the most limited extent. The laws against the Catholics certainly remained largely unenforced.

Secondly, the English Catholics were never without hope of an amelioration of their state at home. The most natural time for a great Catholic exodus was in the later years of the reign of James I. and the early years of Charles I., when the foundations alike of Virginia and New England were being laid, and when Maryland was offering a basis on which either a Catholic or a Protestant community might presumably have been built up; but this was just the period when the influence of the crown was most consistently used in favor of the Catholics at home. They might fairly hope that a better day was dawning for them, when the powerful interposition of Spain and France was willingly accepted by James and Charles in their favor. The special time when emigration seemed most practicable was also the time when the occasion for it was least.

Again, it is to be noted that no American colony ever reached the position in which it could provide a positively secure refuge to Catholics. Maryland wavered from toleration to Catholicism, then to Anglicanism and to Puritanism, and then back to toleration; but never at any time was it a Catholic settlement in the sense in which Massachusetts belonged to the Puritans or Pennsylvania was the special home of the Quakers. English Catholics, hesitating between emigration and the further endurance of their ills at home, would feel no irresistible attraction in the dubious toleration of any of the colonies.[1]

Lastly, it is to be noticed that the great proportion of the English Catholics were not of the emigrating classes. Many of them were of the nobility and gentry, and therefore not of the ordinary stuff of which colonists were made. It is quite possible that the same conservative tendencies which held them to the old church held them to their old homes. If they had been as easily detached from their native soil as the Puritans and Quakers, one cannot doubt that some great migration comparable to that of those two bodies would have taken place.

[1] Tyler, *England in America*, chaps. vii., viii.

CHAPTER XII

THE ENGLISH PURITANS AND THE SECTS
(1550–1689)

THE multitude of Englishmen other than Catholics, who, at the opening of the seventeenth century, were dissatisfied with the church of England as by law established, may be grouped under the general name of Puritans; although as time passed on various newly organized religious bodies formed themselves from among them, so that two more religious classes, at least, have to be differentiated. The roots of Puritanism are to be found in the characteristics of human temperament. Conservatives and radicals will always exist; the Puritans were those who carried or tried to carry the principles and ideas of the Reformation to their logical and rigorous conclusion. Such men as Latimer, Cranmer, and many of the theologians of the reign of Edward VI., were already steadily approaching the fundamental position of the Puritans, as their thought developed, long before the foreign influence of the reign of Queen Mary became effective and the modified Protestantism of Elizabeth was introduced.

If the government had kept its hands off, England

would have divided into two camps, that of the Catholics and that of a Puritanically reformed church. The Anglican system was an artificial one, a compromise established under the influence of the crown and kept in power by royal determination till it eventually won the devotion, the loyalty, or at least the deliberate acceptance of the great body of moderate and conservative Englishmen. Catholics and Puritans were the logical opposites, and not Catholics and Anglicans, nor yet Anglicans and Puritans.

Yet in a more immediate sense Mary gave occasion to the rise of Puritanism by driving into banishment many of the more devout Protestants of her day. At Frankfort, Strasburg, Basel, Zurich, and Geneva groups of these English exiles gathered, formed congregations worshipping together; developed, apart from the restrictions of government, the logical tendencies of their religious ideas; and in many cases came under the powerful influence of continental reformers. Especially at Frankfort[1] and at Geneva was the religious life of these Protestant communities at white heat; and controversies were then begun and principles adopted which dominated all the later life of these Englishmen, and were handed down to their successors in England and America as party cries through more than a century. When the ordeal of Mary's reign was over, the exiled for conscience' sake returned to England, but they

[1] Hinds, *The England of Elizabeth*, 12–67.

formed already a body divergent from the church as it was then established.

During Elizabeth's reign three stages of the development of Puritanism gave occasion for corresponding conflicts with the crown and for making more clear the differences between Anglican and Puritan. During the first decade of the reign, Puritanism meant a protest against certain of the ceremonies and formulas and vestments required of clergymen by the law. The sign of the cross on the child's forehead in baptism, the celebration of saints' days, insistence on kneeling to receive the communion, the use of church organs, the changing of robes during the service, and even the wearing of a surplice or a square cap, were to many earnest souls survivals of "popery" and temptations to superstition. The clergy who held such beliefs tried by resolutions in convocation to change the practices of the church: but notwithstanding the large votes in their favor they were still in the minority and were defeated.[1]

Then individual ministers began to disregard the law, and either to neglect the use of certain requirements of the prayer-book altogether or to change the forms there laid down. The archbishop and the Court of High Commission issued detailed instructions insisting on observance of the authorized form of worship;[2] but the ministers declared that they

[1] Strype, *Annals*, I., 500–505.
[2] Prothero, *Statutes and Constitutional Documents*, 191–194.

owed obedience to God rather than to man, and
either resigned their pastorates or, encouraged by
their congregations, continued to disobey the law
and the archiepiscopal injunctions. It was at this
time and in this connection that the word "Puritan"
came into use, as a term of reproach for those who
insisted on an ultra-pure ritual, purged from all
traces of the old religion. "Puritan" was used as
"Pharisee" might have been.[1]

From 1570 onward Puritanism entered upon a
second stage, in the form of a contest for changes
in the organization of the established church. In
the main the same men who were dissatisfied with
the liturgy of the church began to oppose the system of its government by bishops and archbishops.[2]
The "Admonition to Parliament" of 1572 declares
that "as the names of archbishops, archdeacons,
lord bishops, chancellors, etc., are drawn out of the
pope's shop, together with their offices, so the government which they use . . . is anti-Christian and
devilish and contrary to the Scriptures. And as
safely may we, by the warrant of God's words, subscribe to allow the dominion of the pope universally to rule over the word of God as an archbishop over a whole province or a lord bishop over
a diocese which containeth many shires and parishes.
For the dominion that they exercise . . . is un-

---

[1] Camden, *Annals*, year 1568.
[2] Letter from Sampson, formerly dean of Christ Church, to
Lord Burleigh, March 8, 1574, in Strype, *Annals*, III., 373.

lawful and expressly forbidden by the word of God."[1]

The greater number of those who attacked the episcopal organization of the church advocated the system of Presbyterianism which had been extensively adopted on the Continent and recently introduced into Scotland by the Book of Discipline. November 20, 1572, was erected at Wandsworth, in Surrey, the first presbytery in England;[2] from this time forward presbyteries were established here and there by groups of neighboring parishes. Some ten or fifteen years later the larger group, known as the "classis," was introduced; provincial and national "synods" were contemplated by many of the Puritan clergy; and the English church bade fair to be reorganized on Presbyterian lines, without the authority of the law.

This action met the stern opposition of the queen and the Court of High Commission. In 1583 Elizabeth appointed Whitgift archbishop of Canterbury, and under him the law was enforced with rigor. Individual clergymen were deposed or forced to conform; the devotional practices called "exercises," on which Puritanism throve, were forbidden; and although the contest continued, the introduction of Presbyterianism was held in check.

The latter years of Elizabeth's reign saw Puritan-

---

[1] Prothero, *Statutes and Constitutional Documents*, 199.

[2] Bancroft, *Dangerous Positions*, chap. i., quoted in Prothero, *Statutes and Constitutional Documents*, 247.

ism within the church taking on a new activity, by
turning from questions of ceremony and church government to questions of morals. The Puritans always stood for greater earnestness and for the abo-
lition of abuses in the church, but as time passed on
they brought into greater prominence the ascetic
ideal of life; the strict keeping of the Sabbath borrowed from the Jewish ritual became customary;[1]
prevailing immoralities and extravagances were
more bitterly reprobated in books, sermons, and
parliamentary statutes; and Puritanism took on
that unlovely aspect of exaggerated austerity which
characterized its most conspicuous manifestations
in the seventeenth century.

The great body of men of Puritan tendencies, both
clergymen and laymen, were deeply interested in
reforming the church of England in liturgy, in organization, and in practices; but they had no wish or
intention to break it up, to divide it into different
bodies, or to withdraw individually from its membership. They were as completely dominated by
the ideal of a single united national church, one in
doctrine, organization, and form of worship, as was
the queen herself. Nevertheless, a group of men
arose among them, under the general name of Independents, to whom the very idea of a national
church seemed idolatrous; who found in the Scriptures, or were driven by the logic of their position, to one plan of church government only—the

[1] Eggleston, *Beginners of a Nation*, 123-132.

absolute independence of each congregation of Christian believers. They looked back to the little groups of chosen believers in Syria and Asia Minor, the shadowy outlines of whose organization are found in the New Testament; their imagination gave definite shape and their reverence for the Scriptures gave divine authority to these as examples. According to the analogy of biblical times, they looked upon themselves as a remnant of saints, sacred and set apart from a wicked and persecuting world.

Some of these extreme Puritans were under the influence of Robert Browne, a zealous advocate, whose activity lay principally between 1581 and 1586. Others came under the somewhat more systematic teachings of Barrow and Greenwood. Thus it became a fundamental principle of several thousand persons, between 1580 and 1600, to separate themselves from the established church. They are, therefore, known as "Separatists," though they were more commonly called at that time, as a term of reproach, by the names of their leaders, "Brownists" or "Barrowists." They met in "conventicles," and even strove to form more permanent congregations by gathering in secret places, or sometimes openly, in defiance of the authorities. A churchman of the time says that they teach "that the worship of the English church is flat idolatry; that we admit into our church persons unsanctified; that our preachers have no lawful calling; that our government is ungodly; that no

bishop or preacher preacheth Christ sincerely and
truly; that the people of every parish ought to
choose their bishop, and that every elder, though
he be no doctor nor pastor, is a bishop."[1]

In times when church and state were one, such
teaching could not be endured. If the Puritans
were scourged with whips the Separatists were lashed
with scorpions. Their teachers were silenced and
imprisoned, and Barrow and Greenwood were, in
1587, hanged at Tyburn. Their congregations were
broken up and attendants at their conventicles were
fined, deprived of their property, and thrown into
prison, where they died by the score. Before Elizabeth's reign was over, the Separatists had gone into
exile or become but a persecuted remnant, so far, at
least, as outward manifestation extended; though
one can scarcely doubt that among Puritans generally, and even, perhaps, among those who still ad-
hered to the established church, were many who
shared their convictions. It is to be remembered
that the Independents and all the new sects which
were formed in England later in the seventeenth
century, as well as the Puritans of New England,
organized themselves on the basis of independent
congregations of Christian believers.

The close of the sixteenth century saw the contrast
between the Anglican churchman on the one hand
and the Puritan and Separatist on the other becom-

[1] Paule, *Life of Whitgift* (1612), 43, quoted in Prothero,
Statutes and Constitutional Documents, 223.

ing more harsh, their incompatibility more evident. Fifty years earlier episcopacy and ceremonialism seemed to most Anglicans comparatively unimportant in themselves. They rather blamed the Puritans for making a difficulty about matters indifferent, and for opposing the civil authority in things pertaining to conscience; but did not quarrel with them on religious questions. But a generation of disputes, the development of fundamental principles, the need for justification of a position already taken, drove both parties into a more dogmatic attitude. The high - church party in the established church now began to assert the divine appointment of the episcopal office, to lay stress on the doctrine of the apostolic succession, and gradually to reintroduce much symbolic ceremonial.

The Puritans, on the other hand, were more than ever convinced that the system they advanced was based upon divine authority; and that the church as it stood was founded upon human regulation only and must be forced, if it could not be persuaded, to change its system. Still greater clearness was given to this division of parties by the theological contest that came into existence between 1600 and 1620. The Puritans were almost completely Calvinist, and they claimed that the established church itself had always been so. On the other hand, the Anglican leaders of the early seventeenth century were Arminian, and this form of theological doctrine was asserted by all those who defended the existing organization and ceremonial practices of the church.[1]

Thus the breach between the Puritan and the churchman was now so wide that James I., indolent and arrogant for all his toleration and learning, did nothing — perhaps could do nothing — towards its closing. He said of the Puritans, at the Conference at Hampton Court in 1604: "I shall make them conform themselves or I will harry them out of this land, or else do worse."[2] He disappointed and angered them, drove them into opposition to his civil rule as well as to his church policy, and strengthened their number and their position by his treatment of Parliament, whose interests and theirs had come to be inseparable.

All the antagonisms, religious and political, of the reign of James were intensified in that of Charles I. The new king was more autocratic and more unsympathetic with his subjects; Parliament was more self-assertive and more determined to impose its wishes upon king and ministers; the authorities of the established church were more intolerant towards the Puritans and milder towards the Catholics. The Puritans, on the other hand, were more convinced that the Anglican church was retrograding towards Catholicism, and more determined to destroy episcopacy if they should ever be able to do so.

The freest opportunity of the established church

---

[1] Makower, *Constitutional History of the Church of England*, 75.
[2] Gardiner, *Hist. of England*, I., 157.

to destroy Puritanism came during the period of
the personal government of Charles, from 1629 to
1640, when Parliament had no meetings, and when
the Court of Star Chamber, the High Commission,
and the Privy Council were the all-powerful instruments of an administration sympathetic with
the high-church party. The oppressions of the
Puritans were now at their height, and the prospect of ever obtaining freedom to worship as they
chose seemed the darkest. With the most prominent liberal and Puritan leaders imprisoned for their
political opinions, like Sir John Eliot, or lying in
prison, crushed under enormous fines, like Prynne;
with the courts subservient to the royal will;
with court preachers declaring the duty of passive
obedience to the government; with Laud guiding
the policy of the king in all ecclesiastical matters,—
the state of the Puritans might well seem hopeless,
and they might well look towards some distant land
as a place for the establishment of a purified national church.

Archbishop Laud typified and embodied the spirit
of the dominant church, and in addition he had un-
wearied energy, industry, and determination. Sincere, practical, and brave, but narrow-minded and
unsympathetic, he set about the work of reducing
the church of England to absolute uniformity in
accordance with the law as he interpreted it. The
Nonconformists had no rest; Puritan clergymen
must conform; Puritan laymen must suffer under

the power of the church, which, dominated by its bishops and wedded to its idols, was becoming steadily more powerful and all-inclusive. The reign of Charles was not marked by the passage of harsher laws against the Puritans, but it was distinguished from all periods that preceded or followed it by the continuous, steady, and thorough-going application of those already in existence.

It was under this régime that the great Puritan migration to America took place. The Puritans represented a class of society which was much more ready to emigrate than the Catholics. As early as 1597 some imprisoned Brownists sent a petition to the Privy Council asking that they might be allowed to settle in America; and four men of the same persuasion even went on a voyage to examine the land.[1] In 1608 many Puritans seem to have prepared to emigrate to Virginia, when by Archbishop Bancroft's influence they were forbidden by the king to go, except with his express permission in each individual case.[2]

The Separatists early became wanderers on the face of the earth, a now famous group of them leaving their English homes for Amsterdam, migrating thence to Leyden, and then, after hesitating between a Dutch and an English colony and between North and South America, a portion settling themselves

[1] Eggleston, *Beginners of a Nation*, 167.
[2] Stith, *Hist. of Virginia*, book II., year 1608.

on Plymouth Harbor.[1] In all the history of early
colonization there have been few such occasions as
that of the year 1638, when fourteen ships bound
for New England lay in the Thames at one time,
and when three thousand settlers reached Boston
within the same year.[2] Almost all the Englishmen
who were ever to emigrate to New England left
their homes during the twelve years between 1628
and 1640. Unfavorable economic conditions at
home and the prospect of greater prosperity in the
colony doubtless had their influence; but of the
more than twenty thousand who passed from the
old England to New England during that time, it is
fair to presume that by far the greater number were
more or less influenced by their Puritan opinions.

The most decisive proof of this motive for emigration is the slacking of the tide of Puritan expa-
triation after 1640. When Parliament, after eleven
years of intermission, met in that year at West-
minster in the full appreciation of its power, one
of its first actions was to order the impeachment and
arrest of Archbishop Laud. At last the Puritans
had their turn, and the assembling of Parliament
found them no longer a scattered, disorganized, di-
versified element in the English church and nation;
but, thanks to long persecution, a compact body,
austere in morals, dogmatic in religious belief, ready

[1] Griffis, *Pilgrims in Their Three Homes.*
[2] Authorities quoted in Eggleston, *The Beginners of a Nation,*
344.

to make use of political means for religious ends,
and determined to impose their asceticism and their
orthodoxy on the English people so far as they
might be able.[1]

A majority of Parliament, small but sufficient,
were Puritans, as had probably been true of every
Parliament for many years, had they been free
to act. Their intentions showed themselves in a
prompt inception of reforms in the church, and the
burdens of official ecclesiastical oppression were
rapidly transferred to the shoulders of those who
had previously bound the loads upon Puritan backs.
In 1641 orders were issued by the House of Commons
for the demolition of all images, altars, and crucifixes.[2]
A commission known as the "Committee of Scan-
dalous Ministers" was appointed, and proceeded to
discipline the clergy and to harass the universities.
Demands for the harsher treatment of priests and
Jesuits were soon followed by plans for the diminu-
tion of the power of archbishops and bishops of the
established church. The Court of High Commission
was abolished July 5, 1641.[3] The archbishops and
bishops were removed from the House of Lords
and the Privy Council by the act of February 13,
1642.[4]

The Solemn League and Covenant of September
25, 1643, pledged Parliament and the leaders of the

---

[1] Eggleston, *Beginners of a Nation*, 133.
[2] *Commons Journals*, II., 279.
[3] 16 Chas. I., chap. ii.   [4] *Ibid.*, chap. xxvii.

now dominant party to extirpate "church government by archbishops, bishops, their chancellors and commissaries, deans, deans and chapters, archdeacons, and all other ecclesiastical officers depending on that hierarchy"; and to reform religion in England "in doctrine, worship, discipline, and government, according to the word of God and the example of the best reformed churches." [1]

By this time the quarrel between Charles and Parliament had been put to the arbitrament of the sword, and the distinction of Cavalier and Roundhead to a certain extent superseded that between Anglican and Puritan. In 1645 came the catastrophe of Naseby, then the long series of futile negotiations ending in the execution of the king at Whitehall in 1649. From the general confusion emerged the commonwealth, "without any king or House of Lords," the church organized on Presbyterian lines, the spirit of Puritanism dominating, although there was toleration for every form of Christian belief, "provided this liberty be not extended to popery or prelacy." [2] For full twenty years the Anglican church was under a cloud, first Presbyterianism and then Independency being the official form of the church of England. The ill-fortunes of the royalist party in the civil war and under the commonwealth, and the religious oppression imposed by the Puritans upon churchmen, now combined to send to the colo-

[1] *League and Covenant*, §§ 1, 2.
[2] *Instrument of Government*, § 37.

nies the very classes which had so recently been the
persecutors. From 1640 to 1660 Virginia, Maryland, and the Carolinas received an influx of English
churchmen escaping from conditions at home as
intolerable to them as those which drove the Pilgrims and Puritans to New England during the previous decades.

The commonwealth was not merely a triumph
of Puritanism, it was a birth-time of new religious
sects. The excitement of a period of civil war, the
breaking down of old standards, the disappearance
of old authority, the opportunities offered by the
quasi - democracy of the commonwealth, the pre-
occupation of the seventeenth - century mind with
questions of religion, all combined to cause almost
a complete disintegration of religious organization.
Here and there a man began to preach religious
truth and duty as they looked to him; he obtained adherents, a congregation was organized,
the tenets of this body spread, and branches
were formed; till shortly a new religious society
had come into existence, with its creed, organization, missionary spirit, and more or less vigorous
hope of converting all men and absorbing all other
religious organizations. An almost indefinite number of such religious bodies arose during the middle years of the seventeenth century—Millenarians
or Fifth Monarchy Men, Baptists or Anabaptists,
Quakers, Ranters, Notionists, Familists, Perfectists,
and others. Most of them died out within the brief

period which gave them birth, but some survived to become great religious denominations, extending into America as well as throughout England.[1]

Of these the Quakers are the most interesting in their relations to the New World. The spirit from which they arose was closely similar to that which gave birth to the Baptists of England, the Anabaptists, Mennonites, Pietists, and Quietists of the Continent. Their movement was an extreme revolt against the formalism, corporate character, and externality of established religion. It contained a deep element of mysticism. The Quakers declared all believers, irrespective of learning, sex, or official appointment, to be priests.[2] They asserted the adequacy of the "inner light" to guide every man in his faith and in his actions. They opposed all forms and ceremonies, even many of those of ordinary courtesy and fashion, such as removing the hat or conforming the garb to changing custom.

George Fox, the representative of these ideas, began his public preaching in 1648, and his doctrines at once found wide acceptance. In 1652 there were said to be twenty-five Quaker preachers passing through the country; by 1654 there were sixty, some of whom were women, who, by the principles of their teachings, should preach as freely as men. Their missionary journeys led them to Scotland and Ireland, and later even to Holland and Germany

---

[1] Gooch, *English Democratic Ideas in the Seventeenth Century*, chap. viii.   [2] Fox, *Letters*, No. 249.

and the far east of Europe. Organization among
the Quakers proceeded somewhat slowly. This was
due partly to the individualist character of their
beliefs, partly to the lack of constructive interest
on the part of Fox and the other leaders during
the early period of their missionary work. Nevertheless, "meetings" were gradually organized, took
definite shape, and kept up regular communica-
tion with one another, so that there came to be a
net-work of such bodies over the whole country. In
1659 it is estimated that there were thirty thousand
Quakers in England.

Notwithstanding the religious liberty guaranteed
by the Instrument of Government of 1653, the
teachings and practices of the Quaker preachers
brought them into much turmoil. Their vituper-
ation of the clergy, their intrusion into church services and ceremonies, already reduced only too frequently to confusion by the rapid changes of the
time, their objection to the payment of tithes, their
refusal to take an oath, their outspoken denuncia-
tion of all whose actions they disapproved, the
prominence of women in their propaganda, and, in
early times, suspicions that they were connected
with political plots, could not but subject them to
ridicule, abuse, and actual persecution. They habitually violated numerous laws on the statute-
book, ranging from those requiring good order to
those forbidding what was construed as blasphemy.
They were, therefore, beaten and stoned by the

mob; abused, fined, and imprisoned by the magistrates; ridiculed and prosecuted by the clergy; subjected to starvation, exposure, and other hardships by sheriffs and jailers.[1]

In 1660 Charles II. was recalled to the throne. This event was a restoration of the church even more than a restoration of the monarchy. The royal power could never again be what it had been before the civil war, the execution of a king, and the establishment of a republic. But the church, with the longevity and recuperative power of all religious organizations, arose again to a life apparently as vigorous and despotic as in the times of Laud. The year 1662 found four thousand two hundred Quakers in the jails of England;[2] and the popular reaction against the austerity of the Puritan régime subjected Quakers to much ill-treatment by the rabble.

Yet just at this juncture the dignity of the body was strengthened and its power of self-assertion increased by the adherence to it of men of higher education and social position. The Quakers of the commonwealth period were almost all of the middle and lower-middle or trading classes. Soon after the Restoration a number of men of good family and some means threw in their fortunes with the persecuted sect. One of them, Robert Barclay, reduced to order and system the scattered and incoherent state-

---

[1] Besse, *Sufferings of the Quakers*, I., chaps. iii., iv., xi., xviii., II., chap. i., etc.   [2] Sewel, *Hist. of the Quakers*, 346.

ments of its theology. In his *Apology*, published in 1675, he set forth a logical and consistent statement of beliefs, couched in clear and graceful language and supported by calm reasoning and example.[1] Of the same class was William Penn, an educated, wealthy, polished, and genial English gentleman. Yet he was also a serious-minded and devout Quaker preacher, missionary, and writer, and as he saw and shared in the sufferings of the faithful he might well despair of better conditions in England and think of a "Holy Experiment" in America, where Quakers from 1675 onward were settling in West New Jersey.[2]

Under Charles II. the attitude of the king was favorable to the Quakers, while in the short reign of James II. they had the great advantage of the personal friendship of the king for Penn. Yet no matter what should be the favor of the king, or even their more moderate treatment by the authorities of the established church, Quakers could not hope for material comfort or ease of mind in surroundings so alien to their ideals as England was in the last decades of the seventeenth century. They, still more than the Puritans in the time of Laud or the churchmen in the time of Cromwell, suffered because of the incongruity of the ordinary law and custom with their ideals. It was the realization of

---

[1] Thomas, *Hist. of the Society of Friends in America*, chap. ii., 200, 201.

[2] Fiske, *The Dutch and Quaker Colonies*, II., 99, 167; Andrews, *Colonial Self-Government*, chap. vii.

this incompatibility, along with the attraction of a community under Quaker government, cheap and abundant land, a promise of a growing population and lucrative business opportunities that set flowing to Pennsylvania the tide of Quaker emigration and created in a few years a great Quaker commonwealth in America.

Besides Puritans, Anglicans, and Quakers, another great stream of emigration poured into the central colonies of America—the Presbyterian Scotch-Irish. To understand their coming, it is necessary to return to the early years of the seventeenth century and to consider the policy of James I. towards rebellious Ireland. At the opening of his reign James found in Ireland an opportunity to plant a colony near home.[1] When Englishmen and Scotchmen had been established in Ireland, the Irish sore would be healed, and that restless Catholic community be transformed into an outlying district of England. The "Plantation of Ulster" began in 1611. The titles of the natives were ruthlessly forfeited, the six counties of the province of Ulster were redivided, and the land was regranted to proprietors who engaged to settle colonists from England and Scotland upon it according to a fixed system.

This system was skilfully devised and rigidly carried out. It required the new land-owners to establish freeholders, small tenants, laborers, and

[1] Walpole, *Kingdom of Ireland*, 130–135.

artisans upon the soil in proportion to the amount of land they received, allowing only a certain minimum number of the Irish natives to be retained as laborers. The proprietors were largely merchants of London and merchandising noblemen of the court; the tenants they introduced were mostly from the towns and country districts of the north of England and the lowlands of Scotland. Men of Puritan tendencies showed the same readiness to emigrate to Ireland that they showed soon afterwards as to New England, and as a result the settlers of Ulster, during the first two decades of the seventeenth century, were almost universally Presbyterians.

Under these new and somewhat anomalous conditions a population grew up in the north of Ireland which was almost as distinct in race and religious organization from the people of England and Scotland as it was from the Catholic and Celtic population which it had displaced. Its religion, without being proscribed, was not acknowledged, for Anglicanism was the established church of Ireland, though it numbered but few adherents. Ulster's industrial interests were, from the beginning, subordinated to those of England, as completely as were those of the natives.[1]

As the century progressed the economic evils under which the Scotch-Irish suffered became more pronounced. The navigation acts were so inter-

[1] Cunningham, *Growth of English Industry and Commerce*, **II.**, 136.

preted as to exclude Ireland from all their advantages and to cut her off from any direct trade with the colonies. Tobacco-growing was forbidden, and the exportation of cattle to England placed under prohibitory duties. The wool manufacture was crushed by heavy export taxes, and the linen manufacture neglected or discouraged. In 1642 and again in 1689 came war and new conquests of the country, to add to its disorganization and chronic sufferings. Kidnapping, enforced service in the colonies, and traffic in political prisoners were indulged in by the government. Ireland, as a dwelling-place for Catholics or Protestants, for Celts or Saxons, for natives or English and Scotch settlers, was a country of ever-renewed distress.

To economic disabilities is to be added religious persecution of a mild type, especially after 1689. All the laws that interfered with the religious equality of the Presbyterians in England were extended to Ireland; and they seemed more vexatious there because in Ulster the Presbyterians were in the vast majority and the established church almost unrepresented, except by tithe collectors and absentee landlords. At the close of the seventeenth century there were more than a million Ulster Presbyterians. But soon, as a result of this combined economic and religious oppression, they began to migrate in a narrow stream which by 1720 became a wide river. They formed the largest body of emigrants that left Europe for the American colonies. Before the eighteenth century was over the Presbyterian population of Ireland was reduced by at least a half;[1] and the missing moiety was to be found scattered along the whole line of the Appalachian mountain-chain, at the backbone of the English colonies, extending eastward and westward and forming a prolific and influential element of the American people.

[1] Fiske, *The Dutch and Quaker Colonies in America*, II., 354.

CHAPTER XIII

THE POLITICAL SYSTEM OF ENGLAND
(1500–1689)

AN earlier chapter of this work has been devoted to the political institutions of Spain, France, and the Netherlands, and each had its share of influence on American history; but it is England from which the American nation really sprang, of which it was for more than a century and a half a dependency, and to whose traditions, institutions, and government we must look back for the origins of our own. The oldest political institution in England is the monarchy. Older than Parliament, older than the law-courts, older than the division of the country into shires, the monarchy dates back to the consolidation of the petty Anglo-Saxon states in the ninth century — and these were themselves kingdoms.

At no time in this long course of English history were the claims of the monarchy more exorbitant than under James I. and Charles I., from 1603 to 1642, just when the tide of immigration began to flow towards America, and when the governments of the colonies were being established. "What God hath joined, then, let no man separate. I am the husband and all the whole isle is my lawful wife. I am the head and it is my body. I am the shepherd and it is my flock. . . ." [1] So King James wove metaphors, when he addressed Parliament at its opening in 1604. When disputes had arisen in 1610 he declared: "The state of monarchy is the supremest thing upon earth, for kings are not only God's lieutenants upon earth and sit upon God's throne, but even by God himself they are called gods. . . . As to dispute what God may do is blasphemy, . . . so is it sedition in subjects to dispute what a king may do in the height of his power." "Encroach not upon the prerogative of the crown; if there falls out a question that concerns my prerogative or mystery of state, deal not with it till you consult with the king or his council, or both, for they are transcendent matters." [2]

This absolute prerogative of the king was attributed to him by others, as well as claimed by himself. Dr. Cowell, professor of civil law at Cambridge, declared that the king "is above the law by his absolute power"; [3] and Sir Walter Raleigh wrote that attempts to bind the king by law justified his breach of it, "his charters and other instruments being no other than the surviving witnesses of unconstrained will." [4] But this definition of the

[1] Prothero, *Select Statutes*, 283. [2] *Ibid.*, 293, 294.
[3] Cowell, *Interpreter*, under word "king."
[4] Raleigh, *Prerogative of Parliament*, Preface.

prerogative of the king was an exaggerated description of his real position in the English system of government, and was either academic or argumentative. As properly used, absolute monarchy merely meant an all-powerful not an autocratic government; government was supreme, but the king was not necessarily supreme in the government. As government had been developed in England, in the course of time it had grown up around the monarchy as its centre and found in it its embodiment.

In Anglo-Saxon England government was crude and embryonic, but even then the king held a general oversight over the exercise of its few functions. In the later Middle Ages, when government was somewhat more highly developed, its more numerous functions, in so far as they were not performed by feudal lords or church officials, were fulfilled by the king. It was by the monarchy that the law-courts were formed and commissioned, that Parliament was summoned and given the opportunity for self-development, that the system of taxation and of military life was organized. The great advance in the organization and effectiveness of government which marked the reigns of the Tudor rulers consisted in the elaboration and increased activity of the administrative or royal element in the government.

The royal prerogative might, therefore, be conceived of as the function of keeping the machine of government running. The king was the director and controller of an aggregate of governmental powers. All officials were commissioned in his name, and those of higher rank were actually selected and appointed by him. All foreign intercourse was carried on in his name, and in the main directed by him; Parliament was called, prorogued, and adjourned at his will, and he kept at least a negative control over its actions. All justice was exercised in his name, and his interests and known wishes sometimes influenced decisions. All charters, whether to cities, to guilds, to possessors of mercantile monopolies, or to commercial and colonizing companies, were issued under his name and seal, and the powers granted in them could not be in opposition to his will.[1]

The powers of the king were, therefore, very real, even if the philosophic contentions of James and other theorists be disregarded; but they were powers restricted in every direction by actual conditions, and exercised through ministers whose familiarity with precedent, whose control over the details of administration, whose dignified offices, and whose personal weight of judgment and character made them, though nominally servants of the king, a real power in the government.

Much of the royal power was exercised through the three great law-courts, King's Bench, Exchequer, and Common Pleas; through the courts of equity,

[1] Smith, *The Commonwealth of England*, book I., chap. ix., book II., chap. iv.

held by the chancellor, the master of the rolls, and the master of requests; through the half-administrative, half-judicial bodies, the council of the north and the council of the marches of Wales, and through the circuit courts of assize. Much was exercised through higher and lower administrative officers, through the Exchequer, and through lower offices such as the wardrobe and the admiralty.

But the real centre of gravity of the executive powers of the government at this time is to be found in the Council or Privy Council, two terms which are used indiscriminately.[1] This body was made up of seventeen or eighteen members, including all the great ministers of state, the lord chancellor, or, as he was sometimes called, lord keeper of the great seal, the high treasurer, the two secretaries, the great master and the comptroller of the household, the chamberlain and the great admiral, besides a certain number chosen as members of the Privy Council without otherwise occupying office.[2] There were usually from six to ten members of the council present, the membership of some of the ministers being somewhat perfunctory.

As a body, however, its services were as far from perfunctory as can well be conceived. Its sessions were held almost daily and its sphere of activity was apparently coextensive with the life of England and of all its dependencies. Scarcely an interest,

[1] Dicey, *The Privy Council*, 80.
[2] *Acts of the Privy Council*, 1594-1597.

public or private, escapes its attention, whether it is the organization of a campaign in France or the settlement of a family quarrel between father and son;[1] whether it is "Sir John Norreis, knight, and Thomas Diggs, esquire," or a Lord Morley, or the chief baron of the Court of Exchequer, Lord Manwood, or some merchants or poor artisans or an "Elice Gailer, of Berton, yeoman," that appear before the council at its summons; whether it is engaged in formulating rules for articles contraband of war, or trying to put an end to illicit coinage on the borders of Wales; whether engaged in one or other of a hundred different interests, the council is always active, intrusive, and high-handed.[2]   It regulated manufactures and trade, protected foreigners, disciplined recusants, kept the oversight of customs and other officials, settled disputes between colleges and their tenants, bishops, deans, and government officers, instructed sheriffs and justices of the peace as to their duty, made provision for the keeping up of military and naval forces, and performed other duties so numerous and varied as to defy enumeration or classification.

A special duty of the Privy Council was to keep up correspondence with the officials of outlying districts under the dominion of the crown and not within the systematic administration of sheriffs, assize courts, justices of the peace, or other regular

---

[1] *Acts of the Privy Council*, 1591–1592, pp. 160, 193, 256–258, 292, 327, 414, 476, etc.   [2] *Ibid.*, 231, 305, 314, 378, 449, 572.

governance. These regions included the marches of Wales and of Scotland, certain counties of England, Ireland, and the Channel Islands, the last two of these having been placed under the direct supervision of the Privy Council by statute.[1] As colonies grew up they fell, naturally, under the special care of the Privy Council. The duty of hearing appeals from colonial courts became and is still a duty of the council; to the Privy Council were referred colonial laws for approval or veto; and the successive bodies formed for the oversight of the colonies, culminating in the Board of Trade and Plantations of 1696, were either committees of the Privy Council or boards acting under its control and reporting to it.

Although most of this control over the colonies was still far in the future, the power exercised by the council over England's nearest dependency, Ireland, may fairly be taken as anticipatory of it. Irish matters during the later years of Queen Elizabeth and the early years of James I. demanded much attention and time from the Privy Council, notwithstanding the existence of an Irish Parliament, a lord deputy, various provincial officials, and the whole framework of a subordinate government in Ireland. All the variety of cases that came before the council from England were duplicated from Ireland In fact, Ireland was treated much as if it were an English county, or better, perhaps, one of those regions

[1] Poynings's Act (1495), Dicey, *The Privy Council*, 90.

of England, like the marches of Wales, which had a somewhat peculiar jurisdiction.

The most important form of oversight of Ireland exercised by the Privy Council was that based upon "Poynings's Act" of 1495. Sir Edward Poynings, a type of that class of vigorous officials of middle rank which were such useful instruments of the Tudor government, was sent, in 1494, to Ireland as lord deputy; the next year he called a parliament at Drogheda and obtained its assent to a number of statutes designed to introduce order into that disturbed country, and to make real the power of English government by diminishing that of the turbulent lords of the Pale.[1] As a means of reaching the latter object, the Irish Parliament, which had long been under their control and which had lately made some assertion of its right of independent action,[2] was to be curbed, and that by its own ordinance.

It was therefore enacted that in the future no bill should be introduced into the Irish Parliament unless its heads had first been submitted to the English Privy Council and obtained the approval of that body and of the king.[3] Moreover, this approval must be given before Parliament met. This reduced the Irish Parliament to a mere registering body for royal enactments. In 1556 an explanato v

---

[1] Morris, *Hist. of Ireland, 1496–1868*, pp. 58–63.
[2] *Irish Statutes*, 37 Henry VI.
[3] *Irish Statutes*, 10 Henry VII., chap. iv.

act was passed[1] amending Poynings's Act so far as
to make it allowable for the Irish Parliament to pass
any bills which had received the approval of the
crown and of the English Privy Council at any time
during its session. The regular practice of Irish
legislation under these acts was as follows: any
member of either house of the Irish Parliament
might bring in heads of a bill, which, if approved by
both houses, were submitted to the viceroy, who
referred them to the Irish Privy Council; that body
sent them, altered or unaltered, to the king, who referred them to the English Privy Council; this body
then approved, rejected, or modified them; and they
were returned, through the viceroy, to the Irish Parliament in the form of a bill, to be accepted or rejected as a whole, but not to be further modified.[2]

By this cumbrous method only could the Irish
Parliament legislate. It was, moreover, subject not
only to the English Privy Council, but to the English
Parliament. One of the clauses of Poynings's Act
had provided that all statutes which up to that time
had been passed by the English Parliament should
bind Ireland also.[3] Many laws were subsequently
passed by the English Parliament for Ireland, thus
ignoring the Irish Parliament; but it was not till
later than the period we are considering that a
claim of the superiority of the English Parliament

---

[1] *Irish Statutes*, 3 and 4 Philip and Mary, chap. iv.
[2] Walpole, *Kingdom of Ireland*, 253, 254.
[3] *Irish Statutes*, 10 Henry VII., chap. xxii.

was definitely made. In the eighteenth century a member of the Irish Parliament published a book called *The Case of Ireland Being Bound by Acts of Parliament in England Stated*. This was formally condemned by the English Parliament and ordered to be burned by the common hangman.[1] When still later the Irish House of Lords protested against the reversal of one of its judgments, on appeal, by the English House of Lords, the English Parliament, in 1720, passed an act depriving the Irish House of Lords of any appellate jurisdiction, and declaring that "the English Parliament had, hath, and of right ought to have full power and authority to make laws and statutes of sufficient force and validity to bind the people of Ireland"[2]—a precedent of portentous applicability to the American colonies when a similar question came up in regard to them a half-century later.

The power of Parliament over external dependencies was destined to come into greater prominence in the future. The question at issue at the beginning of the seventeenth century was the extent of its power over England itself. Was it, like the Privy Council, the law-courts, and other such bodies, merely a creation and dependency of the crown? Or was it, although in form an assembly of royal councillors, meeting only when the king summoned it and ceasing to exist when he ordered its dissolution, a branch of the government co-ordi-

---

[1] Walpole, *Kingdom of Ireland*, 252.   [2] 6 George I., chap. v.

nate with or even in certain relations superior to him?

In the organization of Parliament there were several grave deficiencies, if it were to be considered an independent body. It was a composite assembly of two ill-related parts. The House of Lords, which consisted at this time of some fifty members,[1] had an existence as a royal council quite apart from the House of Commons, and there were still many evidences that it was the original body and the House of Commons a later accretion. In 1601, when Elizabeth appeared in the House of Lords to open her last Parliament, the Commons, who were waiting in their own chamber, did not hear of her presence promptly, and when they hastened to the Lords' chamber the door was closed and they could not obtain admission, so they "returned back again into their own House much discontented."[2] The Lords had various privileges and constitutional rights of their own: as individuals, of trial by peers, of being represented by proxies, of entering individual protests, of audience with the sovereign, of certain advantages of procedure in the courts of common law; as a body, of trying impeachments brought by the House of Commons, and of acting as a final court of appeal for all lower courts whether of law or equity.[3]

[1] D'Ewes, *Journals*, 599.   [2] *Ibid.*, 620.
[3] Pike, *Constitutional History of the House of Lords*, chaps. ix., xi.-xiv.

The House of Commons was composed of two knights or gentlemen elected for each shire; and one or two representatives for each of nearly three hundred cities and boroughs. The system of representation was crude and antiquated. The knights of the shire were elected by the "forty-shilling freeholders"—that is to say, by all who had a tenure approaching ownership in lands whose annual rental value reached that sum. This was an electorate that reached far down in the social scale, but it was limited by the tendency of English land to remain in the hands of large owners, and by the influence, legitimate and illegitimate, of the gentry, the great county noble families, and the crown. The knights of the shire, therefore, as a matter of fact, not only belonged to, but were elected by and reflected the interests and feelings of, the great body of rural gentry; while the yeomen exercised little influence in Parliament, as the laboring classes certainly exercised none at all.

There were vast differences in the system of election by the towns which were represented in Parliament, varying all the way from appointment by patrons, in some towns, down through divers grades of extension of the franchise to an almost universal suffrage in a few. Nevertheless, from the towns, as from the counties, it was representatives of the upper and middle classes that sat in the Commons. There was no approach to equality in the constituencies represented in the House of Commons; members were elected often by outside influence and always by a narrow constituency, and no control was possessed by the electors over their representatives.

Yet these defects were more apparent than real. The special powers of the House of Lords were becoming shadowy, and almost the only real significance of the peerage was when it was united with the House of Commons and made a part of the larger whole of Parliament.[1]

In the House of Commons was the real source of power of Parliament. Whatever the imperfections in the method of election, whatever the irregularity of constituencies, whatever the crudity of the idea of representation, the five hundred or more knights, country gentlemen, lawyers, and merchants who made up the Commons at this time[2] were convinced that in some way they stood for the whole nation. When Parliament had been once summoned and organized, it became a body with three hundred years of precedent back of it; and in the days of the Stuarts it confronted the king with claims to a very different position and power from those he was inclined to concede to it. So far from assimilating their position to that of the law-courts, Privy Council, and other such bodies, at the very opening of the reign of James the Commons declared "there is not the highest standing court in

[1] 36 and 37 Henry VIII., f. 60 (Dyer, *Reports*, pt. i., 327).
[2] *Names of Members Returned to Serve in Parliament*, pt. i., 442–448.

this land that ought to enter into competency either for dignity or authority with this high court of Parliament which with your Majesty's royal assent gives laws to other courts, but from other courts receives neither laws nor orders." [1]

The course of time intensified this difference of opinion. "Set chairs for the ambassadors," James cried, mockingly, when the deputies from the House of Commons visited him with a petition during the dispute of 1621. To the king Parliament seemed to be making a claim to sovereignty against which the only proper argument was a jest. Shortly afterwards he wrote to the speaker of the House of Commons, "These are, therefore, to command you to make known in our name unto the House that none therein shall presume henceforth to meddle with anything concerning our government or deep matters of state." He insisted that "these are unfit things to be handled in Parliament except your king requires it of you. . . ." As to the privileges of Parliament James wrote, "We cannot allow of the style calling it your ancient and undoubted right and inheritance, but could rather have wished that ye had said that your privileges were derived from the grace and permission of our ancestors and us." [2]

The Commons, on the other hand, a week later,

[1] *Apology of the Commons*, 1604; Petyt, *Jus Parliamentarium*, 227-247.
[2] *Letter of the king to the House of Commons*, December 10, 1621.

placed this protestation on their minutes: "That the liberties, privileges, and jurisdictions of Parliament are the ancient and undoubted birthright and inheritance of the subjects of England, and that the arduous and urgent affairs concerning the king, state, and defence of the realm, and of the church of England and the maintenance and making of laws, and redress of mischiefs and grievances which daily happen within this realm, are proper subjects and matters of counsel and debate in Parliament; and that in the handling and proceeding of those businesses every member of the House of Parliament hath and of right ought to have freedom of speech to propound, treat, reason, and bring to conclusion the same." [1] It is true that James sent for the *Journal* and tore this page from its records, but he could not tear the belief in its statements from the hearts of a great part of the people of England.

King and Parliament held diametrically opposite views of their relative powers, and both appealed to the past in justification of their opinions. But England's past was a long story, and its successive chapters read very variously. James appealed to the immediate past to justify his possession of the "inseparable rights and prerogatives annexed to our imperial crown, whereof, not only in the times of other our progenitors, but in the blessed reign of our late predecessor, that renowned queen Elizabeth,

[1] Rushworth, *Historical Collections*, I., 53.

we found our crown actually possessed."[1] The leaders of the House of Commons, on the other hand, were looking back to a more remote past, the birth-time and period of acknowledgment by the crown of the parliamentary privileges and English liberties which now seemed to them endangered.

As a matter of fact, Parliament, like all other political institutions in England, had grown up around the monarchy. Primarily, the Houses were a body of advisers of the king, summoned by him to give their counsel in matters in which he needed the advice of the various classes of his subjects; and to give their consent to taxation, which would require sacrifice on the part of the people. Once organized, however, Parliament gathered into itself all the shadowy survivals of self-government coming down from a still earlier period; it reflected the local independence of the towns and counties which sent members to the House of Commons, and the corporate rights of the church and individual privileges of the nobility, which constituted its upper house; it served as the instrument by which the nation at various times protected itself against bad government; it embodied the fifteenth-century ideal of a government conjointly by king and estates of the realm.

Moreover, Parliament gained by repeated use and acknowledgment an established procedure and powers, well - understood rights, and precedents

---

[1] _King's proclamation on dissolving Parliament_, January 6, 1622.

frequently invoked. The four fundamental privileges of members of Parliament were: (1) freedom of elections; (2) freedom from arrest during the sessions; (3) freedom of speech in debate; (4) freedom of access to the sovereign for their speaker, if not for all individually. These were frequently acknowledged by the sovereign at the opening of Parliament and enrolled upon its records, and still more frequently asserted in the House.[1] The powers of Parliament were less clearly defined than its privileges; but its control over taxation and legislation, its right to impeach the king's ministers and to discuss all matters of interest to the nation, were frequently asserted and usually conceded.[2]

Thus Parliament was much more than a royal council; it was a body with claims to co-ordinate powers of government. How far, at any one time, these privileges and powers were conceded, how far they were denied or encroached upon by the crown, was largely dependent on circumstances. These circumstances during Tudor times had been such as to put the initiative and much of the actual power of government in the hands of the king, and parliamentary powers were largely in abeyance. Parliament during this time was a conservative body; the monarchy was the innovating element of the state.

---

[1] D'Ewes, *Journals*, 65, 66, 175, 236, 259, 411, 460, etc.; Petyt, *Jus Parliamentarium*, 227 – 243, quoted in Prothero, *Select Statutes*, 289; *Commons Journals*, I., 431, etc.

[2] Gneist, *Hist. of the English Constitution*, chaps. v., xxxii.

Circumstances changed with the closing years of the sixteenth century and favored an increase of parliamentary participation in government. With all her prestige the old queen herself had to feel it.[1] With the accession of the half-foreign Stuarts, with the cessation of danger of invasion from abroad, with the increasing weight of exactions of an unwise and unpopular personal government, with the growing interest of the seventeenth century in matters of politics, and, above all, with the development of Puritanism, individualistic and self-assertive in its very essence, Parliament was sure to reassert all the powers which it had ever possessed, and likely to seek to extend them. The king was now the conservative element, while Parliament, if recent conditions be taken as the standard, was the innovating party.

It was exactly at this period of contest and of unsettled balance of powers that the early settlements were made in America. The colonists represented almost without exception what might be called the parliamentarian view. It was not the king, the courtiers, the nobles, the judges, the higher clergy, the official classes, and the fellows of the universities that emigrated. Among these the royalist spirit was strong, but they remained in England. It was rather from the middle and lower classes, from those who were on poor terms with the king, whatever their position in society, from the

[1] D'Ewes, *Journals*, 602.

persecuted, the dissatisfied, the restless, that the great body of colonists was drawn; and among these classes the views upheld by the House of Commons were wide - spread. The same thing was true of those companies which, remaining in England, yet had so much influence over the destinies of the American colonies. The most influential elements in the Virginia Company, the Massachusetts Bay Company, and other similar bodies were distinctly opposed to the high claims of the king. Yet unanimity did not exist even among those who left England; and strong as the predilection was among the founders of America for self-government and representative institutions, the Old-World differences of view were transferred to the colonies and played a part in local struggles there.

Much of the disputation between James and the House of Commons concerned the privileges of Parliament, and might be suspected of being largely the natural jealousy of its own rights felt and asserted by an ancient corporation. But Parliament was waging war for larger objects than the rights of its own body; it felt itself to be defending in its own privileges the personal rights of all Englishmen. In the contested election case of 1604 a member declared that "the case of Sir John Fortescue and Sir Francis Goodwin has become the case of the whole kingdom."[1] "The rights and liberties of your subjects of England and the privi-

[1] *Commons Journals*, I., 159, March 30, 1604.

leges of this House," is a formula that appears frequently in the documents of the time, and combines the two objects of the contest, in which the latter were upheld largely because they supported and protected the former.

These ancient rights of the people were less definite than either the privileges or the powers of Parliament. They were, perhaps, attractive and valued somewhat in proportion to their vagueness. They certainly included right of freedom from arrest or imprisonment except on a definite charge and by due process of law; they included exemption from taxation except after consent of Parliament;[1] they included protection against violence and injustice; they included the right of petition to the king against any grievance,[2] and in general a right to have the laws enforced, yet to have nothing done to their disadvantage which was not in the law. It was the spirit rather than the letter of Magna Carta that was valued by the English people.

As time passed and under Charles I. the conflict between the parliamentary and the royal claims became more intense, the upholders of the former fell back more and more on the ancient rights and liberties of the people, and relatively less is said of parliamentary privileges. In the Petition of Right

[1] Hakewell's argument in the Bates case of 1610 (*State Trials*, ed. 1779, XI.); Petition of Right of 1628.
[2] Coke's speech on Petition of Right (*Parliamentary History*, VIII., 104).

of 1629, Parliament appeals to the Great Charter, to the Confirmation of the Charters, and to other early statements of personal liberties. Pym declared that "the liberties of this House are inferior to the liberties of this kingdom." When the civil war was actually imminent, in December, 1641, the Grand Remonstrance was issued as a statement of the contentions of the leaders in Parliament. In this document "the people," "the liberties of subjects," "rights of the nation," and other popular expressions are constantly used or implied.[1]

Ultimately, as a result of the struggles of the later years of the seventeenth century, the more important of such rights were formulated in the Bill of Rights of 1689. Thus the heritage of civil freedom which the people of England had traditionally enjoyed was neither taken from them by the strong monarchy of the sixteenth century nor forgotten in the struggle of Parliament for its own privileges in the seventeenth. It was reasserted with constantly new insistence in England, and was carri to America by the colonists as an acknowled d and valued possession.

[1] *Grand Remonstrance*, §§ 11, 19, 28, 40, 53, 57, 98, ˌo, etc., in Rushworth, *Historical Collections*, IV., 438.

CHAPTER XIV

THE ENGLISH COUNTY AND ITS OFFICERS

(1600–1650)

THE ordinary Englishman in the seventeenth century had much more to do with local than with national government. Only a few score men served the king as ministers, councillors, or judges; only a few hundred attended Parliament; while as lords lieutenant, sheriffs, justices of the peace, constables, church-wardens, mayors, aldermen, and in other capacities of local and limited but real power, many thousands must have taken a part in public affairs. National government was remote from the ordinary man; local government came close to him. The political institutions which surrounded him on all sides, insensibly controlling every action and forming the world to which his outward life conformed, were familiar to him and affected his habits and ideas, whether he remained at home or emigrated to the colonies, far more directly than did the political institutions of the nation.

The oldest, most stable, and most important unit of local government was the shire, or county. The conspicuous official and historic head of the county was the sheriff.   As Camden says, "Every year some one of the gentlemen inhabitants is made ruler of the county wherein he dwelleth."[1]

Though no longer relatively so powerful as in the Middle Ages, his position was even yet one of much dignity and importance.   On occasions of public ceremony he had an imposing personal retinue, carried a white rod of office, and wore official robes.[2] Richard Evelyn, when sheriff, "had one hundred and sixteen servants in liverys, every one liveryed in greene sattin doubliets; divers gentlemen and persons of quality waited on him in the same garbe and habit."[3]   William Ffarrington, sheriff of Lancashire in 1636, kept up the following household: a steward, a clerk of the kitchen, two yeomen of the plate cupboard, a yeoman of the wine-cellar, two attendants on the sheriff's chamber, an usher of the hall, two chamberlains, four butlers and butler's assistants, eight cooks, five scullions, a porter, a baker, a caterer, a slaughterman, a poulterer, two watchmen for the horses, two men to attend the docket door each day by turns, twenty men to attend upon the prisoners each day by turns—altogether a household of fifty-six servants.[4]

[1] Camden, *Britannia* (ed. 1637), 160.

[2] King, *The Vale-Royall*, 40; North, *Examen*, quoted in *Dict. Nat. Biog.*, XII., 121.   [3] Evelyn, *Diary*, 1634.

[4] *The Shrievalty of William Ffarrington*, 17 (Chetham Society). This reference and a number of those which follow I owe to the industry and good scholarship of Mr. Charles Burrows, a young man of great promise, who, after studying at the universities

With the need for such official outlays, it is no
wonder that a long series of statutes should have
provided that the sheriff should be one who had
land in the county "sufficient to answer king and
people." [1]   In fact, he was usually a knight or a man
of such rank as might be made a knight.   A list of
the sheriffs of the county of Chester during the
reigns of James I. and Charles I. shows twenty-
three knights and twenty-three without title, but
presumably of equal rank in society.[2]   Many of the
best-known men of this period, such as Sir Thomas
Wentworth, Sir Ralph Verney, Sir William Selby,
and Sir Anthony Ashley Cooper, afterwards earl of
Shaftesbury, acted at various times as sheriffs of
their respective counties.   They were direct successors of Chaucer's Franklyn, of whom we are told,

"A shir-reeve had he been."

With some exceptions, such as those cities which
had their own elective sheriffs, and those pairs of
counties which were conjoined under one sheriff,
each shire had one sheriff, appointed in the following manner: every year, on November 1, a special
meeting of the Privy Council was held at the exchequer, a number of the higher government officials
being especially required to be present; here a list

of Chicago and Pennsylvania, and beginning the preparation of
a thesis on the subject of this chapter, went abroad for further
study and died in 1902.

[1]   Ed. II., st. 2; 4 Ed. III., chap. ix.; 5 Ed. III., chaps. iv.,
xiii., xiv.   [2] King, *The Vale-Royall*, 233.

of three persons of distinction from each county, qualified to fill the office of sheriff, was made up and submitted to the king, who "pricked" one from each three; the men thus chosen were then bound to seek letters-patent, and take their oaths as sheriffs for the ensuing year in their respective counties.[1]

By law the same man could not be appointed for two successive years.[2] This was probably a welcome restriction, as the appointees bore somewhat unwillingly the burdens and expenditures of the office.[3] In 1630 we find Sir Francis Coke writing to ask Sir J. Coke "to keep my loving neighbour and friend Edward Revell of Brookhill from being sheriff this year";[4] and in 1663 Evelyn enters in his diary, "To court to get Sir John Evelyn, of Godstone, off from being sheriff of Surrey."[5]

It is true that the office brought with it many small fees. A long list of customary payments for the issue of various writs and the performance of various services by the sheriff is given in the manuals of the time.[6] On the other hand, the fees payable by the sheriff to the officials of the exchequer on his appointment and discharge,[7] the expenses of his office, and the requirements of his position for social expenditure were very considerable, and the comment of a contemporary law-writer was, no doubt,

---

[1] Fortescue, *De Laudibus Legum Angliæ*, chap. xxiv.
[2] 14 Ed. III., chap. vii., etc.
[3] Hist. MSS. Commission, *Report VII.*, App., 3–9, 25.
[4] *Ibid.*, *Report XII.*, App. I., 414.   [5] November 6, 1663.
[6] Greenwood, *The County Court*, 183.   [7] *Ibid.*, 122.

in most cases, justified: "But the sheriff is at much more charge, which is laid out and is disbursed during his sheriffwick, as experience will inform him." [1]

Another burden of the sheriff's office was enforced residence in his own county during his term of service. The records are overspread with fines for the violation of this requirement and with requests for dispensations from conformity to it. [2] A personage in an old play says of the ladies of his time, "I think they would rather marry a London jailer than a high-sheriff of a county, since neither can stir from his employment." [3]

The title high-sheriff, frequently used instead of the simple term sheriff, had no especial significance and was probably suggested by a desire to discriminate him from the under-sheriff. The exacting duties of the office led the sheriff very frequently to appoint, at his own cost, such a subordinate and to empower him to perform such services as could be legally transferred to another. He was usually a man of some position, "learned somewhat in the law, especially if the sheriff be not learned himselfe." [4] He was a source of considerable expense

---

[1] Greenwood, *The County Court*, 187.

[2] Hist. MSS. Commission, *Report VII.*, App., 5; Rushworth, *Historical Collections*, II., App., 27; Deputy Keeper of the Public Records, *Reports*, XLIII., 151; *Cal. of State Pap., Dom.*, 1628–1629, pp., 396, 403, etc.

[3] Wycherly, *The Country Wife*, act iv., sc. 1.

[4] Smith, *Commonwealth of England*, book II., chap. xvii.

to his superior, an estimate of annual cost made in 1628 amounting to £352 18s. 6d. He relieved the sheriff, however, of his more onerous and invidious duties. North declared that "Clifford and Shaftesbury looked like high-sheriff and under-sheriff. The former held the white staff and had his name to all returns, but all the business, especially the knavish part, was done by the latter." [1]

The duties of the sheriff were many and varied; some of them old judicial and administrative functions, others new and irregular services demanded of him by the innovating Tudor and Stuart sovereigns. Every month he must hold a county court, at which were brought suits for debts of less than forty shillings, suits for damages, for breach of contract, for non-payment of wages, for not returning borrowed or pledged articles, and a hundred other petty causes.[2] In this court also, and at some other times and places, he must proclaim certain ancient statutes and new laws and ordinances for the information and warning of the people.

The county court as a judicial body was, in the seventeenth century, a waning institution, its competence and functions becoming rapidly obsolete; but occasionally it awakened suddenly to life, took on a new aspect, and became of unwonted importance. This occurred when a summons was issued for a new parliament, for the county court was the

Examen, 8, quoted in *Dict. Nat. Biog.*, XII., 113.
Fitzherbert, *Natura Brevium*, 28 d, etc.

electing body of the knights of the shire, and to the
next session after the writs for the parliament had
been issued came the gentry and freeholders of the
county to elect their representatives.[1] There was
often a great concourse and much excitement, and
the petty disputes of poor suitors and the labors of
obscure officials were for the time completely superseded.

The sheriff, as presiding official at this election,
as the returning officer of the elected members, and
as the official charged with levying money for the
payment of their wages and expenses, had an active and influential connection with the choice of
members of Parliament. A long series of statutes
checked the abuses connected with this influence;
but even yet the sheriff exercised some power over
the selection made, especially when he was a man
of large influence in his county apart from his
office.[2]

There was great irregularity in the process of
election. Sometimes the members were elected by
acclamation, sometimes by show of hands, sometimes by a poll, one voter after another expressing
orally his preference The election should, by law,
be held between eight and eleven o'clock in the
morning, but a sheriff sometimes postponed the
election, or refused to acknowledge the candidate
insisted on by the electors, or threw out votes which
he claimed were not properly given, or closed the

[1] Dalton, *Officium Vicecomitum*, chap. xcii.   [2] *Ibid*

election when his preferred candidate was in an ad-
vantageous position. The journals of the House
of Commons are filled with reports of contested
elections, and sheriffs are repeatedly found kneeling
at the bar of the House to receive censure or pardon
for such offences.[1]

A period of scarcely less responsibility for the
sheriff was the semi-annual assizes, when the judges
in their robes, on their circuit, with all the dignity
of the judicial representatives of the crown, visited
the county.[2] It was the duty of the sheriff to see
that grand and petty juries were ready to perform
the services required of them by these judges, and
to carry out the mandates and judgments of the
court. These judgments, which he had to execute
either in person or by his under-sheriff or bailiffs,
varied in character from the serving of writs or
levying upon property for debt to the infliction of
the death penalty.[3] The sheriff had also the
supervision of the jail and the appointment of jailers. His presence at the two assizes of the year
was considered one of his most fundamental duties,
and heavy fines were imposed when occasionally a
sheriff was absent from his post at that time.[4] He
not only met the judges with his retinue and fur-

---

[1] *Commons Journals*, I., 511, 556, 801, 854, 884, etc.

[2] Rushworth, *Historical Collections*, I., 294.

[3] Greenwood, 133; Fortescue, *De Laudibus Legum Angliæ*,
chap. xxiv.

[4] Rushworth, *Historical Collections*, II., App., 27; *Cal. of State
Pap., Dom.*, 1628–1629, p. 396.

nished them a guard, but feasted them and acted as a sort of local host to the circuit court so long as it was in session in his county.

Closely analogous to this duty of the sheriff was the requirement that he should be present, provide jurymen, and carry out the behests of the justices of the peace at their quarter-sessions; but the justices were, like himself, local officers belonging to the county, not visitors from the capital, so that their sessions had little of the ceremony and excitement of the assizes; and, in fact, the sheriff was usually represented there by the under-sheriff acting as his deputy.[1]

In addition to these and many less conspicuous regular duties the sheriff in the early seventeenth century was utilized from time to time by the central government in irregular and somewhat questionable services. When James revived the distraint of knighthood it was the sheriffs who were required to make out lists of all who had £40 a year of lands or rents and to order them to appear at court and receive knighthood. When Charles I. revived the imposition of ship-money it was to the sheriff of each county that the writ was sent, stating the amount to be paid by his county and ordering him to arrange with the lower officials for its assessment and collection.

The patriotic resistance of Hampden found a par-

[1] Lister, *Two Earliest Sessions Rolls of West Riding of Yorkshire*, 1597–1602, III., 28, 44, 64, etc.

allel in the passive opposition of some of the sheriffs
to this demand upon them. On June 30, 1640, the
King's Council wrote to the sheriff of Huntingdon-
shire: "We have read and considered of your letter
of the 24th of the present, wherein we perceive that
you have been rather industrious to represent the
difficulties which, as you say, you find in the execution of his majesty's writ, than circumspect or
careful, as you ought to have been, in overcoming
and removing them, . . . and we cannot but make
this judgment upon your proceedings, that instead
of doing your duty in person and compelling others
subordinate to you to do theirs, you endeavor to
make excuses both for yourself and them."[1]

Alongside of the sheriff at the head of the shire
was another officer, the lord-lieutenant, whose position, although but recently attained, was in some
ways more conspicuous and in certain exigencies
more powerful than his. No statute or other formal
action provided for the original creation of the lord-
lieutenancy, and it is probable that Henry VIII.
simply began the habit of delegating his military
power in the shires to such officers. Early in the
reign of Edward VI., October, 1549, they are mentioned as existing in the counties, and by 1600 their
office was fully established.[2] This position was
usually held by the greatest nobleman with estates
in the county, and he appointed as his deputies

---

[1] Rushworth, *Historical Collections*, I., 1203.
[2] 3 and 4 Ed. VI., chap. v., in *Statutes of the Realm*, IV., 107.

various knights and gentlemen of high position; as when, in 1626, the duke of Buckingham was lord-lieutenant of Bucks, and Sir Edward Verney and five others were his deputies in that county. Although purely honorary, the appointment was one of much dignity and responsibility in military matters.

It was the duty of the lord-lieutenant in times of peace to see that the musters of the trained bands were regularly held, that the militia-men had their arms, and that men of higher rank who owed military service to the crown were prepared to perform it; in time of war to levy, muster, and train soldiers, fix the quotas of the hundreds and townships, see to the payment of troops, the collection of horses, and equipment generally, until the recruits were actually handed over to their officers. It was also their duty to see that the beacons were kept in order. The lords-lieutenant must be present, by an ord of 1615, nine months in the year[1] in their counties; but there was no such rigorous requirement of constant residence as in the case of the sheriff, nor was the appointment restricted to a single year.

Such an official as the lord-lieutenant was not likely to be left unburdened with other duties when the government was struggling to obtain the enforcement of its laws, and, as a matter of fact, functions quite unmilitary were imposed upon him. In 1637 the council orders the lords-lieutenant of six of the eastern counties to assist in the better enforcement

[1] *Cal. of State Pap., Dom.,* 1611–1618, p. 337.

of the acts for the drainage of the marshes.[1] In
1621 they are to investigate frauds of his majesty's
carters.[2] They are asked to help collect subsidies
and benevolences, to search for popish recusants, to
oversee ale-houses, slaughter-houses, and the assize
of bread and ale, to assist in the administration of
poor relief and the suppression of vagrancy.[3] In
1619 the Lords of the Council write to the lieutenant
of Surrey asking him to urge co-operation in a lot-
tery for the success of "the English colonies planted
in Virginia, to accept the sums adventured, and to
report to the treasurer and council of Virginia."[4]

Much less dignified in position than either the
lord - lieutenant or the sheriff, and yet filling an
old and important office, was the coroner. He
was elected by the freeholders of the county in the
county court, and his oath was administered by the
county clerk. He was, therefore, more distinctly
local and representative than the other county
officers, who were appointed by the crown; and as a
result he was the only officer whose office did not
terminate with the death of the king. Notwithstanding the generality of duties indicated by his
name, "*custos placitarum coronæ*," his functions were
few beyond the fundamental duty of investigating
sudden deaths and binding over for trial such per-

---

[1] *Cal. of State Pap., Dom.*, 1637, p. 92.
[2] Hist. MSS. Commission, *Report VII.*, App., 670.
[3] Chetham Society, *Lancashire Lieutenancy*, I., Int., 19; Camden Society, *Verney Papers*, 37, 88.
[4] Hist. MSS. Commission, *Report VII.*, App., 670.

sons as were indicated by the jury through which he made his inquest.[1]   Under some circumstances the coroner took the place of the sheriff, and in general his position looked back to a time when it was of greater significance than it had become in the seventeenth century.[2]

[1] Smith, *Commonwealth of England*, book II., chap. **xxiv.**
[2] Greenwood, *The County Court*, 258.

CHAPTER XV

ENGLISH JUSTICES OF THE PEACE
(1600–1650)

HOWEVER extensive the duties of the officers whose functions are described above, the real men-of-all-work in the counties at this time were the justices of the peace. The law required that a justice of the peace must have lands and tenements to the value of £20 a year, the amount of the legal knight's fee;[1] but ordinarily he had much greater property. John Evelyn's father, who has been so often referred to as a typical country gentleman of the early seventeenth century, had an estate of £4000 a year when he was successively sheriff and justice of the peace.[2] The justice of the peace, like the sheriff, the lord-lieutenant, and the coroner, was expected to perform his public services as part of his patriotic duty. It is true that certain statutes provided that part of the fines for any violation should go to the justices before whom the violators were prosecuted; two or three others gave small fees to the justice for affixing his seal or signing a

---

[1] 18 Henry VI., chap. xi.
[2] Evelyn, *Diary*, year 1634.

document; but these were apparently casual efforts to secure enforcement, and can have brought no appreciable return to the justices. The law gave each justice 2s. for each day of quarter-sessions up to three days; but this could have produced at most only 6s., and seems to have been usually jointly expended by the magistrates in a dinner.

In an interesting speech by a Mr. Glascock in the House of Commons, December 16, 1601, two equally undesirable justices are described — first, the one "who from base stock and lineage by his wealth is gotten to be within the commission"; the other "a gentleman born, virtuous, discreet, and wise, yet poor and needy. And so only for his virtues and qualities put into the commission. This man I hold unfit to be a justice, though I think him to be a good member in the commonwealth. Because I hold this for a ground infallible—that no poor man ought to be in authority. My reason is this: he will so bribe you and extort you that the sweet scent of riches and gain taketh away and confoundeth the true taste of justice and equity." [1]

But burdensome as the duties of a justice must have been, and almost unpaid as they were, the office does not seem to have been avoided as was that of sheriff. Probably such service was taken as a matter of course by the gentry, and compensation was found in the stamp of social position it placed upon them, and in the sense of power, as well

Townshend, *Proceedings*, 953, 954.

as of a patriotic fulfilment of duty. It was sometimes a matter of complaint that "with us these
magistrates have been so unsuitably appointed that
a county justice is made a jest in comedies, and his
character the subject of buffoonery and laughter." [1]
This is an obvious reference to Justice Shallow and
other worthies of the dramatists. It is dangerous
to make too serious an inference from contemporary
comedies, because certain personages soon became
stock characters and ceased to have any very close
relation to actual life; and in this particular instance Shakespeare was probably gratifying an old
grudge.

Nevertheless, there was evidently some foundation for this picture of the county justice. Dorothy
Osborne, in one of her delightful letters to Sir William Temple, in giving her requirements for a husband,
pokes fun at such ambitions. "He must not be so
much of a country gentleman as to understand nothing but hawks and dogs, and be fonder of either than
his wife; nor of the next sort of them whose aim
reaches no further than to be Justice of the Peace,
and once in his life High Sheriff, who reads no book
but statutes, and studies nothing but how to make
a speech interlarded with Latin that may amaze his
disagreeing poor neighbours, and fright them rather
than persuade them into quietness." [2]

---

[1] Carey, *English Liberties*, 275.
[2] *Letters of Dorothy Osborne to Sir William Temple*, letter 36 (ed. by Parry), p. 171.

With all these criticisms, and in the face of occasional ineptitude, the body of justices of the peace included much ability. It was scarcely possible for a justice to act without some knowledge of Latin, as almost all the records and documents which he would have to make, read, or sign were in that language. A succession of text-books on the duties of the office, the more important of them appearing in many successive editions, proves an intelligent interest and demand for instruction in their duties. Moreover, the men who served as justices were often well known in other ways, many of them as sheriffs, as members of Parliament, and in still other capacities. They were of families who provided the acti-men of enterprise of the period. The list of evonshire justices in 1592 includes Sir Francis Drake, Sir Ferdinando Gorges, Gilberts, Carews, Seymours, Courtenays, and other names prominent among the men who laid the foundations of the maritime greatness of England and of the existence of America. Of the fifty-five, twenty-eight were at one time or another high-sheriffs of the county, twenty more were then, or became afterwards, knights, six sat in the House of Commons, and three in the House of Lords.[1]

The justices of the peace were fair representatives of that great class of rural gentry which exercised so strong an influence over the destinies of England in the sixteenth, seventeenth, and

[1] Hamilton, *Devonshire Quarter-Sessions*, 3, 330–348.

eighteenth centuries. From this class were drawn all the county officials who have been named, except the lord-lieutenant; from it were chosen the county representatives to Parliament; and in it were found the strength and the weakness of the English political system. James I., in appealing to the country gentry to continue to live on their estates in their counties, said to them, "Gentlemen, at London you are like ships in a sea, which shew like nothing, but in your country villages you are like ships in a river, which look like great things." [1]

Out of this body of rural gentry from twenty to sixty in each county were chosen by the lord-chancellor to serve as justices of the peace.[2] The "commission of the peace," by which the justices were appointed and from which they drew their powers, was a formula well known and constantly quoted and commented upon, and added to from time to time until late in the sixteenth century. In was then, in 1590, revised and formulated anew by Sir Christopher May, Chief-Justice, with the advice of all the other judges of the time, and has not been changed from that day to this.[3]

The justices of the peace performed some of their duties separately, acting individually as circumstances required, or as proved convenient to themselves. Other powers they could exercise only when

---

[1] Bacon, *Apothegms*, in *Works* (Spedding and Heath ed.), VII., 125.   [2] Lambard, *Eirenarcha*, book I., chap. v.
[3] *Ibid.*, book II., chap. vii.

two or more acted together and concurrently. Still others, and those far the most important and dignified, they performed in a body at their "quarter-sessions." What things a justice might do singly, what two, three, or four justices might do together, and what they might do only in the formal sessions of the whole body of justices of the peace of the county were defined partly in the statutes, partly in the commission under which they acted.

The regular or quarter-sessions were meetings held four times a year—in October, midwinter, spring, and midsummer—at which all the justices of the peace of the county were supposed to be present. There were, besides, occasional irregular sessions, or meetings of the regular sessions adjourned from one time to another. In corporate towns the city officers acted as justices of the peace, reinforced usually by some others especially appointed; and each town followed its own customs as to meeting in general sessions.

Although the law contemplated the attendance of all the justices of the county at each quarter-sessions, as a matter of fact the attendance was ver' irregular and incomplete, few of the records, so ar as published, showing an attendance of as many as a dozen out of perhaps forty or fifty. Most o' them evidently came riding up to quarter-sessi .s if it suited their convenience and remained a vay if it did not, restricting their services to t ose duties which could be performed in their own neighborhoods, and leaving to a few active, regular, and hard-working magistrates the responsibilities of the higher work.[1]

Of those who made up quarter-sessions one at least must be "of the quorum." This expression is taken from the commission of the justices of the peace, which in the clause giving to the justices the power to inquire and determine by oath of the jurors as to felonies and other offences and to punish them, after naming all those to whom the commission for that county is issued, says, *quorum aliquem vestrum, A, B, C, etc., unum esse volumus* (of whom we wish you, A, B, C, etc., to be one), naming presumably such as were learned in the law or otherwise especially trustworthy.[2] As without the presence of one of the "quorum" no quarter-sessions could be held, to be a "justice of the peace and of the quorum" was to be one of a select list of the justices. One-third or one-half of the list of those in the commission were usually named also in the quorum.

In addition to the justices there should, according to law, be present at quarter-sessions, in the first place, the *custos rotulorum*, or keeper of the rolls of the sessions, the "*cust-alorum*" of Justice Shallow.[3] This was always one of the justices of high rank indicated to the lord-chancellor for appointment

---

[1] *West Riding Sessions Rolls; Manchester Quarter-Sessions,* passim.   [2] Lambarde, *Eirenarcha,* book I., chap. ix.
[3] *Merry Wives of Windsor,* act i., sc. i.

by the king himself,[1] and was very apt to be the
lord-lieutenant of the county. He could be, and
probably was, usually represented at the sessions
by a deputy, who was a person of considerable importance and influence, upon whom much responsibility was placed by the statutes, and whose abilities must have been constantly relied upon by the
magistrates. The title of this deputy was "clerk of
the peace," the predecessor apparently of the American county clerk. He was usually familiar with
the law, and his knowledge of precedents and procedure must often have stood the unlearned justices in good stead, besides the work which he performed in drawing up indictments, writing orders,
and keeping records.

Besides the *custos* and the clerk, the sheriff or his
deputy were bound to be present prepared to em-
panel jurors and execute process; as well as the
jailer ready to produce his prisoners; the superintendent of the county house of correction; all jurors
who had been summoned by the sheriff; all persons
who had been bound over by single justices to appear at quarter-sessions; all high constables and
bailiffs of hundreds; and the coroners.[2] The quarter-sessions should, by law, be kept for three continuous days if there was any need;[3] but, as a
matter of fact, sessions seldom lasted more than a

[1] 37 Henry VIII., chap. i.
[2] Dalton, *Officium Vicecomitum*, chaps. xxxiv., clxxi.
[3] 12 Richard II., chap. x.

day, and a contemporary complains that "many
doe scantly afford them three whole hours, besides
the time which is spent in calling of the county and
giving of the charge."[1]

The powers and duties of the justices of the peace
in quarter-sessions and separately were so considerable and varied as to tax the ability of an Eliza-
bethan or Jacobean text-book writer to reduce them
to simplicity of statement, or to the compass of five
or six hundred pages of enumeration. Many of
these powers were general, arising from the nature of
the office for the "conservation of the peace"; but
the great mass of their duties was placed upon them
by statutes. Ten early statutes are enumerated
in the commission itself, before coming to the inclusive "and cause to be kept all other ordinances
and statutes made for the good of our peace and the
quiet rule and government of our people." From
the middle of the fifteenth century forward, the enforcement of the greater number of new laws was
placed primarily in the hands of the justices of the
peace.

As time passed on legislation became more and
more minute and inclusive. Few interests in human life escaped the paternal attention of government under the Tudors and Stuarts, and this great
mass of enactment it became the duty of the groups
of country gentry in the counties and of the civic
magistrates of the towns to put into force. A

[1] Lambarde, *Eirenarcha*, book IV., chap. xix.

writer of the time enumerates two hundred and ninety-three statutes passed previous to 1603 in which justices of the peace are mentioned and given some jurisdiction or duties.[1] Under Elizabeth alone there were seventy-eight, ranging from the "preservation of spawn and frie of fish" to those "touching bulls from Rome." The infrequent and short-lived parliaments of James I. added thirty-six to the list.[2]

Although many of these laws are repetitions, some others temporary or local, still others insignificant, yet, on the other hand, some of them opened up whole new fields of activity to the justices: as for instance, those placing upon them, after ˙ ˙3, the administration of the Act of Apprenti˙ ˙, and, after 1581, the responsibility for the se˙ ˙n for and punishment of popish recusants. ˙ whole code of law, procedure, and precedent ˙ ˙w up on these two subjects, besides others sca˙ ˙ly less extensive.

Quarter-sessions had ˙ ˙hing to do with civil suits, and cases of treason ˙urder, and certain other high crimes were exc˙ ˙ded from their competence. Apart from this r˙ ˙riction and these offences, there was little di˙ ˙erence between sessions and assizes, between the jurisdiction of the learned judges of the king in their half-yearly circuit and that of the county magistrates in their quarter-sessions. Before them both grand and petty juries were empanelled, indictments drawn up, prisoners tried for

---

[1] Lambarde, *Eirenarcha*, book IV., chap. xix., Table, App.
[2] Dalton, *The Country Justice*, Table of Contents.

assault, burglary, horse-stealing, witchcraft, pocket-picking, keeping up nuisances, cheating, failure to attend church, and almost all other offences of which seventeenth-century Englishmen were capable. If convicted they were placed in the stocks, whipped, or hanged. In Devonshire, in the mid-winter sessions of 1598, out of sixty-five culprits who were tried eight were hanged; at midsummer, out of forty-five eight were hanged, thirteen flogged, seven acquitted, and seven, on account of their claim of benefit of clergy, were branded and then released.[1]

The justices in sessions or singly also performed much administrative work, such as the oversight and repair of bridges, the granting of licenses to ale-houses, the establishment of wages, the binding out of apprentices, and the relief of wounded soldiers. Many laws passed under Elizabeth and James I. admitted of exceptions when approved by one or more justices of the peace, and there was thus con-stant occasion for granting to individual persons or at special times permission to export grain, to turn their barley into malt, to build cottages without land attached, to carry hand-guns, to buy and sell out of market-hours, to beg, and other dispensa-tions from the rigorous application of the law.[2]

The punishing of recusants and the discipline of those who refused or neglected to go to church was, as already stated, an active occupation of the jus-

---

[1] Hamilton, *Devonshire Quarter-Sessions*, 33.
[2] *Ibid.*, 27. 164, etc.

tices. At certain times, such as the period just following the Gunpowder Plot, when the search was
for Catholics, and somewhat later, when the search
was for Puritans and Separatists, the Privy Council brought severe pressure upon the justices to
fulfil these duties, and numerous prosecutions were
brought by them.   In Middlesex during the reign of
James I. the indictments averaged eighty-five per
year for religious offences, and sometimes at one
session there were as many as one hundred and
fifty persons indicted.[1]

The justices were constantly called upon to act in
special emergencies or to give special relief. If a
man's thatched cottage were burned, the nearest
justice might authorize him to make an appeal to
his neighbors for help to rebuild; if a whole village
or town suffered from a more extensive fire, the
justices in their sessions quartered the homeless people in various parishes, announced a subscription,
and, calling constables and leading villagers before
them, exhorted them to liberal voluntary gifts, and
appointed a subcommittee to administer the funds
for relief; if a pestilence appeared, a tax-rate for
immediate assistance was levied, and the justices
supported the sick and enforced the quarantine;
if food became scarce and high-priced the justices
forbade its export from the county or conversion

[1] *Middlesex County Sessions Rolls* II., III.; Hamilton, *Devonshire Quarter-Sessions*, 27, 74, etc.; *Cal. of State Pap., Dom.*, 1633–
1634, p. 531.

into malt, and even announced a maximum market-price for it. When weavers or other artificers were out of work the justices set to work to induce masters to employ them or merchants to buy their goods, or, as a last resort, levied a rate for their support. If news came of the capture of a number of English sailors or merchants by Barbary pirates, collections were taken up by the justices of the maritime counties for their redemption. In all such exigencies it was the justices of the peace who were expected to tide over the special temporary difficulty or need.

Besides the ancient regulative duties of the justices, and besides those that were definitely given them by successive statutes, they were constantly subject to the commands and instructions of the Privy Council. In 1592, soon after the remodelling of the commission, a circular letter was sent by the Privy Council to certain commissioners in each county requiring them to call a special meeting of all justices of the peace, at which the oath of office and the oath of supremacy must be taken by each, or they must retire from the commission of the peace.[1] This seems to have been preparatory to a more strict discipline and oversight of their actions, for communications from the council now became more frequent and more drastic.

[1] Hamilton, *Devonshire Quarter-Sessions*, 36, 48; Nichols, *Hist. of the Poor Law*, 252; Hist. MSS. Commission, *Report XIV.*, App. IV., 42.

In requiring them to fulfil their duties as magistrates the Privy Council spoke categorically in the name of the king in a constant series of letters, couched often in such harsh terms of reproof as to make it hard to realize that the justices were gentlemen of rank and dignity, fulfilling laborious services practically without compensation. In 1598 vigorous letters were sent to the various counties calling the attention of the justices to the recently enacted poor law, and requiring them to see it put into execution.[1] From this time forward to the outbreak of the civil war the pressure of the council on the justices became stronger and stronger. In January, 1631, a *Book of Orders* was issued by the Privy Council giving instructions in greater detail to the justices as to their duties, especially in regard to the poor law, and requiring them to make reports every three months to the sheriffs, who were to transmit these reports to the justices of assize, who were in turn to send them to certain members of the Privy Council deputed for the purpose. The judges of assize were also to report directly to the king if they learned of the negligence of any of the justices of the peace.[2] The *Book of Orders* was reissued from time to time and its requirements followed up.

An attempt was made by these means to introduce a system of "thorough" in the affairs of local government during the period of the personal gov-

[1] Leonard, *The Poor Law*, 143.   [2] *Ibid.*, 158, etc.

ernment of Charles I., analogous to that attempted
in the higher ranges of government by Wentworth,
Laud, and their fellow-members of the Privy Council.
The great instruments of this plan were the justices
of the peace, acting within the limits of their respective counties, carrying out the manifold duties
imposed upon them by law, under constant pressure
from the Privy Council and the king. After even
this partial enumeration of the services of the justices of the peace and of the supervision kept over
them, one can readily appreciate the feeling of the
justices of Nottingham who complained that they
had "little rest at home or abroad." [1]

.The centre of gravity of local government in England was in the county. The power which put its
machinery in motion was that of the central government; but the actual administration was in the
hands of the sheriff, the lord-lieutenant, the coroner,
and the justices of the peace. The county bounded
the sphere of activity of all these officials. The
commission of any group of justices named the
county in which they were to exercise their functions,
and outside of its boundaries all their powers dropped
from them. The coroner could not hold an inquest
outside of his own county, and even the lord-lieutenant could exercise his military functions only
within the shire or shires named in his commission.
When, in 1603, James I. rode southward from Edin-
burgh on the news of the death of Elizabeth, and

[1] *Cal. of State Pap., Dom.,* 1631–1633, p. 18.

crossed the border at Berwick, he was met by the sheriff of Northumberland and escorted by him to the borders of Durham, where he was met by the sheriff of that county, and so from shire to shire through the whole length of England till he reached London.

The basis of representation in Parliament was the county: the counties formed the districts for all the circuit courts; national taxation was largely distributed by counties, and, as has been seen, local jurisdiction and administration were largely in the hands of county officials.

CHAPTER XVI

ENGLISH PARISH OR TOWNSHIP GOVERNMENT
(1500–1650)

NEXT below the county as a political sub-division of England came the hundred, or wapentake, as it was called in the northern shires. One of the oldest political units of the country, perhaps the very oldest, it had become the least important of all. Its ancient significance as the primary organization of the community for judicial purposes disappeared long before the beginning of the seventeenth century, leaving only a desultory practice of holding a sheriff's semi-annual "tourn" through the hundreds of the shire; and some traditional payments of fees to the noblemen who held the hundred court as a "liberty," or to the crown. Apart from its existence as a unit of jurisdiction, the hundred was still put to some use as a subdivision of the county for purposes of taxation, for military organization and service, for the preservation of order, and as the sphere of activity of the high-constable.[1] The high-constables were, indeed, the only officers of the

[1] Lambarde, *Constables*, § 25; *Cal. of State Pap., Dom.*, 1637, pp. 39, 104.

hundreds, one or more being chosen annually by the justices of the peace in quarter-sessions from the same class of rural gentry as we have already seen furnishing the county local officials. The hundred, for some reason, took but slight root in colonial soil, though it was established in a few of the colonies, and in such places many of its English functions reappeared.[1]

An ancient Latin law writer says, "England is divided into counties, counties are divided into hundreds (which in some parts of England are called wapentakes), and hundreds are again subdivided into *villas*."[2] By using the general word *villas* ("vills") he evaded one of the greatest difficulties in the description of English local government in the sixteenth and seventeenth centuries, the confusing and conflicting use of terms for the smallest subdivision of civil government. Shall we use parish, town, township, manor, or tithing when we speak of a neighborhood organized for the affairs of petty government? All these terms are used abundantly in the records of the time and to a great extent are used indiscriminately.

This lack of consistency is quite natural and explicable. In the first place, local organization as it existed at this time was the residuum of several successive systems of custom and law, and contained

[1] Howard, *Local Constitutional History of the U. S.*, 272-286; Wilhelmi, *Local Institutions of Maryland*, 60, *n.* 5.
[2] Fortescue, *De Laudibus Legum Angliæ*, chap. cxxiv.

survivals from the nomenclature of each. "Township" or "town" was a term belonging to a far-distant Anglo-Saxon past, and had been long obscured by the later institution of tithings and the still later manors. Secondly, the union of church and state, the mutual interpenetration of the ecclesiastical and civil systems, served to complicate the matter still further by confusing the word "parish" with terms which applied in a non-ecclesiastical sense to the same little group of people and the same tract of land.

Of all these terms, three—manor, town (or township), and parish—are the most usual. A manor was a group of inhabitants and the land they occupied (usually a single village), so far as these people were connected with and dependent upon a certain "lord of the manor," who had various rights over the people and their lands. Aside from his position as landlord, the most important of these rights was that of holding a court-baron and a court-leet and view of frank-pledge.

Various powers and activities had long gathered around these petty courts, but the whole group of manorial rights and duties of jurisdiction and administration was, in 1600, fast becoming an obsolete and insignificant institution. Yet the terms connected with it had worked themselves inseparably into local life. Courts-baron were held in but few places, and almost solely for the purpose of making land transfers; courts-leet were held only infrequently and irregularly, many lords of manors who possessed the right exercising it but once a year or less frequently; the whole system of frank-pledges had long gone into desuetude. Grants of manorial powers, "court-leet, court-baron, and view of frank-pledge," were made in several of the colonial charters; but these institutions showed little inclination to renew in America a vitality they had lost in England.

The English word town or township is the nearest equivalent to the Latin word *villa* or vill, which i a generic term used in the records, without very exact connotation, for one of those country villages in which the rural population of England was distributed, including the land connected with the village. Town and township meant the same thing, except when the former was applied an urban community. Over and over again to the same locality first the term "town" and then "township" is applied;[1] and a careful search fails to find any distinction drawn between them. In the north of England the term town or township seems to have been especially familiar and frequently used as a subdivision of some of the other local units;[2] and it was in common use everywhere as a synonym for manor or parish.

While all these terms meet us frequently in the records of the seventeenth century, the term parish, notwithstanding its ecclesiastical connotation, was,

[1] *West Riding Sessions Rolls*, passim.
[2] Fishwick, *Hist. of Preston*, 2.

in fact, superseding all others as the most usual appellation to give to the unit of local government. Terms strictly applicable to other phases of the local organization were apt to be applied to the parish. For instance, we hear of the "constable of a parish," [1] although that officer was an official of a township; proprietors of "free" and "copy-hold" lands of a parish are spoken of, though those terms properly applied only to a manor; the same is true of an order for a court to be held every three weeks in certain parishes,[2] the term "court" being properly manorial. These expressions show the tendency of the time to substitute the term "parish" for more exact terms applied to the local governing body in its different aspects. It was the "parish" that was usually sued, taxed, and fined, that received property by bequest, and that was ordered by the government to perform various duties.

Our colonial forefathers, according to the locality of their origin or the particular phase of local government that applied to their new conditions, used sometimes one term, sometimes another; but in this study of English conditions the parish and the officers whose sphere of action was the parish may be taken to include all that is necessary, with the understanding that our use of the term parish is broad, in conformity with seventeenth-century usage.

The knowledge of the boundaries of the parish

[1] *Archæological Review*, IV., 344.
[2] Saalkeld, *Reports*, III., 98.

was kept alive by the traditional ceremony of perambulation. From time to time, usually once a
year, a procession was formed which went the rounds
of the outer boundary, stopping from time to time
at well-marked points for various commemorative
ceremonies. In pre - Reformation times the ceremony was a religious one, the priest leading and the
parishioners following with cross, banners, bells,
lights, and sacred emblems, successive points being
blessed and sprinkled with holy water.[1] When religious processions were forbidden at the Reformation, this ceremony came under the condemnation of
the law; and Queen Elizabeth found it necessary, in
order to perpetuate the useful civil element in it, to
direct by proclamation a certain form of renewal of
the processions. "The people should, once in the
year, at the time appointed, with the curate and
substantial men of the parish, walk about the parish, and at their return to the church make their
common prayers. And the curate in the said perambulation was, at certain convenient places, to
admonish the people to give thanks to God in the
beholding of His benefits, and for the increase and
abundance of his fruits upon the face of the earth,
with the saying of the one hundred and third
Psalm."[2]

The custom survived in this or other forms,[3]
because there were no surveyed boundaries, and re-

[1] Burn, *Ecclesiastical Law*, II., 133, 134.   [2] Gibson, *Codex*, 213.
[3] Shillingfleet, *Ecclesiastical Cases*, I., 244.

liance had to be placed on marked stones and trees, hill-tops, watercourses, and such indications, interpreted and defined only by human tradition. In some remote districts it is still preserved. From the practice of performing the perambulation in rogation week it was often called "the rogation," and conversely rogation days were sometimes called "gang - days" [1] In the seventeenth century, as the men who afterwards practised it in New England and Virginia must have remembered, it was still a festivity. In the church-wardens' accounts for the parish of St. Clements, Ipswich, in 1638, is the item "ffor bread and beare given to the boyes when they wente the boundes of the parishe, 12s." [2] Boys were taken as those whose life and memory would naturally be the longest, and the poorer boys were often especially included as a treat. In Chelsea, Middlesex, at a somewhat later time, a more official feast is suggested by the entry: "Spent at the perambulation dinner, £3 10s." [3]

No material obstacle was allowed to interfere with the progress of the perambulators. They could, by law, enter all dwellings on the boundary and pass through and even break down all enclosures which lay across it. Private persons whose houses lay in the line of march of the perambulators sometimes provided food and drink for them,

[1] Burn, *Ecclesiastical Law*, II., 133.
[2] *East Anglian*, IV., 2d series, 5.
[3] Toulmin Smith, *The Parish*, 473.

and this became so customary that efforts were made, though unsuccessfully, to enforce this custom by law.[1]

In describing the officers of the parish we pass from the class of country gentry, from which the sheriffs, coroners, justices of the peace, and high-constables were drawn, to a group of lower social rank. In the towns they may have been of somewhat higher or at least more varied status, but in the rural parishes the officers were of very humble position. In the invaluable description of England written by Harrison in the latter part of the reign of Elizabeth, from which we have had occasion to quote so frequently, the author says: "The fourth and last sort of people in England are day-labourers, poor husbandmen, and some retailers (which have no free land), copyholders, and all artificers, as tailors, shoemakers, carpenters, brickmakers, masons, etc. . . . This fourth and last sort of people therefore have neither voice nor authority in the commonwealth, but are to be ruled and not to rule others: yet they are not altogether neglected, for . . . in villages they are commonly made churchwardens, sidesmen, aleconners, now and then constables, and many times enjoy the name of head boroughs."[2]

The most active and conspicuous officer of the parish or township was the constable, or petty con-

---

[1] Burn, *Ecclesiastical Law*, II., 133.
[2] Harrison, *Description of England* (Camelot ed.), 13.

stable, as he is often called, to distinguish him from the high-constable of the hundred. He was appointed by the court-leet, where this was still held; in other cases by the steward of the lord of the manor, the vestry of the parish, or, as a part of their residuary duties, by the justices of the peace. The regular form of oath of the constable may be quoted in some fulness to show the nature of his duties. "You shall **swear** that you shall well and truly serve our sovereign lord, the king, in the office of a constable. You shall see and cause his majesty's peace to be well and duly kept and preserved, according to your power. You shall arrest all such persons as in your sight and presence shall ride or go armed offensively, or shall commit or make any riot, affray, or other breach of his majesty's peace. You shall do your best endeavor to apprehend all felons, barrators, and rioters, or persons riotously assembled; and if any such offenders shall make resistance you shall levy hue and cry and shall pursue them until they be taken. You shall do your best endeavors that the watch in and about your town be duly kept for the apprehending of rogues, vagabonds, night-walkers, eavesdroppers, and other suspected persons, and of such as go armed and the like. . . . You shall well and duly execute all precepts and warrants to you directed from the justices of the peace of the county or higher officers. In time of hay or corn harvest you shall cause all meet persons to serve by the day for the mowing, reaping, and getting in of corn or hay. You shall, in Easter week, cause your parishioners to chuse surveyors for the mending of the highways in your parish. . . . And you shall well and duly, according to your knowledge, power, and ability, do and execute all things belonging to the office of a constable so long as you shall continue in this office. So help you God." [1]

The constable, among the other duties prescribed by his oath, had to "raise the hue and cry" when it was demanded—that is to say, if any one were assaulted or robbed and appealed to the constable of the parish in which the injury occurred, the constable must summon out his neighbors, whether it were by day or by night, to seek the culprit. If not successful he must give notice to the constables of the adjacent parishes, who were similarly to raise the hue and cry in their neighborhoods. If the offender was not then discovered the person who suffered the loss might bring suit for its recovery from the whole hundred in which the attack occurred. [2]

In practice hue and cry was a very ineffective method of capturing ill-doers. Harrison says: "I have known by my own experience felons being taken to have escaped out of the stocks, being rescued by others for want of watch and guard, that thieves have been let pass, because the covetous and greedy parishioners would neither take the pains nor be at the charge to carry them to prison,

[1] Dalton, *The Country Justice*, chap. clxxiv.
[2] *Ibid.*, chap. lxxxiv.

if it were far off; that when hue and cry have been made even to the faces of some constables, they have said: 'God restore your loss! I have other business at this time.'"[1]   To prosecute petty offenders, to force laborers to serve during harvest-time, to sign their testimonials when they wished to leave the parish, and to see that innkeepers refused no travellers, gave the constable considerable duties of local supervision.

The constable must, with the advice of the minister and of one other inhabitant of the parish, whip any rogue, vagabond, or sturdy beggar who appeared in the parish, and then send him, with a testimonial to the fact of the whipping, back to his native parish.   The word rogue was a comprehensive term as used in the laws of Elizabeth, including wandering sailors, fortune-tellers, collectors of money for charities, fencers, bearwards, minstrels, common players of interludes, jugglers, tinkers, peddlers, and many others, and adequate whipping of them and starting them in the direct route homeward must have been no sinecure.[2]

A contemporary testimonial with which such a person was provided may not be without interest as an illustration of the manners of the time. "A. B., a sturdy rogue of tall stature, red-haired and bearded, about the age of thirty years, and having a wart neere under his right eie, born (as he confess-

---

[1] Harrison, *Description of England* (Camelot ed.), 247.
[2] Lambarde, *Duties of Constables*, § 45.

eth) at East Tilberie, in Essex, was taken begging at
Shorne in this county of Kent, the tenth of March,
1598, and was then and there lawfully whipped
therefor, and hee is appointed to goe to East Tilberie
aforesaid, the direct way by Gravesend, over the
river of Thamise; for which hee is allowed one whole
day, and no more at his peril; subscribed and sealed
the day and yeare aforesaid. By us" (signed by the
minister, the constable, and a parishioner).[1] It is
no wonder that constables are advised "in every
corner to have a readie hand and whip."

The constable was also the warden of such arms
and armor as each parish kept, or was supposed to
keep, in obedience to the militia requirements. A
writer of Elizabeth's time says: "The said armour
and munition likewise is kept in one several place of
every town, appointed by the consent of the whole
parish, where it is always ready to be had and worn
within an hour's warning. . . . Certes there is almost
no village so poor . . . that hath not sufficient furniture
in a readiness to set forth three or four soldiers, as
one archer, one gunner, one pike, and a billman."[2]

An account of the armor kept in a parish in Middlesex is entered in the vestry accounts of the year
1583. "Note of the armour for the parish of Fulham: first, a corslet, with a pyke, sworde, and
daiger, furnished in all points, a gyrdle only except-
ed. *Item*, two hargobushes, with flaskes and touch-

[1] Lambarde, *Duties of Constables*, § 45.
[2] Harrison, *Description of England* (Camelot ed.), 224.

boxes to the same; two morryons; two swords, and
two daigers, which are all for Fulham side only.
All which armore are, and do remayne in the possession and appointment of John Palton, of Northend,
being constable of Fulhamsyde the yere above
wrytten."[1]   One may easily imagine the nature and
value of such accoutrements, and of the villagers
who were occasionally pressed into the service to
wear them.   Mouldy and Bullcalf, Wart, Shadow,
and Feeble, and Falstaff's whole company of "can-
kers of a calm world and a long peace" may readily
enough have been drawn from the life.

These duties the constable must fulfil at his own
initiation or upon the recurrence of the occasion for
them.   But the great part of his duties were those
imposed upon him from above in special cases—that
is to say, in carrying out the warrants and precepts
of the justices of the peace, or occasionally of the
coroner, sheriff, lord-lieutenant, or still higher officials.   If the justice of the peace was the man-of-all-
work, as has been said, of the government of the
time, the constable was the tool and instrument with
which he worked.   The constable was required to
arrest all persons who were to be bound over by
the justices to keep the peace, and all felons and
other ill - doers for whom a warrant had been
issued, and to bring them before the justices into
jail.   And woe be to him if he allowed such a pris-
oner to escape.   The justices might construe his

<hr>

[1] Toulmin Smith, *The Parish*, 473.

inactivity as participation in the crime of the pris-
oner, or he might be fined to the extent of all his
property.[1]

The constable must carry out the lesser sentences
of the justices, inflicting the punishment ordered and
collecting the fines imposed. For instance, when a
certain poor woman, Elizabeth Armistead, was convicted of petty larceny at the West Riding Sessions,
in 1598, it was ordered by the justices that " she shall
nowe be delivered to the constable of Keerbie, and
he to cause her to be stripped naked from the middle
upward and soundly whipped thorowe the said town
of Keerbie, and by hym delivered to the constable
of Kirkby and he to see like execution within h'
town, and the next markett att Weather⊢' ⸏o de-
lyver her to the constables of We⸴+' ⸏ie, and they
to see like punishment of h⸴ ⸴xecuted thorow their
towns."[2]

In assessi⸴⸴ and collecting taxes and in obtaining
information the constables were at the command of
county and hundred authorities. They were used
as the active or at least the most available intermediaries between the justices of the peace and the
individuals whom it was desirable to reach.[3] They
were by no means ideal instruments; many were
extremely ignorant—as, for instance, the constable
of Collingbourne Ducis, who in 1650 prays to be

[1] Lambarde, *Duties of Constables*, § 15.
[2] *West Riding Sessions Rolls*, 58.
[3] Hist. MSS. Commission, *Report XIV.*, App., pt. iv., 28, 67.

relieved from his office because he can neither read
nor write, and is obliged to go to the minister and
divers others to get his warrants read.[1] They were
constantly being fined by the justices for neglect of
their duties or for inefficiency.[2]

The most important remaining ancient parochial
officers were the church - wardens. Their position
and functions were not so purely ecclesiastical as
the name would suggest. Their duties included, it is
true, the care of the parish church and the provision
of other material requirements for religious services.
But they also included many things which were
quite clearly temporal or civil in their nature.
Coke says of their position, "The office is mere temporal."[3] That is to say, the church-wardens represented the parishioners, not the minister or the
ecclesiastical authorities. They formed a quasi-cor-
poration for the holding of the personal property
that belonged to the parish, and could sue and be
sued as trustees for the parish.[4]

The almost invariable custom was for the body
of the parishioners at a vestry meeting in Easter
week to choose two church-wardens for the next year.
But neither the number nor the mode of appointment was at this time quite fixed. During the first
half of the seventeenth century clergymen were in-

[1] Hist. MSS. Commission, *Report I.*, 121
[2] *Middlesex County Records*, II., 36, 41, 139.
[3] Lambarde, *Duties of Constables*, §§ 57-60.
[4] Lambarde, *Duties of Church-wardens*, § 1.

clined to magnify their office, and the canons of
1603 and 1639 gave to the minister of the parish
some control over the choice of the wardens; although whenever the rights of the parishioners were
asserted and an established custom shown, the
courts upheld this custom against ecclesiastical en-
croachments.[1]

The financial powers of the church-wardens were
considerable, though exercised in most cases along
with the constable, and in many only after the approval of the whole body of parishioners at a vestry
meeting. They had, of course, the duty of providing for the repairs of the church and of taxing their
neighbors for this purpose. Unless previously settled upon by the parishioners themselves, they levied
and collected the local taxes already described as
being imposed by the justices upon the parishes for
various purposes. They had the power to seize and
sell the property of such parishioners as refused or
neglected to pay the amounts assessed upon them.
Many of the parishes also received considerable
sums by gift or bequest, which were invested, and
the income expended for the poor or other parish
objects.[2]

Property in land and houses also belonged to some
parishes, apart from the minister's glebe, and the
renting and accounts fell within the church-warden's
duties. Various means of combining the securing of
funds with much neighborhood merriment, even in

[1] Toulmin Smith, *The Parish*, 78–87.   [2] *Ibid.*, chap. v., App.

those days of militant Puritanism, were used by the parish authorities, such as "church-ales," "pigeon-holes," Hock-tide games, Easter games, processions, and festive gatherings, at all of which farthings, pence, and shillings were gathered.[1] Such accounts of these various funds and the record of the thousand and one petty expenditures for local purposes as were kept were usually the work of the church-wardens and made their office one of real local importance.   In fact, a whole cycle of parish life passes before us in these accounts.   "Paid the carpenters 5s. for a barrow to carry the people that died of the sickness to church to bury them."   "For a coat for the whipper, and making, 3s."   "For too payre of glovys for Robin Hode and Mayde Maryan, 3d."   "Received for the May-pole, £1 4s."   "Paid Robert Warden, the constable, which he disbursed for carrying away the witches, 11s."[2]

The church-wardens, under a law of Queen Mary,[3] with the constables and parishioners, selected the surveyors of highways; and under two statutes of Queen Elizabeth[4] every year appointed two men who should be named "the distributers of the provision for the destruction of noisome fowle and vermine."   A tax was levied upon the parishioners to provide these officers with funds, and it then became

---

[1] Various quotations in Toulmin Smith, *The Parish*, chap. vii., § 12.   [2] *Ibid.*, 465–472.

[3] 2 and 3 Philip and Mary, chap. viii.

[4] 8 Eliz., chap. xv., and 14 Eliz., chap. xi.

their duty to pay bounties for the heads and eggs
of crows, rooks, starlings, and many other birds.
A long list of four-footed beasts is also included in
the definition of "vermine," and rates ranging from
a shilling for a fox to a halfpenny for a mole were
established.[1] The mole-catcher was a regular em-
ployé of some parishes.[2]

Finally, the church-wardens were *ex-officio* overseers of the poor. By the great poor law of 1597
the church-wardens, along with four overseers of the
poor appointed each year at Easter by the justices,
had the whole charge of the relief of the poor.[3]
They were to estimate the annual costs and to tax
their fellow-townsmen for this purpose. From this
time forward taxation for the poor under the control of parish officers became the most important,
as it was the heaviest, of local charges. The constant efforts of the Privy Council, through the justices of the peace, to enforce the poor law, kept
church-wardens and other overseers of the poor up
to their duties and engaged them in constant con-
ferences with the justices and in making reports, as
well as in the actual work of poor relief.

A vestry clerk existed in some parishes, and later
such an office became quite general and influential,
but at this period the records were generally preserved by one of the church-wardens or by the min-

---

[1] Lambarde, *Office of Distributers*, etc., 92.
[2] Hist. MSS. Commission, *Report III.*, App., 331; V., App.,
597.   [3] Leonard, *The Poor Law*, 76, etc.

ister. The vestry - clerk is of special interest as being apparently the prototype of the town-clerk in the American colonies.[1]

Various other petty officers existed, but their duties were either identical with those already described, or insignificant, or so exceptional as not to reward inquiry and description here. Such were the beadle, sexton, haywards, ale-conners, waymen, waywardens, sidesmen, synodsmen, swornmen, questmen, and perhaps some others.[2]

Such being the officers whose sphere of activity was the parish, it remains to describe the general assembly of the people of the parish, the vestry. This name arose apparently from the practice of meeting in the part of the church in which the vestments were kept. Ordinarily, all who held house or land in a parish, no matter on what tenure, were members of the vestry of the parish. All inhabitants, therefore—land-owners, free tenants, copyholders, laborers occupying cottages, even those who held land in the parish but lived somewhere else— were by law at liberty to attend the meetings of the parishioners and to join in the exercise of their functions.

Such a body is of great interest.[3] Those officials whose positions and functions have been discussed

---

[1] Howard, *Local Constitutional History of the U. S.*, 39.

[2] Discussed in Channing, *Town and County Government in the English Colonies* (*Johns Hopkins University Studies*, II.), No. 10, p. 18, etc.   [3] Coke, *5 Report*, 66, 67.

in the two preceding chapters drew all their powers from the crown, and the duties that they performed were imposed upon them by statute law or by royal instruction. The same is true of a considerable part of the activity of constables and church - wardens. But the vestry of the parish existed as a body which within certain limits had powers of government of its own, and could impose duties upon parish officials, appoint committees and require services from them, adopt by-laws which bound all the inhabitants, and impose taxes upon the landholders of the parish which they were bound to pay.

Yet evidences of anything like regular meetings of the parishioners are, in the sixteenth and seventeenth centuries, so scanty as to leave considerable doubt as to whether they occurred at all generally. They are not mentioned in the legal text-books of the time, which were, of course, written by men who looked from above downward and were not interested in local institutions as such. A few accounts of such vestry meetings remain,[1] but the action taken at them was apparently restricted to the choice of parish officers, the adoption of by-laws for the carrying out of necessary taxation and other distribution of burdens, and for matters connected with the building or repair of the church. The attendance probably consisted only of the more substantial members of the parish and of those who

---

[1] E.g., those of Steeple Ashton, quoted in Toulmin Smith, The Parish, chap. vii., § 12.

held office and must present reports. The parish life resided more in the activity of its officials than of its assembly. Vigorous local self-government could not have existed without leaving more distinct traces than it has done, and our study of the political system of the time will have made it clear that much local independence was not suited to the period of the Tudors and Stuarts.[1]

Such was the provision for the carrying out of those matters of local concern in the county, the hundred, and rural parish which were not performed by immediate officials or commissioners of the central government. It is evident that in the early seventeenth century the motive power for almost all government, local as well as general, emanated from the national government—from the king, Privy Council, and Parliament. It was a vigorous, assertive, centralized administration, eager to carry out its will and enforce order, uniformity, and its own ideas upon all persons and bodies in England. No shade of doubt of their own wisdom or reluctance to override local or individual liberty of action troubled the thought or weakened the resolution of the Tudor and Stuart sovereigns and their ministers. Nor were their Parliaments antagonistic to the principle of centralized government, even when they wished to curb unrestrained royal control of it. Strong gov-

[1] See Toulmin Smith, *The Parish*, chaps. ii., iv., vii.; and Gneist, *Self-Government*, book III., chap. ix., § 115.

ernment was in entire consonance with the spirit of
the time.

Yet this ambitious central government was working with very inadequate and unsuitable instruments.   Instead of a body of efficient and responsible
officials, directly and immediately dependent upon
their superiors, receiving wages and hoping for pro-
motion, such as successful centralized governments
have usually possessed, the king and council made
use of the old and cumbrous machinery of local self-
government as they found it.   It was quite unsuit-
ed to their purposes.   Sheriffs, coroners, high and
petty constables, church-wardens, even justices of
the peace, had come down from a period when government was of quite another and more primitive
character, in which the central power counted for
far less, local powers for far more.   Most of the
local officials were unpaid, and the others were dependent on insignificant fees for such money reward
as they obtained.   The labors imposed upon them
were performed only from a sense of duty, loyalty,
or necessity, not as a fair return for remuneration
received.

There was little provision for a wise selection of
office-holders, so far as regarded their suitability to
the objects of the central administration.   The
county and hundred officials were taken from one
restricted class, the rural gentry; the township and
parish officials were chosen by their neighbors from
their own number.   In a word, the government of

Elizabeth, James, and Charles was trying to carry on an ambitious, centralized administration by means of an unpaid, untrained, and carelessly selected group of local officials, whose offices had been established and whose characters had been formed for a system of much more limited powers and of more independent local life.

At certain times, as in the period of personal government of Charles I., something like a hierarchy seemed about to develop itself, in which the Privy Council, speaking in the name of the king, gave instructions to the justices of assize, the justices of assize to the sheriffs and justices of the peace, the justices of the peace to the high-constable of the hundred, and the high-constable to the petty constable, church-wardens, and other township or parish officials. But no such regularity was attained; the council frequently communicated directly with the justices of the peace, the sheriff with the parish officers; and the administration became no more systematic as time went on.

The primary governmental division of the country, the shire, was the sphere of much activity; but it was not automatic, and acted wholly or almost wholly in response to pressure from above. The ultimate unit of local government, the parish, township, or manor, had many and interesting functions, but they were for the most part either declining survivals of earlier powers, or new forms of activity imposed upon it from above. It had the

necessary officials and the political rights to enable
it to do a great deal, but it showed few signs of vigorous life. Thus government in England in the
early seventeenth century was so organized that at
the top was an energetic national government, midway an active but dependent county organization,
and at the bottom the parish with a residuum of
ancient but unutilized powers of self-government.

No greater contrast could be noted in the position of men than that between the Englishman at
home, in the early seventeenth century, and the
Englishman who emigrated to America. Almost
all the conditions that surrounded the former were
reversed in the case of the latter. The pressure of
central government was immediately and almost
completely withdrawn. Many of the most urgent
activities of government in England, such as the
administration of the poor law and the restriction
of vagabondage, almost ceased in the colonies. The
class of settled rural gentry from which most local
officials were drawn in England did not exist in
America. On the other hand, the wilderness, the
Indians, the freedom from restraint, the religious
liberty, the opportunity for economic and social rise
in the New World made a set of conditions which
had been quite unknown in the mother-country.

As a result, the colonists had to make a choice
from among the institutions with which they were
familiar at home, of those which were applicable to
their new needs. Of such institutions of local gov-

ernment in England there were, as has been seen, a considerable number and variety. Naturally, some functions which had been prominent at home were reduced to insignificance in the colonies; some which had been almost forgotten or had remained quite undeveloped in England gained unwonted importance in America. Almost every local official or body which existed in England reappeared in some part or other of the English colonies, although often with much altered powers and duties. All the familiar names are to be found, though sometimes with new meanings and always more or less considerably adapted to new conditions. Moreover, the choice was in the main restricted to familiar English institutions, for in the great variety of system in different parts of the colonies there was scarcely an official or body which did not have its prototype in England.[1]

In this as in other matters, the foundations of America were laid in European conditions and occurrences. European needs sent explorers on their voyages of discovery, and European ambitions equipped adventurers for their expeditions of conquest; the commercial projects of England, France, Holland, and Sweden led to the establishment of the principal New-World colonies; the economic exi-

[1] Howard, *Local Constitutional History of the U. S.;* Channing, *Town and County Government in the English Colonies;* Adams, *Germanic Origin of New England Towns.* Cf. also Tyler, *England in America;* Andrews, *Colonial Self-Government;* Greene *Colonial Commonwealth (American Nation Series),* IV., V., VI.

gencies and the political and religious struggles of Europe sent a flood of settlers to people them; the institutions of Spain, France, Holland, and England all found a lodgment in the western continent; and those of England became the basis of the great nation which has reached so distinct a primacy in America.

CHAPTER XVII

CRITICAL ESSAY ON AUTHORITIES

BIBLIOGRAPHIES

N O general bibliography of the whole field of this volume exists, although two comprehensive publications (both described below) have special bibliographic sections: *The Cambridge Modern History* has full lists of books, less well analyzed than the systematic and useful bibliographies in Lavisse et Rambaud, *Histoire Générale*.

GENERAL SECONDARY WORKS

Several general histories of Europe covering the field of this volume have been published in recent years or are now appearing. The most important are: Lavisse et Rambaud, *Histoire Générale* (12 vols., 1893–1901), of which vols. III. and VI. apply most nearly to the subjects included in this book; *The Cambridge Modern History* (to be in 12 vols., 1902–), especially vols. I.–IV.; H. H. Helmolt, *History of the World*, translated from the German (to be in 8 vols., 1902–), especially vols. I. and VII. Helmolt differs from all other general histories by its arrangement in accordance with ethnographical and geographical divisions rather than historical epochs; he pays also especial attention to economic phenomena. The following three volumes in the series entitled *Periods of European History*, give an account of this period in somewhat shorter form: Richard Lodge, *The Close of the Middle Ages, 1272–1494* (1901); A. H. Johnson, *Europe in the Sixteenth Century,*

1494 – 1598 (1897); H. O. Wakeman, *Europe, 1598 – 1715* (1904).

Two excellent histories of the period of discovery are O. F. Peschel, *Geschichte des Zeitalters der Entdeckungen* (1858), and Sophus Ruge, *Geschichte des Zeitalters der Entdeckungen* (1881). More recent works are S. Günther, *Das Zeitalter der Entdeckungen* (1901), and Carlo Errera, *L'Epoca delle Grandi Scoperti Geografiche* (1902).

SPECIAL QUESTION ON COLUMBUS

The seemingly well - established view that Columbus when he discovered America was in search of a direct western route to the East Indies and Cathay, and that he had been led to form this plan by correspondence with the Florentine scholar Toscanelli, was attacked by Henry Vignaud, *La Lettre et la Carte de Toscanelli sur la Route des Indes par l'Orient* (1901), and in a translation and extension of the same work under the title *Toscanelli and Columbus* (1902). Vignaud considers the letter of Toscanelli a forgery, and the object of Columbus in making the voyage the discovery of a certain island of which he had been informed by a dying pilot. His work elicited many replies in the form of book reviews or more extended works. Of the former may be mentioned those of E. G. Bourne (*American Historical Review*, January, 1903) and Sophus Ruge (*Zeitschrift der Gesellschaft für Erdkunde zu Berlin*, 1902); among the latter, the monumental work, *Christopher Columbus, His Life, His Work, His Remains*, by John Boyd Thacher (I., 1903). Few scholars seem to have been convinced by the arguments of Vignaud, but the whole question must be considered as still undetermined. The last word is E. G. Bourne, *Spain in America* (*The American Nation*, III., 1904).

SOURCES

A large number of the contemporary accounts of the early expeditions of discovery and adventure are published by the Hakluyt Society. These volumes are provided with introductions of great value and with numerous maps, glossaries, and other material illustrative of the time. They cover a long period of time and include many lines of travel not referred to in this book; but many of them refer to the early expeditions to the southeast, west, and northwest which had much to do with the discovery and exploration of America. Some of the most important publications of this character in the series are the following: *Select Letters of Columbus*, edited by R. H. Major (II. and XLIII., 1849 and 1870); *Narratives of Early Voyages to the Northwest*, edited by Thomas Rundall (V., 1851); *India in the Fifteenth Century*, edited by R. H. Major (XXII., 1859); *The Commentaries of the Great Afonso Dalboquerque*, edited by Walter de Gray Birch (LIII., LV., LXII., LXIX., 1875, 1880, and 1883); *The Voyage of John Huyghen van Linschoten to the East Indies*, edited by A. C. Burnell and P. A. Tiele (LXX. and LXXI., 1884); *The Journal of Christopher Columbus*, edited by C. R. Markham (LXXXVI., 1892); *The Discovery and Conquest of Guinea, Written by Gomes Eannes de Azurara*, edited by C. R. Beazley and Edgar Prestage (XCV. and C., 1896 and 1900); *The First Voyage of Vasco da Gama*, edited by E. G. Ravenstein (XCIX., 1898); *Texts and Versions of John de Plano Carpini and William de Rubruquis*, edited by C. R. Beazley (1903).

The standard editions of the narratives of the early land travellers in eastern Asia are those of the *Recueil de Voyages et de Mémoires publié par la Société de Géographie*, including (IV., 1839) *Relations des Voyages de Guillaume de Rubruk, Jean du Plan Carpin*, etc. (edited by M. A. R. d'Avezac); and Schafer et Cordier, *Recueil de Voyages et de Documents pour Servir à l'Histoire de la Géographie*, especially "Voyages en Asie ... du ... Odoric de Pordenone" (edited by Henri Cordier). English translations of Rubruquis and Pordenone also appear as an appendix in *Travels of Sir John Mandeville*, edited by A. W. Pollard (1900). Sir John Mandeville is worthless as an historical source, as his genuine material is

all drawn from these sources and from Marco Polo, and
there is no probability that he ever travelled in the East.
His own additions are usually mendacious. The standard
edition of Marco Polo is that of Sir Henry Yule (2 vols.,
1871). This has just been reprinted with additional
editorial notes by Henri Cordier, under the title, *The
Book of Ser Marco Polo the Venetian, Concerning the
Kingdoms and Marvels of the East, etc.* (1903). A valuable
collection of narratives of early discovery is M. F. de
Navarrete, *Coleccion de los Viages y Descubrimientos* (5 vols.,
1825–1837). Those of particular interest to England are
in Richard Hakluyt, *Principal Navigations, Voyages, and
Discoveries* (1589, reprinted 1903, to be in 12 vols.).

GEOGRAPHY AND COMMERCE

Among the standard histories of mediæval and modern
geography are Joachim Lelewel, *Géographie du Moyen
Age* (4 vols., 1852–1857); Vivien de St. Martin, *Histoire de
la Géographie et des Découvertes Géographiques* (1873); M.
F. Vicomte de Santarem, *Essai sur l'Histoire de la Cosmographie pendant le Moyen Age* (3 vols., 1849–1852); and
C. R. Beazley, *The Dawn of Modern Geography* (vols. I.
and II., 1897 and 1901). A full account of the history
and development of maps, especially of the form known as
portolani, is to be found in the two works translated from
the Swedish of A. E. Nordenskiold: *Facsimile Atlas to the
Early History of Cartography* (1889), *Periplus, an Essay on
the Early History of Charts and Sailing-Directions* (1 vol.
and an atlas, 1897); G. Wauverman, *Histoire de l'École
Cartographique Belge et Anversois du 16e Siècle* (2 vols.,
1895).

The state of geographical knowledge at the beginning
of the period of explorations is well described in C.
R. Beazley, Introduction to the volume of the Hakluyt
Society's publications for 1899. F. Kunstmann, *Die
Kenntniss Indiens in XV. Jahrhunderts* (1863); and G. H.
Pertz, *Der Aelteste Versuch zur Entdeckung des Seeweges nach*

Ostindien (1859), describe two important phases of that subject.

The fullest and best work on the relations between the Orient and the Occident, the trade-routes, the objects of trade, and the methods of its administration is Wilhelm Heyd, *Geschichte des Levantehandels im Mittelalter* (2 vols., 1879). There is a French translation of this work (1885–1887), which is later and has been corrected by the author. There is a valuable article on ancient trade in *Encyclopædia Biblica*, IV., 48, etc. Much that is suggestive and informing concerning Eastern commerce and trade-routes can be found in Sir W. W. Hunter, *History of British India*, I. (1899), and on the products of the East in Sir George Birdwood, *Report of Commissioners for the Paris Exhibition of 1878* (1878). Some information concerning trade organization in the Mediterranean Sea and throughout Europe can be found in William Cunningham, *An Essay on Western Civilization in Its Economic Aspects* (2 vols., 1898–1900). H. H. Helmolt, *General History*, VII., pt. i., pp. 1–139, has a long and valuable chapter on "The Economic Development of Western Europe Since the Time of the Crusades," by Dr. Richard Mayr. John Fiske, *The Discovery of America* (2 vols., 1892), contains an interesting popular account of the trade conditions of the time and of those explorations which were directed westward.

The formation of the later commercial companies is described and the provisions of their charters analyzed in P. Bonnassieux, *Les Grandes Compagnies de Commerce* (1892). This work is somewhat superficial, being based, apparently, entirely on works in the French and Latin languages, and using secondary materials where primary sources are attainable; but it stands almost alone in its subject, and has, therefore, considerable importance.

Naval architecture is described in Auguste Jal, *Archéologie Navale* (2 vols., 1840); and J. P. E. Jurien de la Gravière, *Les Marins du XV. et du XVI. Siècle* (1879); Sir William Stirling-Maxwell, *Don John of Austria* (2 vols., 1883).

The best general account of Italy during the fourteenth and fifteenth centuries is in Lavisse et Rambaud, *Histoire Générale*, III., chaps. ix. and x., and IV., chap. i. For the intellectual and artistic history of Italy as a whole, J. Burckhardt, *The Civilization of the Renaissance in Italy* (1860, English translation, 2 vols.), is the most satisfactory work. J. A. Symonds, *Renaissance in Italy* (7 vols., 1875–1886), takes up many sides of the period. A good general history of Venice in small compass is H. F. Brown, *Venice: a Historical Sketch of the Republic* (1893).

M. G. Canale, *Storia del Commercio dei Viaggi, . . . degl' Italiani* (1866), and *Storia della Republica di Genoa* (1858–1864), contain much information about Mediterranean trade and voyages, especially of the Genoese.

The commerce of Venice is described in H. F. Brown, *Calendar of State Papers, Venetian*, Introduction, I. (1864).

Of the fondaco and the German merchants in Venice a description is given in H. Simonsfeld, *Der Fondaco dei Tedeschi in Venedig* (2 vols., 1887). Many additional sources are in G. Thomas, *Capitolare dei Visdomini del Fontego dei Todechi* (1874). A valuable article on the same subject is W. Heyd, "Das Haus der deutschen Kaufleute in Venedig," in *Historische Zeitschrift*, XXXII., 193–220.

The standard history of the rise of the Ottoman Empire is J. W. Zinkeisen, *Geschichte des Osmanischen Reichs in Europa* (6 vols., 1840). More modern works are A. La Jonquière, *Histoire de l'Empire Ottoman* (1881); and G. F. Herzberg, *Geschichte des Byzantischen und des Osmanischen Reiches* (1883).

An excellent work on the fifteenth century is Edwin Pears, *The Destruction of the Greek Empire and the Story of the Capture of Constantinople by the Turks* (2 vols., 1903). For later history, see L. von Ranke, *Die Osmanen in XVI. und XVII. Jahrhundert* (1827). A short and good popular account is A. Lane-Poole, *Turkey* (1886). Good sections are devoted to the Ottoman Turks in the *Cambridge Modern History* (I., chap. iii., by J. B. Bury); and in Lavisse et Rambaud, *Histoire Générale* (III., chap. xvi., and **IV.,** chap. xix.), by A. Rambaud.

PORTUGAL IN THE FIFTEENTH CENTURY

A short but excellent history of Portugal is H. M. Stephens,. *The Story of Portugal* (1891, *Stories of the Nations Series*).

The interesting character and significant work of Prince Henry the Navigator have made him the subject of many biographies. One of the earliest of these was G. de Veer, *Prinz Heinrich und seine Zeit* (1864). More detailed is R. H. Major, *Life of Prince Henry the Navigator* (1868, abbreviated edition, 1874). A number of other biographies were called forth by the interest in the five hundredth anniversary of Henry's birth, which was coincident with the four hundredth anniversary of the discovery of America. A partial list of these is as follows: C. R. Beazley, *Prince Henry the Navigator* (1890); G. Wauverman, *Henri le Navigateur et l'Académie Portugaise de Sagres* (1890); J. P. O. Martins, *Os Filhos de Dom João I.* (1891); M. Barradas, *O Infante Dom Henrique* (1894); A. Alves, *Dom Henrique o Infante* (1894); J. E. Wappäus, *Untersuchungen über . . . Heinrich* (1842). Two valuable essays, *Prince Henry the Navigator* and *The Demarcation Line of Pope Alexander III.*, by E. G. Bourne, are republished in his *Essays in Historical Criticism* (1901).

The most important original source for the early explorations of the Portuguese is Gomes Eannes de Azurara, *Chronicle of the Discovery and Conquest of Guinea* (2 vols., Hakluyt Society, 1896 and 1899). The voyages of Cadamosto are published by the Hakluyt Society. Long extracts from the accounts of the voyages of Diego Gomez are given in C. R. Beazley, *Prince Henry*, 289–298, and in R. H. Major, *Prince Henry*, 288–298. A number of original documents illustrative of this period are contained in *Alguns Documentos do Archivo Nacional da Torre do Tombo Acerca das Navagacões e Conquistas Portuguezas* (1892). An account of the latest stages of the Portuguese advance to India is given in F. C. Danvers, *The Portuguese in India* (1894). An almost contemporary account of the explorations is J. Barros, *Decadas da Asia* (first published 1552, etc.); the first five books have been translated into German by E. Feust (1844).

SPAIN IN THE FIFTEENTH AND SIXTEENTH CENTURIES

The great collection of sources for the history of Spain is the *Coleccion de Documentos Ineditos para la Historia de España* (112 vols., 1842–1895). Matters more particularly relating to the subjects of this book appear in vols. I., III., VI., XIII., XIX., XXIV., XXVIII., XXXIX., and LI. The proceedings of the cortes are published by the Academia de la Historia, *Cortes de los Antiguos Reinos de Leon y de Castilla* (4 vols., 1861–1884). The records of those called by Ferdinand and Isabella are in vol. IV. (1882). A careful analysis and introduction to these records is by M. Colmeiro (2 vols., 1883–1884).

The three most important chronicles of Spain contemporary with Ferdinand and Isabella are Hernando del Pulgar, *Cronica de los Reyes Catolicos* (1780); and André Bernaldez, *Historia de los Reyes* (1878).

The institutions of Spain are described in detail in two admirable works: J. M. Antequera, *Historia de la Legislacion Española* (1874); and F. M. Marina, *Ensayo Historico-critico sobre la Antigua Legislacion . . . de Leon y Castilla* (1834). There is a short but systematic and valuable account of Spanish institutions in *The Cambridge Modern History* (I., chap. xi., by H. B. Clarke). The most satisfactory general description of the changes in Spanish institutions during the reign of the Catholic sovereigns is J. H. Mariéjol, *L'Espagne sous Ferdinand et Isabelle: le Gouvernement, les Institutions, et les Mœurs* (1892). William H. Prescott, *The Reign of Ferdinand and Isabella the Catholic* (various editions), is less uncritical in character, and consequently more trustworthy, than the other works of this author. An important study of the personal character of Isabella is Clemencin, *Elogio de la Reina Catolica,* in Real Academia de la Historia, *Memorias*, IV. An important and suggestive study of this period is W. Maurenbrecher, *Spanien unter den Katholischen Königen: Studien und Skizzen zur Geschichte der Reformationszeit* (1857). Of somewhat similar character is W. Havemann, *Darstellungen aus der inneren Geschichte Spaniens während des XV., XVI. und XVII. Jahrhunderts* (1850). The more purely political history is best given in M. Danvilla y Collado, *El Poder Civil en España* (6 vols., 1885–1887). The expulsion of the Jews is described in the third volume of J. Amador de los Rios, *Los Judios de España y Portugal* (3 vols., 1875–1876); that of the Moriscos in H. C. Lea, *The Moriscos of Spain, their Conversion and Expulsion* (1901). Much valuable description of this period is also given in H. C. Lea, *Chapters from the Religious History of Spain* (1890). Mr. Lea has also an important article," The Policy of Spain towards the Indies" (*Yale Review*, August, 1899). The military history of Ferdinand's reign is given in P. Boissonade, *Réunion de la Navarre à la Castille* (1893), and in the large general histories of Spain, such as A. Canovas del Castillo, *Historia General de España* (1894), and Vicente de la Fuente, *Historia General de España* (30 vols., 1850–1867).

The organization of the Casa da Contractacion is fully described in *Primeras Ordenanzas . . . de la Contractacion de las Indias*, by J. de Veitia Linage (1672, "made English" by Captain John Stevens, under the title *The Spanish Rule of Trade to the West Indies*, 1702). It is also described in Richard Hakluyt, *Principal Navigations*, IV. Economic conditions are further described in two books by K. Häbler, *Geschichte der Fugger'schen Handlung in Spanien* (1897); *Die Wirtschaftliche Blüte Spaniens im XVI. Jahrhundert und ihr Verfall* (1888).

FRANCE IN THE SIXTEENTH AND SEVENTEENTH CENTURIES

The great mass of contemporary writings for this period is published partly in the great *Collection de Documents*

Inédits (about 280 vols., 1835–), partly in other collections, such as that of Michaud et Poujoulat, *Correspondance d'Orient*, 1830–1831 (7 vols., 1835), and partly as individual publications. The royal enactments down to 1514 are best edited in *Ordonnances des Roys de France* (21 vols., 1723–1849). The *Recueil Général des Anciennes Lois Françaises*, edited by Isambert and Taillandier (29 vols., 1822–1833), extends later in time but is inferior in fulness and accuracy.

A short general history of France during this period is A. J. Grant, *The French Monarchy*, 1483–1789 (2 vols., 1900). Of the excellent work, Lavisse, *Histoire de France*, the latest section to appear is V., pt. i., by H. Lemonnier, which covers the period 1492–1547.

For the commercial history of France valuable works are H. Pigeonneau, *Histoire du Commerce de la France* (2 vols., 1887–1889); Pierre Clément, *Histoire de la Vie et de l'Administration de Colbert* (2 vols., 1846); G. Fagniez, "Le Commerce de la France sous Henri IV.," in *Revue Historique*, May–June, 1881; and F. Bourquelot, *Étude sur les Foires de Champagne* (Académie des Inscriptions et Belles-Lettres de l'Institut de France, series II., vol. V., 1865). For the commercial companies in Canada, see H. P. Biggar, *Early Trading Companies of New France* (1901).

THE NETHERLANDS AND GERMANY IN THE SIXTEENTH AND SEVENTEENTH CENTURIES

The best history of the Netherlands is P. J. Blok, *History of the People of the Netherlands* (1892, in part translated by Ruth Putnam, 3 vols., 1898–1900); J. L. Motley, *Rise of the Dutch Republic* (many editions), still has value and much interest, but the work is uncritical and based on inadequate study of the sources. C. M. Davies, *History of Holland and the Dutch Nation* (3 vols., 1851), is of special value for its attention to the internal organization of the Dutch nation. Robert Fruin, *Geschiedniss der Staatsinstellingen in Nederland* (edited by H. T. Colenbrander, 1901), is a much more detailed and modern work, the first two books of which refer to the period of this volume. In it are to be found abundant references to the sources of Dutch institutions. Douglas Campbell, *The Puritan in Holland, England, and America* (2 vols., 1892), is a vivacious work including much description of conditions in Holland and England during this period. It is, however, written in a spirit of controversial exaggeration which reduces its historical value to small proportions. The long and valuable paper "William Usselinx," by J. F. Jameson (American Historical Society, *Papers*, II. 1888), contains much information concerning political and commercial conditions in the Netherlands. There is a short description of the municipal organization of Holland in an article by J. F. Jameson in the *Magazine of American History*, VIII., 315–330. The charter of the Dutch West India Company is in E. B. O'Callaghan, *History of New Netherland*, I., App. A (1855); and in Samuel Hazard, *State Papers*, I.

The general history of Germany for this period can be studied from the following volumes of the series entitled *Allgemeine Geschichte in Einzeldarstellungen*—viz., F. von Bezold, *Geschichte der deutschen Reformation* (1890); G. Droysen, *Geschichte der Gegenreformation* (1893); G. Winter, *Der dreissigjährigen Krieges* (1893); B. Erdmannsdorfer, *Deutsche Geschichte von westfälischen Frieden bis Friedrichs der Grossen* (2 vols., 1892). The last work contains in its first book a valuable résumé of the results of the Thirty Years' War and the condition of Germany at the time. E. Armstrong, *The Emperor Charles V.* (2 vols., 1902), is an excellent account of Germany during the middle years of the sixteenth century. Anton Gindely, *The Thirty Years' War* (English translation, 2 vols., 1884), is a standard work on the Thirty Years' War.

The religious changes of the time are described in a scholarly but extremely dry fashion in W. Moeller, *History of the Christian Church*, III. (English translation, 1900). L. von Ranke, *Deutsche Geschichte im Zeitalter der Reformation*, translated into English (3 vols., 1845–1847), is

a well - known work. More detailed accounts of the
Anabaptists are given in H. W. Erbkam, *Geschichte der
Protestantischen Sekten in Zeitalter der Reformation* (1848);
L. Keller, *Geschichte der Wiedertaüfer* (1880); and Max
Goebel, *Geschichte des Christlichen Leben in der rheinsch-
westphälischen evangelischen Kirche* (3 vols., 1849–1860).

ENGLAND IN THE SIXTEENTH AND SEVENTEENTH CENTURIES

BIBLIOGRAPHY.—The standard bibliographical guide in
early English history is Charles Gross, *Sources and Literature
of English History from the Earliest Times to about 1485*
(1900).

GENERAL WORKS.—The best general history of the
reign of Henry VII. is W. Busch, *England under the Tudors*
(I., *Henry VII.*, 1895); on the early part of the reign of
Henry VIII., J. S. Brewer, *The Reign of Henry VIII.*
(2 vols., 1884); J. A. Froude, *History of England from
the Fall of Wolsey to the Defeat of the Armada* (12 vols.,
1856–1870). Notwithstanding the criticism to which this
work has been subjected it remains the most detailed,
serious, and valuable history of England in the sixteenth
century. A. F. Pollard, *England under Protector Somerset*
(1900), is a valuable survey of the period 1547–1551. S.
R. Gardiner, *History of England from 1603 to 1642* (10
vols., 1883–1884), *History of the Great Civil War, 1642–1649*
(4 vols., 1886–1891), and *History of the Commonwealth and
Protectorate* (3 vols., 1894–1903), form a series of great
value, covering more than half of the seventeenth century.
Henry Hallam, *Constitutional History of England* (3 vols.,
1829), is serviceable. L. O. Pike, *Constitutional History
of the House of Lords* (1894), and A. V. Dicey, *The Privy
Council* (1895), are valuable monographs.

SOURCES.—The sources for English history during this
period are to be found principally in the *Acts of the Privy
Council* (in progress 1890–), *Calendars of State Papers* (about
300 vols.), *Statutes of the Realm, 1235–1713* (11 vols.),

Journals of the House of Lords (16 vols. to 1700), *Journals of the House of Commons* (13 vols. to 1700), Sir S. D'Ewes, *Journals of the Period of Elizabeth* (1682), J. Rushworth, *Historical Collections* (1703), Historical Manuscripts Commission, *Reports* (106 parts), Deputy Keeper of the Rolls, Public Records, *Reports* (64 vols.), and in a vast number of detached publications of contemporary journals, correspondence, etc.

Many of the most important statutes and other state papers are collected in G. W. Prothero, *Select Statutes and other Constitutional Documents of the Reigns of Elizabeth and James I., 1559–1625* (1894), and S. R. Gardiner, *Constitutional Documents of the Puritan Revolution, 1628–1660* (1889). Each of these collections has an admirable introduction discussing the history and institutions of the period. Other collections illustrating the constitutional history of the time are George B. Adams and H. Morse Stephens, *Select Documents of English Constitutional History* (1901); and Mabel Hill, *Liberty Documents* (1901). The following collections of sources also illustrate social conditions: C. W. Colby, *Selections from the Sources of English History* (1899); Elizabeth K. Kendall, *Source-Book of English History* (1900); Ernest F. Henderson, *Side-Lights on English History* (1900).

COMMERCIAL HISTORY.—The Merchants Adventurers are discussed and illustrated in W. E. Lingelbach, *Laws and Ordinances of the Merchant Adventurers* (1902), and *The Internal Organization of the Merchant Adventurers* (1902); in G. Schanz, *Englische Handelspolitik* (2 vols., 1881); Richard Ehrenberg, *England and Hamburg* (1896); and Charles Gross, *The Gild Merchant* (2 vols., 1890). The commercial companies generally are described in Cawston and Keane, *The Early English Chartered Companies* (1896), a book of slight value and limited extent of information apart from the fact that it is practically the only work covering the field. David Macpherson, *Annals of Commerce* (4 vols., 1802), is a book of old-fashioned learning on the subject. For the East India Company there is a large literature. Some of the sources are *The Charters of the East India Company* (no date or place of publication); Birdwood and Foster, *The First Letter Book of the East India Company, 1600–1619* (1893); Henry Stevens, *Dawn of British Trade to the East Indies* (1886). Of more general histories the most recent and one of the best is Beckles Wilson, *Ledger and Sword* (1903).

Events in England affecting the early history of Virginia are related and the original papers given in Alexander Brown, *Genesis of the United States* (2 vols., 1891). Valuable articles by H. L. Osgood bearing on this general subject are: "England and the Colonies"(*Political Science Quarterly*, II.); "Political Ideas of the Puritans" (*ibid.*, VI., Nos. 1, 2); and "The Colonial Corporation" (*ibid.*, XI., Nos. 2, 3). See also his *American Colonies in the Seventeenth Century* (2 vols., 1904). On general commercial conditions, William Cunningham, *Growth of English Industry and Commerce* (revised ed., 1904).

RELIGIOUS HISTORY.—W. E. Griffis, *The Pilgrims in their Three Homes* (1898); Daniel Neal, *History of the Puritans* (4 vols., 1732–1738); W. A. Shaw, *The English Church During the Commonwealth* (1900); E. Eggleston, *Beginners of a Nation* (1897), gives interesting and unfamiliar details of the religious sects in England. A. B. Hinds, *The England of Elizabeth* (1895), is a careful study of the origins of English Puritanism on the Continent. G. P. Gooch, *English Democratic Ideas in the Seventeenth Century* (1898), throws light on the various sects. William Sewel, *History of the Quakers* (1725), is a standard history on the origin of that body.

C. G. Walpole, *The Kingdom of Ireland* (1882), describes the "Plantation of Ulster" and the conditions that led to the emigration of the Scotch-Irish. Of value also are W. E. H. Lecky, *England in the Eighteenth Century* (8 vols., 1878–1890); J. P. Prendergast, *The Cromwellian Settlement of Ireland* (1865); and H. Green, *The Scotch-Irish in America* (1895).

ENGLISH LOCAL GOVERNMENT.—For local government

the admirable bibliography is Charles Gross, *Bibliography of British Municipal History, Including Gilds and Parliamentary Representatives* (*Harvard Historical Studies*, V., 1897). Contemporary legal treatises concerning county government are Michael Dalton, *Officium Vicecomitum, or the Office and Authority of Sheriffs* (1623), and *The Country Justice* (1681); William Greenwood, *Authority, Jurisdiction, and Method of Keeping County Courts, Courts-Leet, and Courts-Baron*, etc. (1659); William Lambarde, *Eirenarcha, or the Office of the Justices of Peace* (1588); A. Fitzherbert, *L'Office et Authorities de Justices de Peace* (1514), often quoted as "Crompton," an editor who enlarged the original work in 1583; John Wilkinson, *Office and Authority of Coroners and Sheriffs* (1628). All these appear in numerous editions, the above dates being, as far as ascertained, those of the earliest editions.

Few records of county government exist to any large extent, and very few have been printed. Among them are three bodies of quarter-sessions records. John Lister, *West Riding Sessions Rolls, 1597–1602* (Yorkshire Archæological and Topographical Association, *Records Series*, III., 1888); J. C. Jeaffreson, *Middlesex County Records, 1549–1608* (Middlesex County Records Society, 1886–1892); Ernest Axon, in Record Society of Lancaster and Cheshire, *Manchester Sessions*, XLII. Some material for Wiltshire and Worcestershire is published in the Historical Manuscripts Commission, *Reports*, VI., VII.

A. H. A. Hamilton, *Quarter-Sessions . . . chiefly of Devon* (1878), contains much on the subject. E. M. Leonard, *The Early History of the English Poor Relief* (1900), is a scholarly study involving much description of local administration and the central and local governments.

For the parish, Richard Burn, *Ecclesiastical Law* (2 vols., 1763); William Sheppard, *Offices and Duties of Constables, Borsholders, Tythingmen*, etc. (1641); William Lambarde, *Duties of Church-wardens* and *Duties of Constables*, affixed to his *Eirenarcha* (1581); George Meriton, *Duties of Constables* (1669).

For the actual life of the parish, recourse must be had to the few bodies of such records that are printed separately or in local histories. Some of these are as follows: J. L. Glasscock, *Records of St. Michael's Church* (1882); Collyer and Turner, *Ilkley, Ancient and Modern* (1885); W. T. Woodbridge, *Rushbrook Parish Registers* (1903); W. O. Massingberd, *History of Ormsby* (1893); J. P. Earwaker, *Constables' Accounts of Manchester* (3 vols., 1891–1892); John Nichols, *Illustration of the Manners, etc., of England from Accounts of Church-wardens* (1797).

The book that has exerted the most influence on opinion on this subject is Toulmin Smith, *The Parish* (1854). It is, however, written in a spirit of controversy, many of its interpretations of the statutes are quite incorrect, and it must, therefore, be used with great caution. Its most valuable contents are its references to sources, and extracts from local records. Rudolf Gneist, *Self-Government, Communalverfassung und Verwaltungsgeschichte in England* (1871), is almost the sole work covering the whole subject, but it is quite unsatisfactory, being drawn from a comparatively small group of sources. George E. Howard, *Local Constitutional History of the United States* (*Johns Hopkins University Studies*, extra vol. IV., 1889), and *The Development of the King's Peace* (*Nebraska University Studies*, I., 1890); Edward Channing, *Town and County Government in the English Colonies of North America* (*Johns Hopkins University Studies*, II., No. 10), and some other articles by Herbert B. Adams and others in the same series, include considerable information on local conditions in England, though their primary reference is to America.

INDEX